CIVIC VICTORIES

"The masses of people always mean well and will always act well *when they can obtain a right understanding.*"

—George Washington

CIVIC VICTORIES

The Story of an Unfinished Revolution

By RICHARD S. CHILDS
Former President, National Municipal League

With an Introduction by
THOMAS HARRISON REED

HARPER & BROTHERS   PUBLISHERS   NEW YORK

CIVIC VICTORIES

Contents

Part III. Readings: Stories from the Civic Battle Front

*Part IV. Outlines of the National Municipal
League's Model Laws*

Introducing the Author

Before he was thirty years old Richard S. Childs had fathered two potent ideas—the short ballot and its blood brother, the council-manager plan of city government. He has spent much of the next forty years in promoting these and other reforms, with credit to himself and great benefit to his country.

He was only four years out of Yale when he sold *The Outlook* an article entitled "The Short Ballot." It would be too much to say that Childs was the first publicist to note that the burden of electing long lists, mostly of obscure people, to obscure offices, was too much for the American people to carry successfully. It was a fact familiar to students of government. But no one up to that time had explained it to the reading public in moving words. The academic world was perhaps a little jealous that a young advertising man to whom words were familiar playthings could do what we could not. There is no gainsaying, however, that Childs did the trick, and the principles he laid down in that brief article and diligently publicized thereafter have since become the commonplaces of textbook and classroom, universally accepted except by some willfully benighted politicians. Seldom in the history of governmental reform has one short essay produced such a great and lasting effect on the thinking of the time."

Childs, moreover, was not merely creative but persistent and practical. He has been no long-haired, wild-eyed reformer but an increasingly successful businessman and has held top executive positions in important industries such as the Bon Ami Company and Lederle Laboratories. The qualities which have made him effective in business have been applied to his many ventures in the field of civic affairs.

Having set the whole country talking about the short ballot, it was only natural that he was able to swerve the Board of Trade of Lockport, New York, from its consideration of a routine adoption of the commission plan to sponsor his second concept, the council-manager plan, which has since been adopted by more than 1000 municipalities. The New York legislature turned down the proposed Lockport charter but it was given nation-wide publicity through the "Short Ballot Organization," with Governor Woodrow Wilson as president, which Childs had in the meantime constructed. To supply this organization with more effective ammunition Childs produced a small volume called *Short-Ballot Principles*. Its substance, with some improvements as the result of forty years' experience, is repeated as part of the volume to which these lines serve as an introduction.

Governmental changes take place slowly in a democracy like ours, and the short-ballot principle has been by no means universally applied in the United States. The degree of progress in the last forty years has been considerable even in state and county government and it has been almost revolutionary in municipal government. In this battle for more simple, better integrated, and more democratic government Childs has been a consistent and self-sacrificing leader. He has been particularly active in the civic movements of his city of New York. There he was for twelve years president of the City Club and for six years chairman of the Citizens Union. In 1920 he was a vice-president of the American Political Science Association. As chairman of the board of the Institute of Public Administration in New York and as a member of the board of directors of the Public Administration Clearing House in Chicago he has had a hand in the promotion of some of the best research that has been done in state and local government throughout the country.

Childs' first love, however, has been the National Municipal League. He has served continuously on its council for more than thirty years. From 1927 to 1931 he was its president and he has since been chairman of its executive committee. When he retired from business in 1947 he moved into the League offices as a volunteer worker and is to be found there most of his time lending a hand in the League's extensive and far-flung activities.

No man has been more intimately or causally connected with the progress of the council-manager plan and other municipal improvements since the crucial year of 1910, when he woke us up to the essential absurdity of electing county surveyors and city engineers. No one, therefore, is better equipped to write a book recounting the campaigns which have been waged and won—some battles have been lost but the march of progress has never been really halted. The fact that a single continuing organization, the National Municipal League, has been all the time in the center of the fight, does not detract at all from the interest of what he has to tell.

THOMAS HARRISON REED *

Wethersfield, Connecticut
August, 1952

* Editor's Note: Dr. Reed, now a widely known authority in political science, has had a long career as professor in two universities, city manager, author, and draftsman of city charters.

Introduction. The Scope
of This Book ·

There is no such word as "democratics" but there ought to be, so we coin it now to describe phenomena produced when various mechanisms of government are provided for voters to operate. Voting behavior has its own infinite variables, but we have in the United States also a diversity of forms of government and of election procedures in the states and towns, and some of them are more practical than others for operation by clumsy masses of voters. Indeed, we have in the area of elections a prevalence of needless complications which, as we shall see, frustrate voters and to a dismaying extent have the effect of disenfranchising them. So we shall neither concern ourselves here with what elective officers do after they are elected nor invade the techniques of internal management of government called "administration." We concern ourselves here with the problems of selecting our elective officers and follow them and their subsequent activities only to the theshold of the state capitol or the city hall; we will stay outdoors! For "democratics" relates only to that field of law which is confused by voter participation.

Democratics examines such occurrences as these:

The voters of Michigan elected a certain man state treasurer four times while only 4 per cent of them knew his name.

Every one of the 203 voters in a Detroit voting precinct was unaware that, in the case of two offices, he was voting for candidates who were not running in that precinct.

Ohio voters are confronted with the task of selecting candidates for forty to fifty-six offices at one time—with weird results.

In a town of 11,000, seventy-eight persons named all the candidates.

Memphis has been firmly in the clutches of a political boss for a generation, and Dayton has chosen nonpolitical councils for twenty successive elections.

Human nature being much the same everywhere, may it not be that some of our diverse mechanisms of democratics are at fault?

Democracy—etymologically, government by the people—as a description is misapplied to many governments. We have seen the Soviets apply it brazenly to their tyrannies and double in brass by redundantly describing their autocratic setups as "people's democcracies." "Democracy" is misapplied also to numerous jurisdictions in the United States where in reality a self-chosen group, called the bosses, the machine, the party committee, may wield for generations a power that cannot be shaken off without a paroxysm of political revolutionary effort.

What we have here is, in any case, *government by elective officers.* Sometimes this results in democracy and often it does not. Forms of government by elective officers could be deliberately devised that would consign a given city to control by a handful of self-serving politicians; conversely, forms can be and have been devised so simple that they work and respond for decades to local public sentiment without any discernible group of politicians to help manage them. So we must analyze the experience and find the way to set up governments by elective officers that will, in common practice, produce democracy rather than bossism or some similar oligarchy.

To cover our field of democratics, then, is to observe the elective officers throughout the country to see how they get elected—how they *really* get into office as distinguished from the ostensible ways which in Russia (and in America) may be far from the inner realities.

545,000 Elective Officers

We voters elect the elective officers of government and they appoint all the rest. If we pick and install the men we really want, they will control the appointive staffs and all the operations of government, whereupon the whole government can be expected to cater to our wishes.

Here is the table of American elective officers:

1 U.S.A.	533 elective officers
48 states	10,000 elective officers
3,049 counties $\times$ 12 each [1]	36,588 elective officers
16,677 municipalities $\times$ 8 each	133,416 elective officers
17,338 towns and townships in 22 states $\times$ 8 each	138,704 elective officers
63,407 [2] elective school boards $\times$ 3 each	190,221 elective officers
11,900 special districts, $\frac{1}{2}$ with elective boards, $\times$ 6 each	35,700 elective officers
112,420	545,162

As to the national government, we elect only the president and vice-president (via a single mark for a group of presidential electors) and, in most states, a single representative to Congress from our district and two senators in separate years—a maximum of three decisions to be made by each voter at any one time. The states and local governments set up the other 99.918 per cent of our elective officers, so it is there that we must go to inquire into democratics. Furthermore, congressional elections are conducted in various ways by the states along with their local elections, and the national parties and nominating conventions are in effect federations of state groups. Congressmen are merely one group of the products of state and local political institutions and even a president acknowledges his origin in the old Kansas City political machine. This book, therefore, neglects the 533 elective officers of the national govern-

[1] The multipliers are the author's "guesstimate." Ogg and Ray in *Introduction to American Government*, 10th ed., Appleton-Century-Crofts, New York, 1951, p. 149, assign 54,000 to counties (eighteen each?) and 66,000 to cities and other incorporated places (only four each?).

[2] U.S. Bureau of the Census, *Governments in the U.S. in 1951*, reports (March, 1952) 70,452 local school districts (38,127 less than in 1942!); these boards, while more or less independent, are not always elective. *Research Bulletin* of the National Education Association, April, 1946, based on data or estimates supplied by forty state boards of education plus estimates for the other states as of June, 1945, counted 111,895 school boards with only 373,287 members, or 3.3 average membership. A sampling of 3068 boards showed 85 per cent elective; a deeper sampling of the small rural districts would have increased the percentage of elective boards and reduced the average board size; some districts have a "board" of one. Thus 70,452 boards$\times$.90(?) elective= 63,407; three(?) members each=190,221 elective officers.

ment to wander into the vaster democratics of the states and their divisions.

DIFFICULTY IN ACCUMULATING EVIDENCE

Democratics has been amazingly neglected as a field of study despite its obvious vastness and importance. The enormous experience involved in 545,000 elections is almost unrecorded except here and there by individual authors in their home states. Collection of comparative experience involves travel—field inquiry—over great geographical areas before trends and broad conclusions can be substantiated. The university professors of political science can each provide a little source data for his home town or state but they cannot usually travel widely.

No philanthropic foundation has as yet fostered inquiries in this field; it is too political, too controversial, too legislative for them, or so they seem to think.

There have been two exceptions: In 1937–39 the Social Science Research Council financed a survey "to appraise the results of what has sometimes been called one of the most important social inventions in government in the twentieth century"—the council-manager plan of municipal government.[3]

Another such study is V. O. Key, Jr.'s *Southern Politics*.[4] It took that author and a team of five co-workers three years to obtain and marshal the facts including months of full-time field work, made possible only by a grant of the Rockefeller Foundation.

Both studies were superior in the fact that the authors went to the scenes and gathered material from enough jurisdictions to provide comparisons and warrant general conclusions.

And that's about all the field work in democratics that was done in ten years!

When we consider how important in the modern world it is to understand and correct the failures of "government by elected officers," it seems no less than calamitous that science has so neglected American democratics.

[3] *City Manager Government in the United States*, by Harold A. Stone, Don K. Price, and Kathryn H. Stone, *City Manager Government in Nine Cities*, by the same authors, and *City Manager Government in Seven Cities*, by several authors, Public Administration Service, Chicago, 1940.

[4] Alfred A. Knopf, New York, 1949.

So in this volume we must proceed with such flotsam evidence as has drifted into print from local observers who happened to feel like writing up local experiences. In the mass of these experiences, gathered mostly by the editors of the *National Municipal Review* since 1912, we can discern important patterns.

OBJECTIVE: DEMOCRACY—NOT "GOOD" GOVERNMENT

Our objective is not good government exactly but democratic government. Good government includes economy of tax funds, expertness in the technical departments, efficiency of administration. You might have all these without democracy. Boss Crump belligerently asserts that the fortunate citizens of Memphis, Tennessee, obtain all these under his beneficent and paternal domination. "Memphis is the only honestly run city in America," says he! But as long as he or any successor boss continues to wield autocratic power over Memphis, that city is no democracy even if the procedures of government by elected officers are faithfully observed. Contrariwise, a city where no trace of perversion of the democratic process is observable may be incompetent in all its operations by any modern standard, and dishonest besides. But in the latter case, self-serving forces in its government will not be found deeply entrenched against correction whenever public opinion wakes up and gets critical.

We cannot devise a system of government that will automatically produce good administration but we can and shall undertake in these pages to identify systems which will almost inevitably be democratic. And if we achieve a practical working of the democratic process, the self-interest of the voters can be appealed to for correction of lapses in performance, and sensitive responsiveness of the mechanism will facilitate the ability of such self-interest to prevail.

So our goal is democracy in a truly workable form, free of such oddities as bossisms, rings, or tight self-renewing cliques of politicians, regardless of whether taxes go up or down!

In the concept of good government we seek the nobler part, the part that represents the aspiration of the ages and which in spots now and then we do achieve—the concept of a government that will diligently cater to the sovereign people!

Part I

The Three Rules for Democracy

Chapter I

THE SOVEREIGN? PEOPLE

> The preachers who tell corrupt cities that the people
> are steeped in sin are the descendants of those who used
> to associate sin and plagues.
>
> —*National Municipal Review,* 1936

THE people—pronounced by the orators "pee-pul"! Or "the plain people," who, we are to understand, have certain supernatural virtues not possessed by "the people"! It is in some minds *lèse-majesté* to allege that there are limitations to the people in either morals or learning. Rounded periods are out of fashion on every other subject, but rhetorical vaporings still enshroud "this great people." And if you should have the temerity to opine that most of the people vote for a state treasurer blindly without adequate knowledge of his qualifications, editors (after having looked up the name of the state treasurer themselves to be sure of it) will explode in paragraphs of scorn—"Doesn't he trust our people?" In the same editorials, after exalting the virtue of the people, they may proceed to deplore their wanton "apathy."

Apathy is assigned as the reason for every failure of the democratic process. Tie upon the backs of the people a triple burden of duties and if they do not carry it well, if they do not do the tasks which writers of state constitutions and city charters assigned to them, bewail their "apathy"!

SAME PEOPLE—DIVERSE RESULTS

But we see in the United States some clear phenomena that upset the notion that the people are always to blame when things go wrong. The government of New York City has been over a period of some years markedly better than that of Chicago in the view of both informed New Yorkers and Chicagoans. Must we then assume

3

that there is some great moral difference between the two populaces? Isn't it a fact that they are indistinguishable in any candid light?

The people of Dayton have had good government for thirty-eight years unbroken through twenty biennial elections, but if its population moved to Chicago, would those people be distinguishable?

Cincinnati in the 1920's was commonly described as our worst-governed city; after 1926 it began calling itself the best governed and is still plausibly doing so. The governmental mechanism changed, but Cincinnatians remained the same people before and after!

Kansas City has had good government for twelve years—ever since it got rid of the 60,000 phantom voters who used to pervert its elections under Boss Pendergast—but, as noted in a later chapter, the government of Jackson County, of which that city's population is 80 per cent, continues backward, inefficient, and suspect under a government of antique design.

If such differences of performance are not to be found attributable to long-run differences in the morality or civic energy of those constituencies, they must be due to differences in the mechanism.

So let us admit that the people are men and women, not demi-gods; men and women, not moral delinquents! If we thus concede to the people the merits and faults possessed by men and women, we can proceed calmly to consider them as the great underlying base of our government-by-elected-officers, with certain familiar and, so far as we are concerned, unalterable characteristics to be reckoned with as we erect the political superstructure.

Think of the people as you would of a brook when building a water mill! You would waste no time in deploring its lazy tendency to slip downward through every crevice in your dam; you would admit the fact and build a tight dam. You would not plan to have the water flow uphill, knowing that you would inevitably be disappointed. If your mill finally failed to work, you would still not blame the water but only the mill, and would strive to adapt its gearing to the force of the stream. Yet you would have just as much right to sit by the motionless mill and curse the characteristics of water (which consistently fails to fulfill your man-made requirements) as has the Charter Revision Committee to devise a city charter that imposes requirements on the people which ample experience demonstrates that the people will not fulfill, and to curse the people for apathy when they fail to live up to these arbitrary man-made duties.

So let us consider the people in the same candid scientific spirit in which we would consider the millstream, ascribing to them no unnatural virtues, no powers that have not been revealed in practice, no halo! Consider them as a phenomenon of nature, which in a given set of circumstances will actually do this and rarely do that.

POPULAR CAPACITY IS NOT UNLIMITED

"In the past we have approached the people as a pagan approached the waterfall—to worship and peer around for nymphs. We must today approach the people as the mill builder approaches the waterfall—open-eyed, unafraid, expecting no miracle, measuring its capacity, making allowance for its variations, and irreverently gauging its limitations in order that our mill shall not exceed them."

In considering the people thus we need not become cynics. A cat may look at a queen and a student of the American political panorama may apply a steel tape to the people and develop a discriminating admiration.

HOW TO GET RESPONSIVE DEFERENTIAL GOVERNMENT?

Human nature being what it has always been through the ages, the problem is: Given the American people, as they actually are, how may a government be organized among them which will be impelled promptly and anxiously to learn their desire and perform it?

This does not mean merely that the government will obey on those occasions when the people in a paroxysm proclaim from press, pulpit, and mass meeting that a certain thing must be done (though even that would be substantial gain in some American communities). It means that the government will be so sensitive to the currents of public opinion that it will even anticipate the popular wish.

There is nothing fanciful in such an ideal. Commerce is no less sensitive than that. Every taste of the public in food, art, and comfort is catered to without any conscious public inquiry for such satisfaction.

IMAGINARY OVERLOADS TO ILLUSTRATE THE PRINCIPLE

Democratic government has three important variations of form.

First: the town meeting where the people themselves gather in conference and, after debate, decide for themselves upon their laws and communal activities. This form of democratic government is suitable only in a limited field of application and is impracticable in large cities, or sparsely settled communities of large area, or communities where the governmental activities are complex and technical in their nature.

Second: the referendum, wherein laws are devised by some committee, official or otherwise, and submitted for approval to popular vote. This form of democratic government also has its limits of practicability; to have *all* the laws of a state made in that fashion would be quite out of the question.

Yet what would happen if some limitations of these forms of democratic government were ignored? Suppose Chicago were forced by the terms of an ancient village charter to submit its vast governmental activities to the tender mercies of an annual public meeting of all the citizens! Of course all the citizens could not get into a single hall or within sound of a single voice, and the few thousand who could do so by trick or violence could gain control and keep it year after year. That would be oligarchy—the rule of the few—although any politician armed with a few carefully selected catch phrases could indignantly argue that it was exactly the same form of government which, when used in little New England towns, had proved a triumph of pure democracy! Inasmuch as it looked as if it *ought* to be a democracy, thousands of citizens would actually believe that it must be one and that the true remedy for the resultant ills of the system lay in "more civic virtue," "a more militant good citizenship," and "the education of the people" so that they wouldn't shove and yell so at the meeting.

Does the picture of such stupid opposition seem overdrawn? It is actually the present condition of American political thought, except that I have imagined it applied to the town-meeting form, instead of to the third form of democratic government, namely, *government by elected officers.*

Government by elected officers, which of course is by far the most important of the three typical mechanisms for ascertaining and effectuating popular will, is supposed to work as follows:

It is known that a certain office in the government will on a certain day be filled by popular vote. The office is made attractive by salary and honor. Several eligible men covet the position and accordingly go among the voters seeking favor. If any considerable section of the voters want a certain policy adopted in that office, either the need of securing their support will lead candidates to announce concurrence in that desire or the opportunity to obtain office by means of their support will produce new candidates who do concur in it. Thus, any important demand among the people is automatically reflected in the list of candidates whose names appear on the ballot on election day. Then the voters go to the polls and, knowing which candidate best represents their individual desires, mark his name on the ballot. The officer thus elected is the one who has successfully catered to the wishes of the greatest number. The necessity that every elected officer shall thus find favor with the people gives the people ultimate control.

That is the theory. We are far from it in practice. It is a sound, workable theory nevertheless. But it has its limitations, just as town-meeting democracy has. And if these limitations are overstepped, oligarchy automatically results.

It would be easy to invent many an ostensibly democratic form of government by elected officers that would in all normal conditions result in oligarchy. Knowing that the people are obliged by natural economic pressure to work to their maximum efficiency at gainful occupation, it is only necessary somehow to elaborate the voters' duties beyond the amount which the bulk of the people have the time and disposition to master, whereupon, being in effect disfranchised, they automatically become the political slaves of those who do have the time and disposition.

Suppose, for example, that the polls, instead of being placed at every barber's shop, were placed in the center of the county, so that the bulk of the people had to travel considerable distances to get there. Suppose also that elections came every month instead of once or twice a year. Sheer inability to spend so much time on their unpaid duties of citizenship, when these interfered with the nearer duty of getting bread and butter, would automatically exclude the majority and throw control of the government into the hands of those few who lived near the polls. That form of government would, of course, be oligarchy; yet again the catch phrase makers could argue that it was genuine democracy and would work if the people were not so indolent.

The whole outcome of a failure to keep within this limitation of "convenience of voting" can thus be easily seen to be wholly unrelated to the "civic virtue" of the people.

If It Doesn't "Democ" . . .

Now for the conclusion based on this reasoning.

No plan of government is a democracy unless it is a democracy! The fact that those who planned it *intended* it to be a democracy and argue that it would be one if the people would only do thus and so, proves nothing—if it doesn't "democ," it isn't democracy!

So we emerge from this chapter of fancies which have demonstrated that democracy is hedged in with many limitations of practicality and that overstepping some of these limitations may result in oligarchy.

We peg the rest of this book on the fact that constituencies are human and too sovereign to be whipped into performance of all conceivable man-made "duties." Now we move nearer to the realities of American politics to see how that fact has been neglected in the inconsiderate and unsuccessful attempts to impose on clumsy constituencies prodigious and preposterous burdens of participation in government.

Where she catches most of the microbes that undermine her civic health.
(McCutcheon in Chicago *Tribune;* copyright, 1914.)

OFFICIAL PARTY COLUMN BALLOT
USE X ONLY IN MARKING BALLOT

OFFICIAL NON-PARTISAN BALLOT
USE X ONLY IN MARKING BALLOT

REPUBLICAN TICKET	DEMOCRATIC TICKET
For Governor	For Governor
THOMAS J. HERBERT	FRANK J. LAUSCHE
For Lieutenant Governor	For Lieutenant Governor
PAUL M. HERBERT	GEORGE D. NYE
For Secretary of State	For Secretary of State
EDWARD J. HUMMEL	CHARLES F SWEENEY
For Auditor of State	For Auditor of State
ROGER W. TRACY	JOSEPH T. FERGUSON
For Treasurer of State	For Treasurer of State
DON H. EBRIGHT	HARRY V. ARMSTRONG
For Attorney General	For Attorney General
HUGH S. JENKINS	HERBERT S. DUFFY
For Representative to Congress (At-Large)	For Representative to Congress (At-Large)
GEORGE H. BENDER	STEPHEN M. YOUNG
For Representative to Congress (22nd District)	For Representative to Congress (22nd District)
FRANCES P. BOLTON	JACK G. DAY
For State Senator	For State Senator
ALLEN N. CORLETT	JOSEPH W. BARTUNEK
HARRY E. DAVIS	WILLIAM M BOYD
ARTHUR W. FISKE	MARGARET A. MAHONEY
JOSEPH R. NUTT, JR.	HOWARD M. METZENBAUM
JACK A. PERSKY	EDWIN F. SAWICKI
EDWARD H. ROGERS	FRANK J. SVOBODA
For Representative to the General Assembly	For Representative to the General Assembly
MARGARET E. BARKLEY	JOSEPH H. AVELLONE
JAMES J. BARTON	MARIE BABKA
OLIVER P. BOLTON	ALBERT A. BENESCH
WILLIAM S. BURTON	JAMES M. CARNEY
LESSLIE G. CAMPBELL	EDWARD A. CIPRA
JOHN A. CORLETT	MICHAEL J. CROSSER
MILES D. EVANS	JOHN T. DUFFY
THOMAS E. HANN	GEORGE E. FEDOR
ROY F. McMAHON	JOHN J. GALLAGHER
WILLIAM E. MINSHALL, JR	ELIZABETH F. GORMAN
E. M. ROSE	WILLIAM J. HART
WILLIAM B. SAUNDERS	BERNARD V. MALIKOWSKI
KENNETH W. THORNTON	MARK McELROY
WM. R. VAN AKEN	JAMES J. McGETTRICK
GEORGE V WOODLING	JOHN F O'BRIEN
RICHARD H. WOODS	FRANCIS D. SULLIVAN
FRANCIS E. YOUNG	STEPHEN A ZONA
For County Commissioner	For County Commissioner
JOHN S. GILBERT	JOHN F. CURRY
EARL R. HOOVER	JOHN J. PEKAREK
For Prosecuting Attorney	For Prosecuting Attorney
HARRY T. MARSHALL	FRANK T. CULLITAN
For Clerk of Court of Common Pleas	For Clerk of Court of Common Pleas
THOS. C COOK	LEONARD F. FUERST
For Sheriff	For Sheriff
THOMAS F. McCAFFERTY	JOSEPH M. SWEENEY
For County Recorder	For County Recorder
JOHN M. LEWANDOWSKI	DONALD F. LYBARGER
For County Treasurer	For County Treasurer
RAYMOND J. TAYLOR	JOHN J BOYLE
For County Engineer	For County Engineer
EDWARD W CHADLAYNE	ALBERT S. PORTER
For Coroner	For Coroner
JOSEPH EDWARD SVOBODA	SAMUEL R. GERBER

For Judge of the Supreme Court (Full Term Commencing Jan. 1, 1949) (Vote for not more than one)
CHARLES H. HUBBELL
EDWARD C. TURNER

For Judge of the Supreme Court (Full Term Commencing Jan. 2, 1949) (Vote for not more than one)
ROBERT M. SOHNGEN
KINGSLEY A. TAFT

For Judge of the Supreme Court (Unexpired Term ending Jan. 1, 1953) (Vote for not more than one)
JAMES GARFIELD STEWART

For Judge of the Court of Appeals (Full Term Commencing Feb. 9, 1949) (Vote for not more than one)
JOY SETH HURD

For Judge of the Court of Common Pleas (Full Term Commencing Jan. 1, 1949) (Vote for not more than one)
GEO. P. BAER
EDWARD BLYTHIN
ARTHUR KRAUSE

For Judge of the Court of Common Pleas (Full Term Commencing Jan. 2, 1949) (Vote for not more than one)
ALVA R. CORLETT
JOSEPH H. SILBERT

For Judge of the Court of Common Pleas (Full Term Commencing Jan. 2, 1949) (Vote for not more than one)
HARRY A HANNA
HUGH A. McNAMEE
DAVID C. MECK, JR.

For Judge of the Court of Common Pleas (Full Term Commencing Jan. 4, 1949) (Vote for not more than one)
BURT W GRIFFIN

For Judge of the Court of Common Pleas (Full Term Commencing Jan. 5, 1949) (Vote for not more than one)
SAMUEL E. KRAMER

For Judge of the Court of Common Pleas (Full Term Commencing Jan. 6, 1949) (Vote for not more than one)
JAMES C. CONNELL

For Judge of the Court of Common Pleas (Full Term Commencing Jan. 7, 1949) (Vote for not more than one)
ADRIAN G. NEWCOMB

For Judge of the Court of Common Pleas (Full Term Commencing Feb. 9, 1949) (Vote for not more than one)
ARTHUR H. DAY

For Judge of the Court of Common Pleas (Unexpired Term ending Jan. 2, 1953) (Vote for not more than one)
WILLIAM F. BURNS
BENJAMIN D. NICOLA

For Judge of the Probate Court (Full Term Commencing Feb. 9, 1949) (Vote for not more than one)
NELSON J. BREWER

The longest ballot in the world. Cuyahoga County, Ohio, 1948.

Chapter II

THE LONG BALLOTS

The long ballot is the politician's ballot; the Short Ballot
is the people's ballot!

—Slogan of the National Short
Ballot Organization, 1910

GETTING a government that will normally obey the people is
a matter of making it feasible for the people to put into public
office the men they really want there. This, in turn, is a matter of
exposing candidates to adequate public examination before election,
so that when the voters go to the polls they will have had ample
information to enable them to decide which man they want as their
representative and servant. Their only protection is to see what they
are getting. Arrange for the fullest, most intensive scrutiny, and you
have done all that can be done. Scrutiny at election is vital to democracy. Failure to provide the people with full opportunity to
scrutinize the candidates leaves them fighting blindly and futilely
in the dark.

CONCEALMENT IN LONG BALLOTS

One method of concealing the candidate from the public gaze is
to have *so many* elections at one time that each candidate is sheltered by the confusion.

Notice I use the plural—"elections." The habit of saying "election
day" instead of "elections day," and "election" instead of "elections,"
has caused us real trouble. When we fill ten offices by popular vote
in a single day it is really ten elections.

When Ohio holds forty-seven elections on one day, does the
average citizen read the names, casting a straight Republican ticket
only when finding that each Republican candidate is to his liking?
Or does the average citizen ignore the individual names for the

11

most part and place his dependence on the party management? To find this out, demand of the average citizen on the evening following elections day, "Whom did you vote for?"

"Dewey for president and Lausche for governor," he will answer.

"Who else?"

"The Republican national ticket and the Democratic state ticket."

"But what men? You voted for forty-seven, you know, and you've only named two! Whom did you vote to send to the state legislature? And whom did you pick for county clerk? And for coroner?"

"Oh, I don't know—I'm not in politics."

In 1950 Dr. Gallup, pursuing his usual methods for getting a fair sampling, asked 1500 voters after the November election:

Some people say election ballots are too long and it is difficult to know the names of all the candidates. Could you tell me the names of all the candidates you voted for in the recent election of November 7? Or do you only remember the candidates running for the most important offices?

Nineteen per cent *said* they could remember all the candidates but their confidence in the matter was not tested by calling upon them to prove it by reeling off the names or to answer a test question as to a typical secondary contest, and their say-so was undependable. The range was from 14 and 15 per cent for manual workers and union members to 27 per cent for college men; 76 per cent admitted they could remember only the most important.

When the ballot is long, i.e., when there are many offices to be filled simultaneously by popular vote, the people (except in small village elections where they can recognize every name) will not scrutinize every name but will give their attention to a few conspicuous ones and vote for the others blindly. In voting blindly for any name the politicians select, the people are simply delegating their choice to a few half-known, possibly irresponsible men whom they had no voice in choosing. The attempt to get the people to say who shall be county clerk, for instance, has failed. It is like asking a question of a crowd and accepting the few scattered answers as the verdict of the whole mob. This is not democracy, but oligarchy, just as in the imagined case of a county that held incessant elections at an inconvenient polling place. Here it is not the inconvenience of *voting* which practically disfranchises the bulk of the citizens but the inconvenience of *voting informedly*. In the test of practice it has thus been demonstrated that, if the people are asked forty-seven questions at one time, they will not give back forty-seven answers of their own but will let others make most of these answers for them.

This statement is no reflection on the morals or intelligence of the people. (Even if it were, in planning a workable democracy we should have to cut our cloth accordingly.) It is simply evidence that there is such a thing as asking the people more questions than they will answer carefully.

Go into Politics?

To "go into politics," impossible as this generally is, is the only way our typical citizen can gain any direct information regarding most of the men on whom he is to pass judgment at the polls. His newspaper perforce barely mentions the candidates for minor offices; its limelight flits over them fitfully and, finding nothing picturesque, leaves them in darkness. Candidates sometimes campaign and get elected on the tail of the ticket without ever getting a line of newspaper publicity. They can get no individual hearing because the public is hardly aware that their little office is being contested for. A candidate for clerk of courts who tried to explain to the people the work of his office and the improvements he proposed to install would be classed as "eccentric" and his efforts would be futile. This or that audience might listen respectfully enough, but he could never force the issue to a point where his opponents would feel obliged to reply. The people, unable to oversee so many separate contests, simply allow sets of candidates to be tied together for them in bunches like asparagus and then vote them by the bunch. A hopeful independent candidacy in Ohio for one of these minor offices is almost unheard of. An independent contestant would be utterly lost in the shuffle and could not secure any public attention.

How Much Shorter Must the Ballot Be Made?

If forty-seven places is too long, then how much shorter must the ballot be?

If the people are not to rely blindly on ready-made lists prepared for them, they must rely on individual lists of their own. That fact reduces us to the psychological question: How many candidates will the average man remember for himself? How many separate contests will he keep clearly defined in his memory? How many mental images or impressions of contesting candidates will he hold without confusion? For on election day he is to see their names before him on the ballot and to choose for himself on a basis of his knowledge regarding them.

We are near enough now to the end of the problem to establish a rule:

To keep a government by elected officers from becoming an oligarchy, *the ballot must be short!*

How short?

Short enough (!) so that the number of choices to be made by the voters will not be so great as to conceal individual candidates from adequate public scrutiny.

BRITISH BALLOT NOW AND FORMERLY

The British system manages to do this.

The British voter is commonly asked to vote for one, his district member of Parliament, and, in another year, for a local councilman from his ward. His ballot does not bear party labels; if he knows anything, he can identify the name of his party candidate without a label. All other public servants are appointed. There is democracy in its most feasible and simple form!

It was not always so. Prior to 1888 Britons elected a considerable array. Graham Wallas in his wise classic, *Human Nature in Politics*, relates:

. . . Since 1888, parliament, in reconstructing the system of English local government, has steadily diminished the number of elections, with the avowed purpose of increasing their efficiency. The Local Government Acts of 1888 and 1894 swept away thousands of elections for Improvement Boards, Burial Boards, Vestries, etc. In 1902 the separately elected School Boards were abolished, and it is certain that the Guardians of the Poor will soon follow them. The Rural Parish Councils, which were created in 1894, and which represented a reversion by the Liberal Party to the older type of democratic thought, have been a failure, and will either be abolished or will remain ineffective because no real administrative powers will be given to them.

In the twenty years after that was written, simplification advanced as predicted, lagging in the rural districts. In the county-borough areas comprising almost all the large cities there is now

1	**HOGG** (Quintin McGarel Hogg of The Corner House, Heath-view Gardens, Putney Heath, London, S W. 15, Bar-rister-at-Law.)	
2	**KEELING** (Ernest Keeling of 57 New Road, Headington, Oxford, Organiser.)	
3	**PAKENHAM** (Lady Elizabeth Pakenham of 10 Linnell Drive, Hamp-stead Way, London, N.W. 11, Married Woman.)	
4	**TWEDDLE** (Donald William Tweddle of 13 Scillonian Road, Guild-ford, Organiser.)	

A parliamentary election ballot in England, 1950. Party labels not needed.

only one local authority for all purposes, namely, the county-borough council, and then the voter has only to select his councilor and his member of Parliament. In the administrative counties there are two layers of elected bodies in the urban parts, i.e., county councils and county-borough councils. And in the rural parts there may be as many as three layers by reason of there being also a parish council. Thus a rural English parish voter may conceivably be called on to make as many as four choices in a year though not on the same day. That is the rare and theoretic maximum. When a councilman's term expires, however, he goes on automatically for another term unless a contestant appears, and such perfunctory renewals of tenure are common, greatly reducing the frequency of elections.

Likewise in almost all nations but ours, elections are only for legislative bodies—parliaments or local councils.

FIVE SIMULTANEOUS CONTESTS IS FEASIBLE

We do not need to get the ballot down to a contest for a single office, but five may be the proper outside limit. In many municipal governments five councilmen are elected at large at one time on nonpartisan ballots at elections separate from those for other elective offices. Voters seem usually to develop their respective individual opinions and select each his own pet five from the array of aspirants listed without sponsoring labels on the ballots. Indeed, voters under such circumstances may resent as officious an attempt by party managers to guide their pencils to candidates whom the managers support as "regular." Voters, having informed opinions, make their own slates.

BUT NINE IS TOO MANY, AS SHOWN IN FIVE CITIES

In the cities of Richmond, Virginia, Dallas and Fort Worth, Texas, Long Beach and Sacramento, California, under the council-manager plan, the councils of nine are the board of directors of the city, not overshadowed by the dramatic single figure of a powerful mayor. But the enhanced importance of those councils is not enough to induce most voters to learn enough about the candidates to pick out nine individual choices and remember them long enough to find them and mark them on the nonpartisan ballot. The voters on the contrary accept ready-made tickets supplied to them by committees or associations of sponsors and, with the aid of pocket memos or otherwise, install one slate or another intact. These slates are not put forward by the local committees of the national parties, to be sure, but by local civic groups or self-arranged groupings of candidates for mutual support. In the two Texas and two California cities [1] tickets have been the outstanding

[1] Omitting the Richmond experience, which has been identical but covers only two elections up to date, and San Antonio, which had its first election under the plan in 1951.

feature of the municipal elections and hardly any "independent" ever gets into the council, as shown in Reading A (in Part III of this book). As that story of fifty-three elections shows, nine is just too many to elect at one time.

Thereby, for good or ill, power gravitates from the voters to the ticket makers, who may be high-minded or otherwise and whose power is capable of great abuse.

Chapter III

ONLY ATTENTION-ATTRACTING OFFICES
SHOULD BE ELECTIVE

Simplification—simplification—simplification is the task
that awaits us.

—WOODROW WILSON, 1909

IN any examination of the phenomena of overlong ballots, we find
the evidence inextricably entangled with a second cause of invisibility—namely, the *unimportance* of many elective offices.

INSIGNIFICANCE AS A SECOND CAUSE OF INVISIBILITY

We might have a short ballot that covered only one office; but if
it were that of coroner, the people at large would shrug their
shoulders and pass on indifferent. There are and ought to be other
things more important to the people than the question, "Who shall
be coroner?" It is no slight thing to ask all the citizens of a county
to bestir themselves all at one time regarding *any* question. The
question may be too trivial. The average man's share of interest in
getting the better candidate for coroner elected is so infinitesimal
as not to warrant the slightest exertion on his part. The powers of
the coroner in a small community are insignificant. In a large city
the coroner may have a busy office, but in proportion to the community he is insignificant still. If 90 per cent of the people are indifferent to the issue, the remaining 10 per cent will have their way
in the matter. And there we have a bit of oligarchy. If the coronership were the only office to be filled on a certain day, only a few
of the people would go to the polls, and the attempt to make the
people stand up and be counted on the issue would be a failure. If
the mayor and the coroner were the only two offices to be filled, the
people would be drawn to the polls by the mayoralty contest, but

18

their votes on the coronership would represent no clear or adequate information and would be easily influenced by the few citizens who *were* interested. A full vote for coroner under these circumstances would be no more a real verdict of the people than in the other case.

NATURE OF OFFICE MAY MAKE IT INVISIBLE

An elective office may also elude public scrutiny by being uninteresting in *nature*. Public scrutiny has to be attracted; it cannot be directed to dull matters by admonitions written into law or implied by the writers of constitutions and charters. When an elective office thus retires into approximate invisibility, the voting of most voters thereon becomes blind and perfunctory, leaving a few political professionals in undisturbed control.

JUDGES, FOR INSTANCE

Judgeships are examples of an office that commonly fails to attract public scrutiny. Especially in the presence of contests for more dramatic offices or amid the confusions of a metropolis! Here is a vignette from the *World Telegram*, May 15, 1948, showing how the people "choose" elective judges in New York City:

Here's the deal on the King's County Court vacancy created by the recent death of Judge Franklin Taylor, a Democrat. Governor Dewey will NOT make an appointment to fill his term, which expires December 31, 1949. Instead, in the November election, City Court Justice George J. Joyce (D., ALP), a former law partner of Mayor O'Dwyer, will be the candidate of both Democrats and Republicans. In return, the Democrats will endorse Supreme Court Justice John MacCrate (R.), whose term expires this year.

Also, City Court Justice Sylvester Sabbatino (D.), running for re-election this year, will receive GOP endorsement. Payoff for that OK will come when Democrats nominate City Magistrate Francis X. Giaccone (R.) for City Court to fill the vacancy left by Justice Joyce's elevation.

CASE OF STATE TREASURER

Many other offices lie outside the spotlight. Technical administrative offices, for instance, are habitually in obscurity. What, for instance, can the candidate for the post of state treasurer do to demonstrate his superiority over rival claimants for the position? He can claim that he will be honest and systematic and intelligent —but so can his rivals. If the accounting system of the state is out of date he can promise reform—but he can't stir the people to strenuous partisanship on his behalf by talking about bookkeeping. Nothing he can do can alter the fact that there is little or nothing in the state treasurership out of which to make an issue that will fire the imagination of a million voters.

Into this classification of undebatable offices fall many that are now elective in the United States. To retain them on the elective list is undemocratic. Nothing is so undemocratic as government in the dark, and to put on the elective list offices which are naturally and inevitably invisible is compelling the people to delegate power to officials cloaked in darkness. The more obscure the office, by reason either of its insignificance or of its undebatable character, the weaker is the control of the people over it, and the stronger is the control of the politician.

The net result of all these considerations is to show a need for the elimination from the elective list of (1) all offices that are not large enough in themselves to stir the people to take sides; (2) all offices that determine no policies large enough to stir the people to take sides.

Such Offices Must Be Dropped from Ballots

For if the people won't settle the question you put to them, some few self-seekers will. To shout at the people questions which the people either will not or cannot answer carefully is not doing the people a favor. It is only making certain that the questions will be answered by someone else.

We must confine the participation of the people to questions which they want to decide. *Each elective office must be interesting.*

Test Is: Does the Office Attract Scrutiny?

The test to apply to an office to ascertain whether it is "interesting" is, of course, to inquire whether it does actually interest the people. Your opinion or mine as to whether the office of judge *ought* to interest the people is of no importance; the question is, Does it? If the bulk of the people are interested enough to divide on the question and stand up and be counted on the issue, then the judge may properly be made elective. If only a few of the people develop opinions clear enough to impel them to take sides on the contest, then your plan of having all the people select the judge has failed to work. You have created oligarchy instead of democracy. You must then make the judge appointive by someone whom the people did select.

The people must take an interest in all their electoral work if they are to be masters. If they do not take an interest in a given ballot there are two solutions: change the people or change the ballot. As the people are too big to be spanked, and since human nature in the mass responds but slowly to prayer, it is good sense to shorten the ballot.

Don't forget our major premise—if it doesn't "democ," it isn't democracy!

Chapter IV

THE PHENOMENA OF BLIND VOTING

> You cannot get good public service from the public
> servant if you cannot see him, and there is no more effec-
> tive way of hiding than by mixing him up with a mul-
> titude of others.
>
> —THEODORE ROOSEVELT, to
> Ohio Constitutional Convention,
> 1912

AS an example of universal experience there comes to mind the
time I prepared to cast my first vote. I was twenty-one years
old then and Abraham Lincoln, a little round man, captain of
my precinct for the Republicans, invited me to join the Republican party club. I demurred that, being rather independent in my
views, I might not be much of a party man, for I had resolved to
vote for the best man for each office regardless of party. He looked
at me with hurt reproachful eyes and said gently, "Well, of course,
that wouldn't be right!"

However, some weeks later I entered a polling booth and un-
folded my first ballot. I found to my dismay that I was hopelessly
unprepared. There near the top were the four principal candidates
on whom my ardent hopes were fastened, but there were fifteen
other officers to be elected—judges of several kinds and the county
officers, sheriff, register, clerk, and four coroners. On these latter
fifteen I had no information, and the ballot printer could have put
the Democratic candidates into the Republican column without my
detecting the error. With mortification I voted blindly for the word
"Republican" in each of the fifteen contests and thereby, of course,
accepted without scrutiny the offerings of the party leaders, as they
knew I would. Walking home with my father, I had the presence
of mind to withhold confession of my shortcomings and ask him
whom he voted for. He named the same head-of-the-ticket candidates who had been my choice. "But whom did you vote for for

judge of general sessions?" I persisted. "For the Republican, who-
ever he was," said Father. "And for sheriff? And coroners?" He
looked toward me, puzzled. "How should I know?" he said.

PROOFS OF BLINDNESS IN VOTING

In the decade after that, Charles W. Eliot, then president of
Harvard, and Woodrow Wilson, then president of Princeton, found
occasions to make public avowal of their practice of voting 80 per
cent of their ballot lists in complete ignorance of the candidates.

In many audiences of voters I have asked for a show of hands.
"How many of you know the name of the governor?" Every hand,
of course, went up. "How many know the name of the secretary of
the state?" The response would be of the order of magnitude of two
per hundred. Likewise as to attorney general of the state or the
various county officers.

THE MICHIGAN POLL

The extent of blind voting—following, usually, a party label without information about the candidates—has been scientifically meas-
ured only once. The procedure requires selecting some minor
elective offices and asking an adequate sample array of voters
whether they can name the incumbents. Or whether they can name
the candidate they have recently voted for. The careful modern
methods of public opinion surveying were utilized thus in Michigan in October, 1950, when the Legislative Committee on Reorganization of State Government made the unique study exhibited
in Reading B. Michigan elects twenty-five administrative officials
and board members in its state government; not all of them, however, in any one year. With careful adherence to the best polling
techniques, Bay County was singled out as an area exhibiting typical voter behavior in the past in which to examine the "impossible
task that voters are expected to perform with our long ballots."
Interviews in rural and urban sections produced 323 usable answers,
all obtained on one day, seventeen days before the well-attended
state election. To encourage frank answers some easy questions of
no importance to the inquiry were asked in each interview. The
first key question was, "Which of the state offices do you know
most about?" Twenty-six per cent picked the state highway com-

missioner, but 75 per cent of them could not name him. The secretary of state had recently run for governor. Of those who picked the secretary as the most familiar minor officer, 73 per cent could not name him. Seven-seven per cent could not name the superintendent of public instruction, 81 per cent could not name the attorney general, and 96 per cent could not name the treasurer although he had been in office four terms, the longest of the incumbent minor officers. Another test, of 500 college students, was confirmatory, with as high as 96 per cent unable to name certain of the minor officers.

The inquirers did not go on in the traditional way to denounce the condition as apathy. "The conclusion," says the report correctly, "would seem to raise a serious challenge against the validity of electing officers to fill such positions."

GALLUP POLLS, 1944, 1945, 1947

Modern techniques of public opinion polling have otherwise ventured only slightly into this subject and there is justification for much more investigation. *The Gallup Political Almanac* of 1946 reports that in October, 1944, just before the presidential election, 33 per cent could not name the Republican candidate for vice-president (Bricker) and 38 per cent could not name the Democratic candidate (Truman). Forty-two per cent of the voters checked in January, 1945, could correctly name both the U.S. senators of their state, 24 per cent more could name one, and 34 per cent could not name either! In August, 1947, Gallup published a poll in which only 38 per cent could correctly name their representative in Congress. These, of course, are offices which must always remain elective, and the indications can only make us more pessimistic as to the showing the same voters would make if checked on minor offices.

VOTERS NEGLECT MINOR OFFICERS—VOTE FALLS OFF

Voters who, as they mark their ballots, reach a string of candi- • dates they know nothing whatever about are commonly encouraged to give their proxy to their party managers, in effect, by the facility on the ballot known as the party circle (or square); one mark there votes a whole party ticket from president to coroner. Countless American voters live and die of old age without ever venturing to split a ticket. But the total vote for the minor offices nevertheless always falls off from that of the top officials despite the party circle's enticement to easy regularity. Thus Illinois has seen 300,000 fewer voters voting for candidates for the office of clerk of the Supreme Court than for the presidency, and a Pennsylvania comparison exhibited 120,000 voters who voted for president failing to vote for auditor general.

WHEN PARTY CIRCLE IS OMITTED, VOTE FALLS OFF FURTHER

When, as in eighteen states having the Massachusetts office-group ballot form, the party circle is omitted, the voter is required to make a separate X mark (or move a separate voting machine lever) for every candidate he votes for. Most voters reaching the obscure minor offices on such ballots also follow a party label slavishly and undiscriminatingly all the way down the sheet, but others in great numbers do not vote at all for these minor posts. When in 1950 Ohio dropped the party circle and adopted the office-group ballot, there was a widening of the gap between the total vote for governor and the total vote of the two lowest opposing candidates for state representatives. In its most populous county (Cuyahoga) the latter total was 72 per cent of the total gubernatorial votes in 1946 and 77 per cent in 1948, with party-circle voting; in 1950, on the new office-group ballot, only 56 per cent of those who had voted for governor voted also for one or the other of the lowest pair of the seventeen state representatives from that county located thirty items down the sheet. But it is not to be concluded that all, or indeed any, of that 56 per cent could have defended all of the forty-seven votes they cast that day or could have even identified that evening all the men they "selected" if the pairs of names had been read to them.

TOP POSITION ON OHIO BALLOTS

In 1948 two men were running in the Republican primary for the party's nomination for the state Senate from a certain district of Ohio. With no opinion to express and no label to guide them, voters on such occasions are believed to vote for the top name, so the law required rotation in that position and thus one William Tyrrell had top position on 144 voting machines and his opponent was at the

top in 128. Tyrrell got 59.5 per cent of the votes when at the top and
38.5 per cent when not. Of the 13,980 votes, top line won 60 per
cent, and of the 272 precincts, top line carried 85 per cent.[1]

The office of representative in Congress, of course, must always
be elective. The task of political reform is to clear away the other
ballot clutter which obscures it. In August, 1951, there was produced this informative bit of evidence in the House committee report on the election contest between Walter B. Huber (D.) and
William H. Ayres (R.) in an Ohio congressional district. Mr. Huber,
defeated by 1921 votes, demonstrated incontestably that some of
the county boards of elections in his district had failed to rotate his
name properly to the top of the list of three candidates in the office
group on the ballots an approximately equal number of times.
Trouble had arisen because there were eight candidates for state
assembly subject to the same requirement and the press would have
had to be stopped twenty-four times to give each assembly candidate and each congressional candidate top position on an equal
number of ballots. The board of elections rotated the congressional
candidates crudely so that Mr. Ayres got top position in two counties 50 per cent of the time, middle position 25 per cent, and bottom
position 25 per cent, whereas Mr. Huber got top position only 25
per cent and bottom position 50 per cent of the time. Likewise on
148 voting machines. The official count gave Ayres 102,868, Huber
100,947, and Brenneman, the Independent, 7246.

As to the influence of this disparity in advantage of top position,
the legal requirement of itself is testimony, supported by what
proofs from past elections we do not know. The congressional committee's minority statement pointed out that Mr. Brenneman received a total of 1144 votes in the thirty-seven polling places where
his name was on the top line on the voting machine and only 161
votes on the thirty-seven voting machines bearing his name on the
third line. In publicity immediately subsequent to the election,
Huber claimed that his name was at the bottom twice as many
times as Ayres' name in Democratic precincts where Huber could
have been expected to make a good showing, but that he got a poor
vote when his name was at the bottom; also that each time a candidate was in third place he received a smaller percentage of the vote

[1] *National Municipal Review,* March, 1950, p. 110.

than he received when in first place. Huber believed the evidence indicated that ballot position had made a critical difference, more than enough to offset the 1 per cent lead of Mr. Ayres.

The majority report of the committee seated Mr. Ayres on the ground that his opponent had failed to exhaust remedies available to him under state law.

The case exhibits how infirm are the convictions of many voters in a congressional election under long-ballot conditions.

Another approach to the measurement of the extent of blind, uninformed voting is found in the dearth of information issued and published about candidates for minor offices. Let us suppose a voter clips from his newspapers every mention of the two leading candidates for secretary of state for review on the eve of election day; he will accumulate almost nothing.

SYMMETRY OF ELECTION RETURNS

Still another index of the prevalence of blind voting is to be found in the election returns. Look at the November, 1948, Wayne County (Detroit and environs) ballot reproduced on page 28. Observe the minor offices on the state ticket: lieutenant governor, secretary of state, attorney general, state treasurer, and auditor general! They are minor as compared with the governor in power, patronage, and budgetary importance. Although, of course, each must operate a department of some size—bigger, for example, than that of the mayor of a good-sized city—the work they direct is technical and fails to attract public scrutiny on any state-wide scale. The voter may mark such a ballot by thirty-nine separate discriminating X's in thirty-nine of the little boxes spread over the spacious (18″ × 24″) sheet.[2] Or, by an easy single X in a party circle at the top, he can vote the whole column. From 85 to 90 per cent of the voters in 1944 did the latter according to a reexamination of 10 per cent of the ballots. Ballot clerks, counting the vote, sort out these

[2] There were four other ballots presented to those voters on that day, covering presidential electors (one decision to be made by each voter) (1), a by-election for a vacancy in the city council (1), a nonpartisan ballot for eight judicial positions (8), a referendum ballot posing five state constitutional amendments and one question re the voiding of a certain pending law (6). Total simultaneous questions for the voter, fifty-five! Not a record, however! The number in Cleveland, Ohio, on that day, including nineteen bond issue and other referenda, was seventy-five. Replica on Page 10.

OFFICIAL BALLOT—County of Wayne—General November Election
Tuesday, November 2, 1948

INSTRUCTIONS—To vote a straight party ticket make a cross (X) in the circle under the name of your party. Nothing further need be done. To vote for a candidate not on your party ticket, make a cross (X) in the square ☐ before his name.

If 2 or more candidates are to be elected to the same office, and you desire to vote for candidates not on your ticket, make a cross (X) in the square ☐ before the names of the candidates for whom you desire to vote on the other ticket, and strike out an equal number of names on your party ticket, for that office.

If you do not desire to vote any party ticket, do not make a cross (X) in the circle at the head of any ticket, but make a cross (X) in the square ☐ before the name of each candidate for whom you desire to vote.

If you wish to vote for a candidate not on any ticket, write or place the name of such candidate on your ticket opposite the name of the office.

Before leaving the booth, fold the ballot so that the initials of the inspector may be seen on the outside.

NAMES OF OFFICES VOTED FOR:	REPUBLICAN TICKET ○	DEMOCRATIC PARTY ○	PROHIBITION TICKET ○	SOCIALIST LABOR PARTY OF AMERICA ○	SOCIALIST WORKERS PARTY ○	PROGRESSIVE PARTY ○	SOCIALIST PARTY ○
STATE Governor	KIM SIGLER 1	G. MENNEN WILLIAMS 59	GORDON PHILLIPS 115	ARTHUR CHENOWETH 166	HOWARD LERNER 173		EMANUEL SEIDLER 211
Lieutenant Governor	EUGENE C. KEYES 2	JOHN W CONNOLLY 60	PERRY HAYDEN 116	JAMES HORVATH 167			LEONARD KLUE 212
Secretary of State	FREDERICK M. ALGER, JR. 3	JOEL P FOX 61	F. HAROLD MUNN 117	JAMES SIM 168	WILLIAM H. YANCEY 174	ROBERTA BARROW 176	HELEN KING 213
Attorney General	STUART B. WHITE 4	STEPHEN J. ROTH 62	LEROY B. McNALLY 118	MARION L. WALBRIDGE 169		ERNEST GOODMAN 177	SAMUEL SILVERSTEIN 214
State Treasurer	D HALE BRAKE 7	JOHN J. KOZAREN 63	CECIL CLAPP 119	GRACE HAMILTON 170		NANCY CARTER MORSE 178	ANTHONY KRAWULSKI 215
Auditor General	MERL K. ATEN 8	MARGARET PRICE 64	BEN R. WILLIAMS 120	CHARLES SCHWARTZ 171		A. JOHN ZAREMBA 179	JAMES H. STITES 216
CONGRESSIONAL United States Senator	HOMER FERGUSON 9	FRANK E. HOOK 65	HAROLD A. LINDAHL 121	THEOS A. GROVE 172	GENORA DOLLINGER 175		MICHAEL MAGEE 217
Representative in Congress FOURTEENTH DISTRICT	HAROLD F YOUNGBLOOD 12	LOUIS C. RABAUT 68	A. L. LEACH 124				A. H. SUPPUS 220
LEGISLATIVE State Senator FIRST DISTRICT	CHARLES N. YOUNGBLOOD 16	HAROLD M. RYAN 72	ARTHUR VALADE 128				AUGUST KERBER 224
Representatives in State Legislature FIRST DISTRICT	SHERMAN LITTLEFIELD 23	TRACY M. DOLL 79	SIDNEY A. SHORT 134			FRANCIS GUTHRIE 185	LEATRICE BRAZEAU 230
	EDWARD W. FREY, 24	MICHAEL J. O'BRIEN 80 Public Works Inspector	JOHN K. WILLIAMS 135			CLEAVON GOVAN 186	ERNEST BROWN 231
	HARRY A. McDONALD, JR. 25	THOMAS C. O'BRIEN 81 Juvenile Court Guard	DONALD C. MARTIN 136			BEN KOCEL 187	MARGARET FERGUSON 232
	D. NEIL REID 26	FRED R. DINGMAN 82	CASPER CASAN 137			EDMUND BUCZAK 188	BELLE GOLDSMITH 233
	JOHN P FITZGERALD 27	PATRICK J. O'MALLEY 83	WALTER ALLIE 138			ANN LEMMONS 189	ANTHONY JANUSZYN 234
	HUGH J. WOOD 28	JOSEPH J. KOWALSKI 84	LUCILE A. MARTZ 139			ARTHUR McPHAUL 190	ALLAN KATZ 235
	HENRY T GAGE 29	PETER J. KELLY 85	ALBERT SHORT 140			PATRICIA MURPHY FRANK 191	MANNY KREINIK 236
	CLARENCE E. HOFFMAN 30	JOHN J. FITZPATRICK 86	PETER WISEMAN 141			SAMUEL LIFSHITZ 192	GEORGE LAFOREST 237
	THOMAS Q. QUINLAN 31	STANLEY NOVAK 87	AARON B. JANES 142			PAUL A. HENLEY 193	DAVID LIFSHITZ 238
	L. W. METCALFE 32	ED CAREY 88	ROBERT McLIVE 143			WALLACE D. McLAY 194	MARVIN DEBS MELTZER 239
	JOHN EDWARD ROWLAND 33	MICHAEL NOVAK 89	LEE COY 144			JOSEPH GULVEZAN 195	LEROY MITCHELL 240
	HAROLD V FIELD 34	DAVID L. LINDSAY 90	A. M. LEWIS 145			JAMES G. COUSER 196	MINT NAUTA 241
	DAN MILLS 35	JOSEPH G. O'CONNOR 91	BERTHA KIDD 146			SOPHIE STEMPKEY 197	OLGA PIONTKOWSKY 242
	PAUL ARNOLD 36	N D. EDWARDS 92	FOXYE ANN HIGGS 147			PAUL BOATIN 198	W ROSS 243
	J. R. JEFFRIES 37	FRANK A. MAHONEY 93	ERNEST C. VALADE 148			OTTO CAPP 199	JEAN SEIDEL 244
	JOHN MAURER 38	JACK FULLER 94	FRANK H. LOCKER 149			DEAN ROBB 200	MURRAY SEIDLER 245
	PHILIP S. WILLIAMS 39	MARTHA W. GRIFFITHS 95	ALICE B. COY 150			JOHN R. GERLACH 201	CELIA STERN 246
	WILLIAM J. HAYES 40	EDGAR CURRIE 96	CLYDE WATTS 151				ALBERT WARZYCKI 247
	JAMES B. COGHRAN 41	CHESTER LEWANDOWSKI 97	GEORGE W CAMPBELL 152				ANNA WEINSTEIN 248
	WALTER W. AMES 42	JOHN J. PLOCZAK 98	CARL NOTON 153				DAVID WILTERSEN 249
	FRED E. DUNN 43	THEODORE J WILA 99	RAYMOND R. LAMB 154				ANTHONY ZARCZYNSKI 250
COUNTY Prosecuting Attorney	JAMES N. McNALLY 50	GERALD K. O'BRIEN 106					
Sheriff	EDWARD BEHRENDT 51	ANDREW C. BAIRD 107	OTTO SATERDAK 160			EDWARD PERRY 207	
County Clerk	ARCHIBALD LEADBETTER 52	EDGAR M GRAVGIN 108	CHAS. C. VALADE 161				
County Treasurer	WILLIAM A. LAU 53	HAROLD L. STOLL 209	MOBY N. BLATCHFURD 162				
Register of Deeds	WILLIAM C. COMSTOCK 54	BERNARD J YOUNGBLOOD 110	DON TAYLOR 163			DEVERA STOCKER 208	
County Auditor	JAMES L. MASON 55	ANTHUR A. SLMERACKI 111				WILLIAM H. JOHNSON 209	
County Drain Commissioner	HARRY B. BRADLEY 56	GEORGE A. DINGMAN 112	RAY W. TUER 164			DON CHRISTIE 210	
Coroners	LLOYD K. BABCOCK 57	ALBERT A. HUGHES 113	M. M. AMES 165				
	ALBERT L. FRENCH 58	SAMUEL D. MILTON 114					

straight ballots, count them, and then with a sigh turn to the ballots of those ultra-particular individualists who made extra work for them by pick-and-choosing.

The symmetry of the returns exhibits the prevalence of the straight voting.

Here is the outcome in Wayne County (November 2, 1948):

	Democratic	Republican
Lieutenant governor	509,445	304,235
Secretary of state	482,061	322,943
Attorney general	494,269	299,026
State treasurer	499,519	299,001
Auditor general	492,888	300,745

The trifling percentage of variation in the respective party votes is significant and typical of such elections everywhere in America.

Going further down that same ballot we see that list of representatives in the state legislature—twenty-one to be chosen. Now legislatures are certainly important *in toto* and legislators must always be elective. But divide the power of the legislatures into small enough bits and the individual memberships can be reduced to pettiness and obscurity, eluding public scrutiny. Did the voters in this bailiwick have, each of them, twenty-one choices among the galaxy of talent offered? No; the amount of discrimination was hardly enough to show in the votes, which came out as shown in the chart on page 31.

That ballot was partisan, and the voters, by voting in 85 to 90 per cent of the cases a straight ticket by a cross mark in the circle, voted for twenty-one; the range of votes from 399,147 for the highest Democrat to 379,491 for the lowest compared with 540,105 for governor and 489,654 for president. Among the Republicans, the range for state representatives from 234,689 to 217,285 compared with 303,078 for governor and 311,773 for president. So, given the party label as a guide, about 75 per cent of those who voted for president and governor voted for all twenty-one.

In the preceding party primaries, however, with a 30 per cent attendance at the polls but consisting as it presumaby did of those most interested in politics and best informed, there was, of course, no party or factional label for these twenty-one state representatives.

"For Experts Only"

Then only 23 per cent of those voting used their full quota of twenty-one choices.

But it cannot be plausibly pleaded that the 75 per cent who followed the party label to the extent of voting for all twenty-one candidates at the final election were demonstrating any greater knowledge of what they were doing than the 30 per cent of the eligible voters in the dominant party who turned up at the Democratic primaries with no label to guide them. The latter condition furnishes the real test. In a study of the 1944 primaries Donald S.

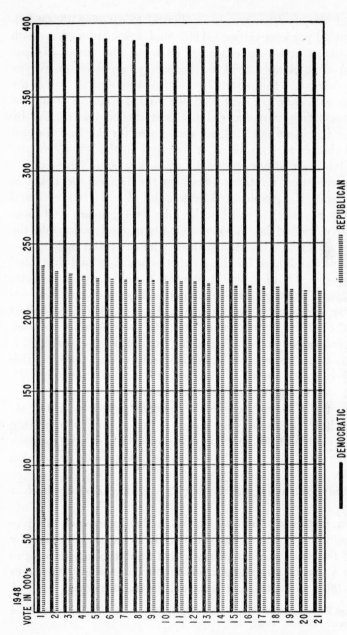

Outcome of the vote for twenty-one representatives in state legislature, Wayne County (Detroit +), Mich., November 2, 1948 (ballot on p. 28), showing lack of discrimination by voters of both parties and their blind acceptance of the tickets intact. Figures on p. 29.

Hecock of Wayne University was allowed to examine 18,569 ballots, about 10 per cent of the 194,602 total, taken from every tenth voting precinct across the city map. Of those who voted, 15.6 per cent marked no choices at all for the twenty-one places on Wayne County's delegation to the state house of representatives, and at the other end were 22.8 per cent who achieved the feat of voting for twenty-one. Of the remainder, 1 per cent spoiled their ballots by voting for too many, and 9.3 per cent voted for one and the rest recorded choices for two, three, or four and all the way to twenty. In total, they cast 43 per cent of the votes they could have cast.

Now nomination for these offices on the Democratic ticket in Wayne County is equivalent to election. But of every 100 registered voters, only twenty-four voted in the July, 1944, primaries. Of these at least one spoiled his ballot or put his marked ballot into the wrong receptacle. Of the twenty-three who cast valid ballots, four voted for no candidates for these twenty-one offices and five voted for twenty-one. Of these five, two were Republicans whose votes were "wasted," leaving three—i.e., 3 per cent—whose votes were determinative for twenty-one candidates. In a check of 383 ballots cast for the full twenty-one candidates, fifty were found who voted as follows: thirteen voted mechanically for twenty-one consecutive candidates or for every other candidate, seven voted only for Irish names, five voted for all candidates with names ending in -ski, -czyk, or -wicz, and twenty-five voted according to a list of ten issued by the Citizens League or eighteen issued by CIO-PAC union leaders. "If those who clearly avoided foreign-appearing names were added to those who made positive use of a set formula, the number indulging in this type of name voting would be doubled at least." [3]

The study concludes gravely that "21 are too many to elect at large."

Another feature of Detroit elections is the appearance of frivolous candidatures. When the situation is so nearly a lottery by reason of the absence of opinion, why not fulfill the easy formalities and take a chance on getting a public job and a salary? Hence as many as 967 candidates have appeared in the primaries.[4]

[3] *Election Without Representation* (pamphlet), National Training School for Public Service, Detroit, 1945.

The story goes that one Detroit saloonkeeper as a sporting proposition files on behalf of some unknown each time, choosing a man with a name likely to attract votes on racial or nationality lines, and that one such candidate survived the primary election and became party nominee!

Similar figures on state-wide offices for a whole state would show a little more variation because individual candidates may have in their home counties regional followings large enough to add a variable factor.

NEW YORK CITY'S "ELECTIVE" JUDGES

Consider the judges "elected" in New York City! There are seventy-seven appointive judges and 136 elective ones in New York City; thirty of the latter came up for election in November, 1947.

Twenty-four of the thirty, however, received their flowers and congratulations months before when the Republican and Democratic party leaders announced their joint selections. For on May 19 Frank J. Sampson "announced" that "the organization" would support certain persons for these offices. The next day another citizen, Thomas J. Curran, corresponding spokesman for the other principal party, announced concurrence in twenty-four of the choices.

Thenceforth those twenty-four candidates were practically assured of perfunctory ratification in the party primaries—there were in fact no contests—and thereafter, enjoying both Democratic and Republican nominations, they needed to do nothing more to be overwhelmingly "elected."

This amiable system provides judges who have taken pains to stand well with the party machines, a severely limited choice. Each judge has a political secretary, and millions of dollars a year of judicial patronage in receiverships, refereeships, trusteeships, etc., are dished out to a certain political 10 per cent of the bar.[5] Thus New York has a mediocre, precedent-bound judiciary; it is a wonder that it is no worse.

Who made these 1947 selections? The party officers did not meet

[4] Harold M. Dorr, "Candidates Won't Stay Out," *National Municipal Review*, May, 1949.
[5] *Political Patronage in the Courts* (pamphlet), report of the Chamber of Commerce, New York, 1937.

in public; they did not report where they met or who was present or what other candidates were considered or why these joint nominees were preferred. Nor what the nominees did to secure consideration. Yet their decisions were conclusive!

In 1932 under this amiable system Brooklyn and Queens needed more supreme court judges to end calendar congestion, but Democrats controlled these boroughs and the Republicans controlling the legislature demanded a share of the jobs before they would create the new positions. Unable to agree upon a proper division of four places, the party leaders thought they might solve their difficulties by creating six. But the difficulties persisted and the number was increased to ten. At length they compromised upon twelve, of whom the Republicans were to name four.

Thus the matter rested from the signing of the bill until the eve of the judiciary convention in September. Then news was spread that Boss McCooey, of Brooklyn, had in mind to pick for one of the Democratic places his thirty-one-year-old son, who had never held public office and could hardly be said to have distinguished himself at the bar.

So preposterous was this suggestion that few were disposed to take it seriously. The boss kept his own counsel, and the names he had selected were not announced until a few minutes before they were offered to the convention. The Democratic convention, which met first, took the slate which McCooey gave it, including the name of this son, and four Republicans. The Republican convention, meeting the next day, placed the same names in nomination.

Fourteen years later the surviving judges of this group available for renewal in office were perfunctorily nominated again by both parties and took office for another fourteen-year term.

Who can say that the people had anything to do with that?

Here is another. The New York *Herald Tribune*, August 6, 1951, reported:

In return for giving Justice Breitel bi-partisan support the Democrats will win Republican endorsement for three sitting Democrats and a Democrat seeking a Municipal Court post. . . .

It is understood that the impetus for the two-line endorsement came to Edward J. Flynn, Bronx Democratic leader and chief leader of the party in the state, from the aids of Governor Dewey. Since New York

County is also in the 1st District, Carmine G. DeSapio, New York
Democratic leader, also had to be consulted and it is understood that he
also gave his word.

Being thus on both of the two principal party tickets is equivalent to election, so the party primaries later in the month and the
final election in November became merely perfunctory, the nominees could plan their future without further waiting or uncertainty,
and the voters were spared any need of considering the merits of
the candidates; a half-dozen private persons conferring at some
time and place had—why pretend?—appointed five New York City
judges for terms running up to fourteen years!

Now judges are important and in the upstate counties of New
York the elective process works well for county judges and judges of
the supreme court.[6] The posts come up for election one or two at a
time and not often, the terms of upstate county judges being six
years and supreme court judges fourteen years. The candidates are,
under these circumstances, visible to the voters, and leaders of the
bar win nomination and election to the bench amid a widespread
appreciation of their dignity and merits.

But no such attention can be consistently focused on the metropolitan judgeships. The press, with the whole metropolitan scene to
cover, including suburbs in three states, can give only fitful attention, and a typical newspaper reader may conscientiously look in
vain for a word of print characterizing those of the thirty sets of
candidates who are running in his county. The newspaper coverage
does not follow political boundaries; radios are silent on the contests; the candidates make no public addresses in their own behalf
and universally rely hopelessly or otherwise on the blind party vote.
Other more dramatic contests for president, governor, U.S. senator,
or mayor overshadow the judicial contests. The verdict at the polls
on the latter represents neither information nor conviction. The city
voters and the city press could handle any one of those thirty contests but each contest is lost in the shuffle when so many are simultaneously conducted under metropolitan conditions. The facts are
that the New York City judges, ostensibly elected, are, in simple

[6] This despite its name is a district court outranked by its appellate division
and by the court of appeals.

reality, appointive in the city, although corresponding judgeships upstate are genuinely elective.

Similarly the Illinois Chamber of Commerce in a 1950 brochure laments that in Cook County (Chicago) "the voters have had little voice in the selection of judges. In all elections of Superior and Circuit Court judges since 1927, one or both major parties have presented 'coalition tickets' and in a number of elections, the two parties have presented a single unopposed slate giving the voters no choice whatever."

Odd Cases

Philadelphia in times past had a practice of electing by precinct votes the 1170 inspectors of elections; the voters sometimes found they had elected empty names, and men chosen later appeared from outside the state in due time to serve under those names, falsify the count, and vanish beyond the jurisdiction.

In Detroit the obsolete offices of constables, two from each of the twenty-two wards, linger on the ballots; in the November, 1951, election in one voting precinct ballots intended for another ward were delivered and the error was not discovered until after the polls closed; all of the 203 voters had voted unaware for candidates listed for the two constable posts who were actually running in another ward.[7]

In 1938 the mayor of Milton, Washington, according to press report, contrived to enter "Boston Curtis" on the opposing ticket for town committee. "Boston Curtis" was elected and was disclosed to be a mule!

The point that on large sections of any long ballot the typical American voter votes blindly, with or without party "guidance" on the ballot, need not be labored further.

Curiously, everybody knows about the practice of blind voting and has always known, yet the enormous fact that Americans vote for a major part of their elective officers without even knowing the names of the men they are voting for has been little studied or appreciated.

And the consequences are massive.

[7] Detroit Citizens League, *Civic Searchlight*, November, 1951.

Chapter V

THE CONSEQUENCES OF BLIND VOTING

We don't know anything about politics but neither do our husbands!

Women's suffrage cartoon, 1910

OBVIOUSLY if 90 per cent of the people refrained from voting the remaining 10 per cent would govern. But if they all vote without knowing what they are doing on 90 per cent of the offices submitted to them on election day, a similar relegation of power to a small minority must occur. Ordinary citizens go to the polls and vote for, say, twenty candidates; they register genuine personal judgment on several of them and no opinions at all about the rest, on whom their voting is blind. Some citizens, however, know about all of the twenty, usually because they have participated more or less actively in advancing candidates. Which leads us to our definition of a politician—a citizen who knows what he is doing on election day! He knows that a coroner is to be elected next November and is concerned about it in August whereas the ordinary citizen is unaware that any such question is brewing. The politician can usually—not always—tell you something about both candidates for the coronership and what groups engineered the nominations; such facts are a part of his equipment and shop talk.

TICKETS

When the ballot is *long,* a prime function of the politicians is to make up tickets of candidates, tying together complete sets of candidates like asparagus so that the ordinary voters can vote them by the bunch. A couple of good stalks on the outside of the bundle will help, but the voters can be relied upon to look no further into the bunch to detect rotten stalks. Hence the voter who eagerly supports a dramatic and fearless reformer for governor may in the

same election unknowingly or helplessly send to the legislature representatives who will thwart every project the governor advances.

NONPARTISAN ELECTIONS FEASIBLE WITH SHORT BALLOTS

When the ballot is *short,* with only *five* (or less) equally important offices at one time, the voter can get along nicely without

---

CONGRESSIONAL ELECTION

Tuesday, November 7, 1950

FOR HOUSE OF REPRESENTATIVES
IN CONGRESS
From the SEVENTH District in Virginia

(Vote for One)

☐ B. P. HARRISON

☐ J. A. GARBER

An election in Virginia frequently submits only two or three offices—in this
case, only one!

the politician and his asparagus string. Or if a ticket be offered, he
can and will examine the individual stalks in the bunch and perhaps discard it in favor of a personal ticket of his own, with easy
freedom. Under these conditions nonpartisan ballots become feasible. These confer no adventitious advantages on the candidates in
the way of position or voter guidance on the ballots; ticket labels
do not appear on the ballot at all but only in the campaign literature
and advertisements of the sponsors. Nor do sponsors of tickets have

much grip on the situation beyond the influence which they possess by reason of their personal reputations.

Nonpartisan municipal elections prevail at present writing in 59.4 per cent of our 2434 cities of 5000 population or over.[1] It was 56 per cent in 1940. When nonpartisan elections are combined with a short ballot of five important offices constituting, under the council-manager plan, the whole board of directors (council) of the city and being the only elective officers, the voters can do their whole task, and often do, without the intervention of ticket makers. On the other hand, if candidates band themselves together for mutual support or if civic leaders come forward to select citizens and induce them to run for office with their civic backing, the conditions may be improved thereby. For leadership or even attempted leadership is always welcome in the democratic process if it be based simply on the character and standing of the leaders and not on any kind of power and compulsion.

Reading D shows how this actually is working. In the 500 such elections there reported, the Republican and Democratic parties had practically never been observed to throw their weight or invoke blind allegiance to their party name. Candidates sought votes from both parties and got them on other grounds than party advantage. In about half the cities there was no organized leadership coming forward on its own motion to select and sponsor candidates. In the other half, leadership was offered, sometimes successfully and sometimes not. And there stands Dayton (whose politics are described in another Reading, H), where, with some responsible volunteer leadership at each election, the so-called professional politicians have been left out of the democratic process for a generation without any breakdown of the process!

BUT WITH LONG BALLOTS, TICKETS DEVELOP IMPORTANCE

But when the sound conditions of a short important-office ballot are not provided, we get different results.

The asparagus-ticket principle involves a tremendous transfer of discretion from the voter to the ticket makers. Suppose on that first ballot of mine I had been privileged to vote for the four candidates

[1] *Municipal Year Book,* International City Managers' Association, Chicago, 1952.

I knew about and to write on the ballot, "Let the Republican County Executive Committee cast my vote as to the remaining fifteen offices!" Would it have been really any more of a blind delegation of power than what I did? The party leaders who drew up that ticket knew—and knew better than I did that first time—that I would ratify their selections for those fifteen minor officers and they proceeded accordingly. The risk that I might be effectively rebellious about the sheriff or the assemblyman was negligible. Indeed, the moment the party label was, beyond recall, attached to a candidate, the party leaders, if they changed their mind, might have been unable to alter the vote or stem the momentum of the mass vote which follows the party name in minor contests.

As in the Aurelio case! Mr. Aurelio was a candidate for judge in 1943 in Manhattan and the Bronx. After he had been nominated by both Republicans and Democrats and after it was too late to remove the party labels, it was brought out that he was acknowledging to certain notorious gambling interests his "undying gratitude" for their help in getting him the Democratic nomination. The leaderships of both parties promptly withdrew their sponsorships of Aurelio and publicly besought their party members to give him no vote, each party however suggesting a different candidate in substitution (there were seven to be elected out of eleven candidates). But in the big metropolitan political panorama this was only one office, a minor one, in one vast district and it was not easy to reach the consciousness of the party ranks on that issue. So Aurelio coasted through to victory with 92,473 Republican votes, 50 per cent of those given to other comparable judicial candidates of that party on the Republican line, and 174,686 Democratic votes, 73 per cent of those given to others on that party's lines. The incident measures the unawareness of the metropolitan voters in those circumstances and the momentum of the solid party voting which, lacking other information, blindly follows the party label.

Politician Control of New York City Sheriffs

The office of elective sheriff in the five counties of New York City provides the most entertaining of our Readings, C. Prior to 1942 New York's sheriffs, elective for four-year terms in each county, controlled considerable patronage unencumbered by any merit system. Indeed, only one employee in the five counties, a telephone girl, was taken from civil service lists. The sheriffs' establishments exceeded in total pay roll that of many a mayor in good-sized cities, but in the metropolis the contests for sheriff were lost in the shadows. The office, relatively at least, was minor, one of a string of dull jobs on the lower end of the party ticket. So the officers of the dominant party in each county could and did hand out nominations for sheriff under the party label as rewards to their most unquestioningly loyal members. The deputy sheriffs, when vacancies developed, were selected from the party clubhouses and most of them were party officials. When it came a district leader's turn to put one of his captains on the public pay roll in the sheriff's office, he would sometimes take his man down and get him sworn in without bothering to tell the sheriff. The bulk of the jobs were sinecures and the real work of the employees was to build and maintain the district activities of the party. The pay roll totaled $1,000,000 a year and the party leaders were thus manning their organization at public expense to maintain themselves in power while their opponents were doing what they could with unpaid volunteers and voluntary subscriptions. Two former sheriffs have testified that even the job of the sheriff himself left ample time for the main tasks of politics. "Al" Smith, later governor, helped to abolish the system altogether, confessing that as sheriff he had been unable to find anything to do to earn the salary. Boss Flynn of the Bronx describes in his autobiography [2] how he utilized the patronage of the office to capture the position of boss of the Bronx, which he held thereafter for a generation. He admitted afterward that the sheriffs deserved abolition but, unlike "Al" Smith, did not turn up on the firing line to clear out the abuse. When after many a year of exposures and scandals the political elective sheriffs gave way to the first civil service sheriff in the country with a new staff selected with a single exception from civil service lists, the county leaders of the larger party were deprived of the $1,000,000 a year in sinecure jobs which they had been dividing among their junior party workers, and their power in local politics has been relatively anemic

[2] Edward J. Flynn, *You're the Boss*, New York, The Viking Press, 1947, chap. 4.

ever since. No one but the politicians mourned the disappearance from the ballot of the sheriffs or the other minor offices of the counties—county clerks, registers and coroners—which have in various ways been replaced with competent appointive officers, as related hereafter. No power was taken away from the people; these offices like the judgeships had always been in reality appointive—hand-picked—by the ticket makers for their own ends.

POWER IN TICKET MAKING PERVERTS DEMOCRACY

Our target is not ticket makers but ticket-makers-with-power. There is no crime in getting up a ticket, sponsoring it, and trying to elect it as a whole. The so-called "Charter" group under the council-manager plan in Cincinnati does it at every election and with a high degree of success. But the Charter group has no power save the town's respect for its selfless leadership, and its nominees, when installed in office, are free men and not agents of an invisible government working out of a party headquarters for its own continuance in importance.

Ticket-makers-with-power are sometimes called "bosses," but that term is variable for we usually describe a leader in the organization of the opposite party as a boss whereas the head of our own party is a "leader." Sometimes the leadership is vested in a coterie of key figures of the party who trade and cooperate as a team and get called "the machine." But even so, it is not their existence or their organization we object to but the power they so often possess—a power not ordained in charter or constitution and yet often arrogant, self-serving, and entrenched against dislodgment.

Essentially our complaint against politicians is not that they are sometimes corrupt or extravagant but that they pervert the processes of democracy and tap the public purse to entrench themselves in power. The processes of election can be perverted by a dishonest count, as in those Latin-American "republics" where the "ins" count the votes and always win. But when elected officials use their opportunities in office to reward their supporters and to strengthen their party organization, they are doing an equivalent thing and falsifying the outcome. The condition becomes a frustration of democracy.

Chicago *Record-Herald.*

Nor does the principle change much when we see one group of honest ticket makers contending in honestly counted elections with another group of honest ticket makers. If it remains a fact that no one can in practice be elected unless he is on one or another of two tickets, we have an uneasy binopoly which is not much better perhaps than the monopoly of the ticket makers in a one-party constituency.

"Yes," said the secretary of the Democratic City Committee of Stamford, Connecticut, to me years ago, "when the Democrats carry this city, the whole personnel in Town Hall is ousted and Democrats replace Republicans all the way down the line."

He was a little shaken at my astonishment that such antediluvian practices still survived, but went on in dead seriousness:

"Oh, yes—a land of settled government!"

Aside from the unsettlement which such whipsawing must bring to technical administration, the groups who put together the two party tickets are in each case small and their offerings are not all scrutinized when the ballots are long and include numerous relatively dull and obscure offices. The real rulers of the city may be as few as fifty, or twenty, or even two, and whether they rule nobly or foully is of no moment in this discussion—they possess an unscrutinized power that is in its very existence incompatible with democracy. "Power corrupts." Unwatched power is doubly dangerous. It is wonderful that our politicians are no worse than they are!

BOSSES

In the country-wide scene the ticket-makers-with-power are as varied as human nature and range the whole gamut of quality from unselfish high-mindedness to self-serving obscenity. Huey Long of Louisiana, Flynn of the Bronx, Crump of Memphis, Pendergast of Kansas City, Curley of Boston, Hague of New Jersey were diverse in character and methods but alike in being safe against all but a paroxysm of citizen effort. So too with the less personalized ticket-maker groups in Republican Philadelphia or Democratic Chicago—when public sentiment rises against them, the problem is how to dislodge them without installing another group of ticket makers acquiring power by similar devices and promises of patronage and holding it thereafter by equally improper use of the opportunities of office.

Below those great "machines" we have almost everywhere the milder situations wherein amiable and honest men like my Abraham Lincoln cooperate to do the endless work of a political party, to fight the other party for good reasons or no reasons, and to value loyalty to the group beyond loyalty to the government. To discriminate when the other party makes an exceptionally good nomination? To withhold support when a rascal gets on our ticket? To vote or work for the best candidate? "Of course, that wouldn't be right!"

When minor elective offices are left out in the dark, unscruti-

nized by the voters and constituting treasure of power, salary, easy
jobs, graft, a scramble for them is likely to ensue. Not always, for
such offices, in rural county governments, for example, are sometimes so poorly paid and so unattractive that vacancies are unfilled
altogether. Or the contests are languid and the ticket makers find it
arduous to dig up some passable candidate to bother with a given
post. But when, as in the usual case, the minor elective office can
be used to reward party supporters and strengthen a party, and can
be kept out of the hands of the other party, the rivalries develop
and victory seems desirable.

SOLIDARITY OF PARTY MACHINES

Organization develops almost automatically, for it will help toward victory. Organization brings men together in warming contact
for a common cause. It may not be much of a cause; it may be no
more than a herd instinct of one class against the other but it bears
the name and dignity of a party and cements the active spirits together in a team. The members lose their freedom of opinion and
dissent. The politicians come from all classes and ranks and the
higher intelligence and morals of the community may contribute
their full quota. But once in an organization they move as a bloc.
Good men who see their organization go wrong on a nomination
continue to stay in and lend their strength, not bolting unless conditions become intolerable. Voting for an outsider, "bolting the
ticket," means withdrawal entirely—it happens rarely—and is regarded as treason to the clan no matter how well justified. So the
party develops a solid core, which works as a team, discards principle and divides up the plunder of the minor offices, and as much
more as it can get, and uses it to insure its own continuance. It can
all be done without any graft or dishonesty and often is. Prove
that the Erie Canal is a dead loss these days on any basis of valua-
tion and try to abandon it! The array of county Republican machines across the state with their supporters on the canal pay roll
will adduce a cloud of reasons, except the real one, to keep it
going. Reorganize the state government of Connecticut to save several millions a year? That would tamper with comfortable party
jobs and every old-timer gets out his microscope in a hunt for flaws

in the plan and few Republicans can see virtue in it since it came from a Democratic governor. Did we not see intelligent Republicans *en masse* swing against our joining the League of Nations in an instinctive aversion to anything propounded by a Democratic president? And in little cities can one political clan ever secure anything but sneers from the other? So, whether through "the cohesive power of public plunder" or a meaningless, purposeless clannishness of contending honest-minded groups, the politicians organize and become a phalanx to seek victory.

Victory for what? Victory as a rule for no principle, just victory —possession of the seats of power. Victory over the other side!

Unscrutinized Power of the Machines

As long as party managements thus possess unchecked power to perform numerous unscrutinized activities in the election processes, the sugar of the unguarded power will attract flies. Party managements as organized in America are unfit to exercise discretion unseen because they are wide open to contamination. The party's doors are, in our practice, open to every voter—testing of his purposes is impossible—and greed and altruism enter together. Any voter may scramble for a captaincy in the party hierarchy. Greed has most to gain in a factional dispute and is least scrupulous in choice of methods. Consequently corruption finally dominates any machine that is worth dominating and sinks it lower and lower as worse men displace better until the limit of toleration is reached and the machine receives a setback at election. That causes its officers to clean up a bit, discredit the party workers who went too far, and restore a standard high enough to win—which standard soon begins to sag again by the operation of the same natural principle.

The essence of our usual complaint against our government is that it represents these easily contaminated party managements. Naturally, when practically none but the politicians in his district are aware of his activities or even of his existence, the minor elective officeholder who refuses to cater to their will and to let his authority be used to entrench the "ins" against the "outs" is committing political suicide. The officeholder himself may be upright—he usually is, indeed—but the shadowy unofficial figures in the party managements to whom he kowtows can privately sell or misuse their influence, and it is rather wonderful that they do not do it to a greater extent than they do.

Obviously the remedy is to get the eggs into a few baskets—the baskets that we watch!

RULE ONE (THE SHORT-BALLOT PRINCIPLE): ELECTIVE OFFICES MUST BE VISIBLE

I believe the short ballot is the key to the whole problem of the restoration of popular government in this country.

—WOODROW WILSON

Out of the helter-skelter of the previous chapters we now deduce: *Rule One. Elective Offices Must Be Visible.*

Not concealed from public scrutiny by being too numerous.

Not concealed by sheer unimportance.

Not concealed by dullness of character.

Commonly this triple-barreled principle has been called "the short ballot," a name which I coined for it and used as title for my pioneer essay in this field in 1909.[3] Experience with this phrase in the forty years since shows that it has led people to think merely of the *number* of offices on the ballot, missing the other points that each elective office must be *important* enough or *interesting* enough to attract scrutiny. We tried in vain to avert the neglect of the second and third factors by putting them first in the condensed statement which has been used in the pamphlet reprints of that 1909 *Outlook* article all through the decades since. (See p. 85.)

Failure to conform to Rule One frustrates the application of public opinion.

[3] "The Short Ballot," *Outlook*, July 17, 1909.

Chapter VI

THE FACTOR OF GREAT CONSTITUENCY SIZE

IN a city of, say, 25,000 voters with a short ballot and an important office to fill, a candidate who has no organized backing can run for that office with an improvised organization of friends and with a modest campaign fund that may indeed come within his personal pecuniary resources. He can get free hearings before various groups of voters; he can issue a mailing or two to every voter, get some newspaper editorial space without expert aid, and pay for some advertisements in the local press. And if he really has some right to be considered, he can be heard and can win.

But, in a prospective constituency of 500,000 voters, how vastly more difficult is his task! A single mailing to all the voters will cost $10,000 for the 2¢ postage stamp alone. The reasonable cost of a modest campaign to get the attention of such a horde can easily run to far more than the salary of the position he is seeking for the entire term. In a nonpartisan election or a primary intraparty contest for a party nomination, the cost falls on the individual candidate and his personal backers. For a state-wide office in a populous state, the legitimate expenditures can and do run to hundreds of thousands of dollars, or even millions.

HEAVY ORGANIZATION AND EXPENDITURE INEVITABLE

In a three-cornered primary election fight for the Republican nomination for U.S. senator in 1926 in Pennsylvania, over $2,000,000 was expended. It is not uncommon in hotly contested races in primaries for congressional nominations for expenditures of $25,000–$100,000 to be made by contestants. "In one constituency of approximately 500,000 population," says Harris,[1] "a publicity firm specializing in political campaigns will not undertake a campaign

[1] Joseph P. Harris, *A Model Direct Primary Election System*, National Municipal League, New York, 1951.

for a leading office at less than $200,000. Notwithstanding official campaign reports to the contrary, the cost of political campaigns in large and populous states and cities comes high." The cost will run beyond the means of all but men of considerable wealth. And victory cannot be achieved by money alone. The task calls for friendly man power and political know-how, for committees and subcommittees, for localized neighborhood contacts and the ringing of countless doorbells by an array of volunteers. For big constituencies are inevitably insensitive as compared with small ones and vastly harder to dent.

Now, among all the democratic nations, we are almost the only one which attempts to elect to public office from constituencies of more than 75,000 voters or 200,000 population.[2]

BRITISH CONSTITUENCIES

In England, for instance, the 1948 reapportionment of parliamentary districts, dividing 484 seats among 28,706,999 electors outside the City of London, arrived at an average district constituency of 59,312 electors and then, striving to vary no more than 10,000 to either side of that figure, ended up with forty-four districts of 70,000 or more including eight exceeding 80,000, the largest being 87,100 electors (or about 150,000 population). The Boundary Commission was led to remark, "We are not unmindful of the disadvantages of such large electorates. . . ."[3] In the boroughs and cities of England there are no elections at large, borough-wide or city-wide; all council members (the only elective officers) are chosen from wards.

But we elect representatives in Congress from populations ranging supposedly around 350,000 but varying in 1950 from 148,000 to 908,000. Similarly, our state-wide elections for U.S. senator, governor, and other state officers set up constituencies of a vastness hardly known elsewhere in the world. In our metropolitan cities, election at large is provided for mayors and some other offices, e.g.,

[2] Except unhappily and recently in Japan, whose new structure of government under the Occupation has led to imitation of our system with elective governors and mayors! The mayor of Tokyo (6,270,000 pop.) in 1950 had been elected by 800,000 votes over an opponent's 680,000. Brazil and Mexico elect presidents at large and the Austrian constitution so provides, although up to 1952 there has been no election there.

[3] Initial Report of the Boundary Commission for England, 1947.

New York, Chicago, Philadelphia, Los Angeles, Boston, and others; likewise, in the populous counties which include such cities, some or all of the offices like sheriff, county clerk, coroner are chosen at large.

Finally we have the spacious spectacle of the national elections for president and vice-president, exhibiting a series of strange phenomena attributable to the simple vastness of the constituency.

DEFINITION OF UNWIELDY CONSTITUENCIES

Unwieldy constituencies may be defined as those which are so large that their mere size frustrates efforts to canvass them adequately on behalf of insurgents, civic groups, or newcomers in the face of the veteran perennial organizations of the two parties.

BINOPOLY CONTROL

Commonly these two standing armies of political mercenaries enjoy a binopoly of hopeful nominations in such constituencies.

The founding fathers were not unaware of the difficulties of selecting a president directly from a far-flung constituency although the slowness of communications among and within the first thirteen states was doubtless more consciously within their thought than the size and deafness of large voting populations. They expected that their Electoral College device would provide presidential electors selected in wieldly districts who would use their discretion in selecting a president. And senators, instead of being elected state-wide, as since 1913, were for a century chosen by district-elected legislators.

THE PROGRESSIVE PARTY EPISODE

In the vast unwieldy constituency of the national elections for president, the nearest to success was achieved in 1912 by the personality of Theodore Roosevelt and the genuine revolt represented by his Progressive party. There seemed a chance that, having captured so much of the Republican rank and file, the new party might replace the Republican party. But the Republicans had experienced party workers almost everywhere, supported often by patronage and by the fact of high local importance, whereas the Progressive party by 1916 became too feeble to accomplish in many states even the technical drudgery of getting up the necessary petitions for placing its presidential candidate on the ballot, to say nothing of conducting effective campaigns in over 3000 counties.

Imagine if you can a successful independent candidacy (i.e., neither Republican nor Democratic) for governor of Ohio! Or still more unimaginably for the obscure state-wide office of state treasurer! Likewise in metropolitan constituencies! In Chicago in 1951 the *Tribune* reported, "Both the Republicans and Democrats figure it will take about $400,000 each to run their April 3 campaign for mayor." When William Randolph Hearst tried in New York City for the mayoralty he enjoyed the support of his own two powerful newspapers and their conditioned readers, but he was outmatched by the Democrats, who had their experienced captains at work in every block. Newbold Morris attempted it in 1945, inducing a minority of the Republican vote to bolt the Republican ticket of that year but exhibiting clearly the utter impracticality of mustering enough volunteer helpers, soliciting adequate subscriptions for campaign funds, and hastily improvising adequate staffs of district workers for a single few-weeks' campaign on so vast a scale. About $120,000 was spent on his behalf that year. It was the mere hugeness of the task in the absence of a nucleus of organized professional political support which made his brave effort futile from the outset. He got 408,278 votes, 20 per cent of the total 1,974,622 votes cast in that three-cornered race of 1945, whereas in 1949, running again, this time with the Republican party and Liberal party nomination, he got 956,170 or 37 per cent of the total vote of 2,577,203.

Boston's "Nonpartisan" Elections

For a less confused example of the effect of bigness, turn to the experience of Boston. In 1910 Boston adopted nonpartisan local elections providing a city-wide elective mayor (and an elective council and school board). With neither the Democratic nor the Republican name attached to candidates, the blocs of unthinking followers of the party names were left free to vote for candidates on the merits without any sense of apostasy or disloyalty to the party with which they were associated by conviction and habit in national elections. Some mighty battles thereupon ensued every four years, and valiant efforts were made to shake off the locally dominant machine of the Democratic party. All nominations were by petition, but the shrewd emissaries of shrewd editors buzzed about the doors of the Democratic City Committee at a certain stage of each campaign to learn which candidate would receive the committee's official (but nonlegal) blessing. And when that was announced, the candidate thus blessed could be sure of the diligent and unquestioning support of experienced and highly capable political patronage-paid workers in every district throughout the city and he would become overnight the prime favorite in the betting.

The Southern State Primaries as Unwieldy Constituencies

The eleven southern one-party states elect their governors, U.S. senators, and state tickets at large, providing examples of unwieldy districts with the equivalent of nonpartisan elections, since the only real contests are in the Democratic primary elections. Here, as described in Key's *Southern Politics*, the candidates commonly come forward with some regional backing and scramble for votes, including ready-made blocs of votes under the influence of local machine leaders. They try to capture the attention and support of local leaders by treaties and trades, but, except in Virginia, the scene is turbulent and wide open to all comers. Frantic efforts to catch the attention of a million voters, more or less, spread over the whole state, have led to queer methods of picturesque demagoguery and the crude characters thus thrown up have sometimes reached the Senate or governor's chairs. Such extreme buffoonery may be one fruit of the discrepancy between the heaviness of the task of appealing effectively to so big a constituency and the slender financial resources of typical candidates at the stage when they are on their own. In the case of Virginia, the Byrd machine within the dominant party is described by Key as successfully exercising a state-wide influence which makes politics in the Old Dominion much less of a free scramble and more of a simple line-up between that machine and its intraparty opponents. Whether the influence of the Byrd machine will long outlive its central and locally much respected character is yet to be known; Virginia may revert to the scramble condition of the other southern states.

The southern picture does not, I think, upset the idea that unwieldiness in size of constituencies provides basis for the existence of political machines and gives to machines a considerable power to control the outcome of elections. Rather it appears to me from Key's studies that each southern state exhibits several machines, each safe in its own section and federating in a loose fashion from time to time with others when state-wide elections come along. Thus Crump's machine in Memphis reaches out for aid in the eastern end of the state in the effort to win state control, but the size of the state-wide constituency is greater than an organization based on personal leadership can usually cover.

State Machines Are Federations

Indeed, in two-party states like New York, the unwieldiness of the constituency begets state party organizations which are merely loose federations of local organizations, and the occasional Boss Platt or Barnes has been an exception to the rule that the natural unit even for professional political organization is a city or county rather than a state.

Likewise in the United States as a whole there is no national boss, and the national committees are collections of agents of local groups and hold few powers that the local units of the party feel impelled to recognize.

Unwieldy districts thus are sometimes not only too big for ordinary insurgent candidates to deal with but too big even for single political machines as distinguished from federations of local machines.

Clumsiness Invites Control

All this is only saying that large electorates are hard of hearing, and they can be so large as to be almost deaf. This deafness of a big electorate to all but expert organized political noisemakers gives to the experts an influence which amounts to virtual control.

To express it another way: An electorate may be so large that it cannot perform even a simple task without organizing for it. A committee can easily do in half an hour the work that a convention of a thousand men can only do in a stormy, blundering fashion in a whole day. In fact, a convention can hardly get anywhere except with the aid of committees. The clumsiness of a convention is nothing to the clumsiness of 100,000 voters scattered through a great city; and if concerted action is required of them, there must be organization. In huge electorates it will have to be more elaborate and costly organization than we can ask the candidates to construct; and if the support of these standing armies is essential to the success of candidates, it follows logically that the armies (or the captains of them) will hold an unassailable monopoly of the hopeful nominations.

Democracy requires that there shall be reasonably free competition for elective offices. To give to any set of men power to exclude various candidates from the contest may often result in barring the very men the people would like. It is not possible to suppress permanent political organizations when they will be of help in winning the great prizes of office, but it *is* possible so to arrange the battleground that there will not be enough advantage in permanent political organizations to confer on them power to dominate.

Let the constituency be not so large but that an adequate impromptu organization can be put together at short notice! Permanent committees or political organizations may then exist without controlling the situation, since the threat of opposition, if their nominations are unsatisfactory, will be truly serious.

It makes no difference whether it be one political machine or two competing ones or a federation of machines that live on the advantages which permanent organizations enjoy by virtue of the fact that the constituency is unwieldy. In unwieldy districts the advantages of permanent political organizations of any kind are excessive and confer monopoly or binopoly of hopeful nominations on the compact little standing armies of political mercenaries who man such mechanisms.

It is not possible to define a wieldy constituency precisely by establishing a limit of, say, 100,000 voters, for other things besides size combine sometimes to frustrate the impacts of public opinion. Many congressional representatives will testify that their districts are too big and clumsy, but others see no trouble. A congressional constituency's unwieldiness may be aggravated by further factors of enormous area, diversity of character of population, lack of any press in common, unnatural boundaries, immersion in a vaster metropolitan political complex, etc.—factors which sometimes bedevil politics and frustrate the democratic process in small constituencies too. Another district may be a natural coherent community of like-minded people with identical traditions and its own press and constituting a natural constituency. Bigness will make more trouble in the first case than in the second.

The voters in an unwieldy constituency can be completely frustrated in their support of a given candidate if the managers of neither party are willing to put their organization and experience at his disposal; no alternative may be available to the candidate in an unwieldy district unless he possesses extraordinary resources of friends and funds. If in a southern state he cannot enlist some of the important local party leaders, if in Indiana he cannot obtain the support of either the Democratic or the Republican machine, if in New Hampshire he cannot win over the Republican party chiefs, his hopes are probably vain no matter how much he may have captured the popular fancy! And so are frustrated the voters who were disposed to vote for him!

The problem has rarely been faced or even recognized by those who frame state constitutions or the charters of large cities and metropolitan counties. Only rarely, of course, do circumstances or events provide occasion for bringing it up in the field.

THE SMALLER CONSTITUENCIES OF LEGISLATORS IN OTHER LANDS

	Membership of Legislative Assembly	Average Constituency
Australia	121	66,000
Belgium	202	42,000
Britain	625	81,000
Canada	262	52,000
France	619	66,000
Israel	120	11,000
Italy	574	80,000
Mexico	147	166,000
Netherlands	100	100,000
Sweden	230	30,000
Switzerland	194	24,000
U.S. House of Representatives	435	350,000

U.S. Senate constituencies run up to 14,741,455 (New York).

Rule Two: The Constituency Must Be Wieldy

The constituency must be wieldy, i.e., not so large in voting population that the task of canvassing it goes beyond the power of ordinary independent candidates and leaves a monopoly of hopeful nominations in the hands of permanent standing armies of organized political mercenaries.

The questions that must arise as to how on earth some of our immovable practices—election of president, governors, and senators—can be reconciled to this Rule Two are tackled at various points in later chapters on "Progress in State Administration," large cities, and "Progress in Intraparty Organization."

Chapter VII

FRUSTRATING DEMOCRACY BY SCATTERATION OF POWERS

> . . . There are some people who have a vested interest in confused government. They like to keep it confused. I don't believe that many of them think that out deliberately or carefully, but when they come right down to staring into the face of effective government, one really reflecting the will of the people, they honestly don't like it.
>
> —GOVERNOR CHESTER BOWLES of Connecticut at the 1950 Governors' Conference

THE prevalent type of American city charter lodges the powers of the municipality in a list of elective offices such as mayor, comptroller, treasurer, auditor, city clerk, council, and some separate boards. A modern city charter under the council-manager plan lodges all the powers of the municipality in a single elective body, the council. When the latter is proposed in substitution for the former, opponents cry out that the project "takes away from the people" the power to choose the mayor, etc., themselves directly and leave unsaid the implication that the people have less total power in consequence. A more candid reflection would show that the total powers of the people are the same in either case, that the voters are to elect a more powerful council than was their privilege before, and that the powers have merely been combined in a single package. Combined, indeed, as a man ties together his load of little Christmas packages to assure his control—he then counts only one package instead of a dozen! But he has not thereby lost eleven! On the contrary, integration of powers of government is essential to effectiveness of popular control so that all the little packages come along when the voter lifts the string.

A government divided into numerous elusive bits defies control, and the dropped packages become the unobserved perquisites of the politicians, not only because they are too numerous and too small (violating Rule One), but because they are not properly tied in.

LOOSE-JOINTED MECHANISMS RESIST CONTROL

A city so organized may be a wieldy constituency and may have, and often does have, a short ballot with no obscure offices. But without a reasonable unification of powers to enable it to move all its parts in proper unison, it may simply clash gears under the jerked levers and fail to move as directed.

The series of men who sit on separate statutory municipal pedestals, called "Council," "Mayor," "Board of Works," "Tax Commission," "Comptroller," etc., each have power to slap the face of the others, and when the people fail to secure obedience to their will from such a cluster of authorities, they must burrow through a labyrinth of detail to find out who is responsible for the holdup. The blocking power of honest disagreements is so great that the government is almost incapable of that orderly, disciplined harmony which is necessary for response to mass opinion.

In that typical city plan of government, responsibility is obscured. When something goes wrong, the people blame the mayor, the mayor tells them to blame the council, the council tells them to blame the board of works, and the board of works blames the mayor, thus sending the people around a circle without giving them any satisfaction. Each officer in the circle may really have a valid excuse and might conceivably ask and secure reelection year after year while the people are vainly trying to enforce their will. Making an officer's responsibility invisible is as undesirable as making the officer himself invisible. The desperate solution sometimes is for the people to secure unity of control by allowing a boss to put in power puppets who will yield to his dictation!

The people lose the ability to hold an official accountable if they themselves choose his subordinates. The stockholders of a corporation who chose not merely the directors but also the business manager would not thus gain additional control over the business, but would lose. In choosing the manager they would be diminishing the power of their other servants, the directors, and would be furnishing the latter with an opportunity to say "It's not *our* fault" when things go wrong. Likewise, in our cities which elect a council and mayor the people have no more "power" than the people of a city which elects only a council. In the latter case the people's council is more powerful, that's all, and the *control* by the people, which is the real thing we are after, is the more complete in the simpler plan.

Such conditions increase the friction in the government, increase the frictional resistance to popular demand, and make the government less obedient, less sensitive to the controlling levers. And thus the people find themselves balked and baffled, get discouraged, make fewer demands, and make them more halfheartedly in a spirit of speculation as to whether this time the shaky ramshackle may not happen to respond. And in taking this attitude, as in everything else, the people are quite possibly right. The trouble of getting an improvement or stopping a graft may, in some circumstances, actually be greater than the resulting advantage warrants.

To be sure, if we have elected the right men they may waive their differences, may not take advantage of opportunities to block and check when they are in the minority, may not use their chances to betray the people without getting spotted. But in a complete democracy the mechanism must be designed so that harmony of action can be compelled—not merely urged.

The Case of Ann Arbor

Professor Arthur W. Bromage relates how, as an articulate and trained observer of political method, he examined with the fresh eyes of a novice in public office the waste of human energy required by the weak mayor form of government in Ann Arbor, Michigan (pop. 53,000). A council of fourteen members elected from seven wards plus a president separately elected at large, and subject to mayor's veto, functioned through eighteen committees in direct relations with operating departments, five of which were headed by boards! Professor Bromage found he had to put in 300 to 400 hours a year to pilot a few measures through the tedious labyrinths of successive consents. Noncontroversial matters took weeks and controversial ones took months to conclude. Aside from the cost of such involved procedure and the difficulty of recruiting councilmen with patience enough to try to make progress, there remains the greater factor that such a complex mechanism resists public control by its sheer inertia and loose-jointedness! [1]

WATERTOWN'S TWENTY-EIGHT LITTLE GOVERNMENTS

Watertown, Connecticut, provides a pertinent and perhaps extreme case. With a population of 11,000 it elects three selectmen, nine members of the board of education, three members of the board of assessors, town clerk, town treasurer, six members of the board of finance, fire district committee in each of two separate districts, tax collector, board of tax review (three), seven constables, eight justices of the peace, from whom the selectmen choose one to be judge, four registrars of voters, one judge of probate, and six grand jurors, from whom the selectmen choose a prosecutor and assistant prosecutor—a total of fifty-six elective town officers.[2] They are not all elected at one time; twenty-two were elected at the 1948 election. They constitute twenty-eight little governments. Making the number so large diminishes the importance of each. The number is too large to permit a complete and adequate scrutiny at the final election. Most of the offices are too slight in importance to attract adequate scrutiny to the individual candidates. Of the 11,000 inhabitants actual registration in 1947 was 3807 (2154 Republicans, 854 Democrats, 799 unaffiliated). Nobody gets elected who is not on either the Republican ticket or the Democratic ticket, so we must inquire how candidates get on those tickets and who puts them there. This inquiry leads us to the party caucus.

The 2154 Republicans are privileged to go to the Republican caucus—an open meeting—vote their way through the long list and set up the Republican ticket and authorize their officers to convey the ticket to the election authorities to be printed on the election ballot. The proceeding, however, is all informal and unembarrassed by official oversight or regulations. The 1947 Republican caucus in Watertown brought out sixty-one persons, including no doubt candidates for the various offices, their relatives, official subordinates, and friends, providing a nucleus of actively interested party per-

---

[1] *On the City Council,* Geo. Wahr Publishing Co., Ann Arbor, Mich., 1951.

[2] But the record may be held by Greenwich, Conn. (40,000 pop.), with 268 elective offices.

sons ready to exchange strength with one another, a coherent and experienced bloc within the sixty-one.

By an amiable custom of long standing the Republicans do not nominate a full ticket but leave three members of the board of finance for the Democrats; one selectman and three of the board of education are, by law, left to the minority party. So we go to the Democratic caucus and find eighteen persons out of the 854 there (1947). The seven Democratic officers, if they and their wives attend, would be sufficient to arrange the Democratic ticket.

The people then going to the polls on election day vote in most cases for the whole Republican or Democratic ticket without much discrimination or thought unless there happens to be some big scandal or ruction.

The result seems likely to be a list of presentable characters manning the highly disintegrated series of twenty-eight little governments, a disposition to follow old traditions and to reelect incumbents over long periods, and a great deal of mediocrity, unprogressiveness, poor cooperation between the little governments. And needless expense and man power for lack of ability to switch man power flexibly from one office to another as seasonal variations of the work load may require to keep all paid employees busy, as could be done if all the money-spending departments were under a single town manager.

Whatever the quality of government resulting from such a ramshackle structure, it is obviously not democracy when one-quarter of one per cent of the people pick all the officers in a characteristic election!

Stamford's Attempt to Integrate a Function

For a more common case, witness the inherent difficulty of imposing a certain measure of efficiency on the government of Stamford, Connecticut. The local Good Government Association in 1949 rallied expert office managers from local manufacturing staffs to reduce the cost of certain paper work in the town hall. It was plain enough that incoming mail and phone calls should be centrally received and distributed to the appropriate departments and that the latter should benefit by a variety of other services supplied as needed from a common center. So a reasoned program for shifting

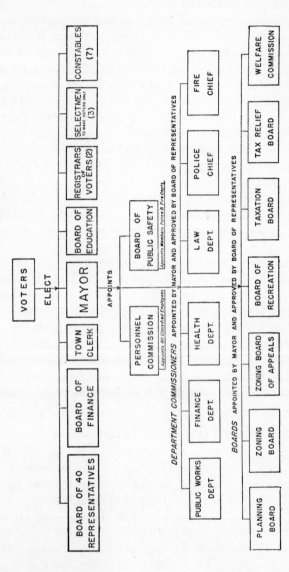

STAMFORD

ORGANIZATION CHART OF THE MUNICIPAL GOVERNMENT

VOTERS

ELECT

BOARD OF 40 REPRESENTATIVES

BOARD OF FINANCE

TOWN CLERK

MAYOR

BOARD OF EDUCATION

REGISTRARS OF VOTERS (2)

SELECTMEN (3) TO MAKE VOTERS ONLY

CONSTABLES (7)

APPOINTS

DEPARTMENT COMMISSIONERS APPOINTED BY MAYOR AND APPROVED BY BOARD OF REPRESENTATIVES

PERSONNEL COMMISSION Appoints All Classified Employees

BOARD OF PUBLIC SAFETY Appoints Members Police & Fire Depts.

PUBLIC WORKS DEPT

FINANCE DEPT.

HEALTH DEPT.

LAW DEPT.

POLICE CHIEF

FIRE CHIEF

BOARDS APPOINTED BY MAYOR AND APPROVED BY BOARD OF REPRESENTATIVES

PLANNING BOARD

ZONING BOARD

ZONING BOARD OF APPEALS

BOARD OF RECREATION

TAXATION BOARD

TAX RELIEF BOARD

WELFARE COMMISSION

A 1949 charter but an 1880 type of structure, with sixty-nine elective offices, two boards to limit the mayor, boards intervening between the mayor and some operating departments, and scatteration of powers with corresponding frustration of popular control (Stamford, Conn.).

staff and rearranging partitions vested this central service logically enough under the city clerk. Logically enough except for the fact that the city clerk is independently elective—a little separate government by himself, as the diagram of the charter shows! And in a position to perform his increased duties according to his own concept of speed and priority and, indeed, according to his own convenience, exempt from day-to-day discipline or appeals to a common superior, the only common superior being the 70,000 people of the city!

The city clerk may be a stubborn old crab or an eager, willing collaborator—who is to decide? The people, speaking through the volunteers of the Good Government Association, may undoubtedly want teamwork at that point, but the setup facilitates frustration and defiance!

While that diagram of the Stamford charter is before you, observe the mutual independence of the mayor and the finance board! The mayor, with departments to operate, finds his budgets cut down by the finance board. "That's money enough!" says the finance board, which, in the mayor's view, is a group of inexperienced amateurs. As I write this, an argument concerning accounting takes the form of acrimonious 500-word letters back and forth for weeks, written for publication in the local newspaper, which, with unusual conscientiousness, does publish them. But I, for one, as a local summer resident, have no confidence in my ability to judge the issue thus thrust upon the voters, and others feel the same way; hence public opinion does not go to the succor of either party.

Nor is calling it apathy any solution. Rather, the inability of the voters to solve the issue thus presented is an example of throwing at the people an issue which they are in no position to settle. The situation demonstrates defects inherent in a multi-headed government—or rather a loose collection of several governments—with a total of sixty-nine elective offices. The voters are invited to learn so much about municipal details, to watch so closely the interaction of its highly independent parts, and to muster a concerted and articulate public opinion about a dozen issues a month that they cannot conceivably do the jobs thus assigned to them. And they don't. The result inevitably is a balky, ramshackle mechanism at times. Its waste motion and inefficiency are often visible enough and may often be nobody's fault, but the more fundamental defect is the fact that ramshackle mechanisms can make futile the efforts of even the most alert constituency to secure obedience.

RAMSHACKLE COUNTIES

The worst cases of ramshackle organization are the typical county governments, consisting usually of an elective board and a series of independently elected county officers—sheriff, clerk, treasurer, register, coroner, and prosecuting attorney. Each county officer, on his separate statutory pedestal, is in for a fixed term and beyond correction or discipline. Each must get his pay and expenses from the board, but his cooperation cannot be compelled, and such a thing as pooling the stenographic service in the county courthouse or shifting employees from office to office with the seasonal work burden may be harder to arrange than an international treaty. The typical county is headless and in reality no more than a loose cluster of independent officers who, because of their fractional responsibilities, can go their own ways for decades regardless of public impatience and immune from effective discriminating scrutiny or criticism. Any such county government is protected from any degree of control by the voters by its scatteration of powers and the impossibility of dealing with it as an adequately organized team.

FEARS OF INTEGRATION PROPOSALS

But when you try to secure unification of powers, you encounter superficial theory at every point. There was, for instance, an effort begun in 1915 in the New York constitutional convention to shorten the ballot. Elihu Root, "Al" Smith, Charles E. Hughes, and other top figures in both parties supported the effort. The party routineers, accustomed to parcel out the minor state officers among the county machines at the state conventions, were forced to concede that the elective secretary of state, state treasurer, and state engineer and surveyor could be made appointive under the governor, but they stuck resolutely and successfully to keeping the attorney general elective. The office is appointive in the federal government and in some other states. "But," it was pleaded, "the attorney general practically makes law for all the departments. They protect themselves by relying on his interpretations of the law. He must be independent of the governor lest the governor dictate his legal opinions in the interest of some improper project." Etc. Plausible and implausible theoretic "what-ifs" to enable a secondary officer to protect the sacred cows of politics and upset unwelcome invasions of old routines by a progressive governor!

Again, in charter commissions, arguments which to a layman sound learned are brought in to justify retaining the city clerk on the elective list—such arguments as that "he must keep the records from being distorted by the administrative head in the latter's interest" or "he must certify the correctness of the ordinances." All regardless of the fact that the voters will pay almost no attention to that obscure routine office at the polls whether the position be well administered or not. Or again, here come the "practical" men to head off the transfer of the city treasurer from the elective to the appointive list. For the dull post has always been easily within their gift for some party worker. The new city manager, it seems, must not be permitted to appoint the treasurer; the treasurer must be independent, chosen separately by the people to keep their money and to see that the manager does not spend it without due authority. Whereby a city manager later in one case finds the co-operation of the independent treasurer so leisurely, insubordinate, and indifferent to the departmental needs that the manager has to set up and run his own duplicate books at duplicated cost so as to secure day-by-day fiscal control!

SCHOOL DISTRICT GOVERNMENTS ARE UNIFIED

In contrast, close at hand are our 63,000 school district governments each with its single elective board, which appoints the professional superintendent. If these familiar institutions are correctly organized to raise and spend about 40 per cent of the local tax money on schools, then the typical city hall setup is wrong. So, following Euclid, let us propose that the school structure be made parallel to that in the city hall! We would then elect the school superintendent separately and endow him with power of appointment over some of the staff and give him veto power over the actions of the school board. The clerk of the board and the treasurer might be made separately elective, and some reason could be found for electing also a separate board of adult education and a board to operate the high-school auditorium. Which, as Euclid—or anybody—would say, would be absurd!

CONSTITUTIONAL CONVENTIONS ARE UNIFIED

Or let us arise at the opening session of an elective state constitutional convention (or a charter-drafting commission) and offer a resolution: "Whereas our state is governed by a governor, other elective state officers, and a two-house legislature, be it resolved that this convention proceed to realize the advantage of such a structure by empowering our chairman to veto our acts, making our secretary and our fiscal officer independent of our direction and dividing ourselves into two bodies for separate duplicate consideration of each proposal on the floor and in two sets of committees. Thus, if 75 per cent of the members favor a measure, the remaining 25 per cent will have multiple opportunities to stifle it by obstruction in either of two committees, in either of two houses, or by disagreement on details between the two houses or by veto. And the people who later stand aghast because of the feebleness of the few measures which survive the gantlet will never know who killed the rest."

GOVERNMENTETTES!

The realization that each independently elected officer or board is a little government by itself compels another look at the number of governments—112,420—counted up in the Introduction. If each county is actually, on the average, six little governments because it has that many separate elective boards and officers, our 3049 counties become 18,244 governmentettes! Similarly, the 16,667 cities with one to ten officers or groups become about 100,000 governmentettes.

If political reform accomplished its orthodox purpose of bringing to county, city, and town governments the simple oneness seen in the elective school board systems, each of those governments would become a unified organism and correspondingly easier for the voters to control.

HAVING TOO MANY GOVERNMENTS FRUSTRATES DEMOCRACY

But beyond that correction lies the further frustrating fact that in many American areas there are far too many governments. In Maryland there is one unit of local government for each 10,000 of population, in New York 6.1, in Michigan 15.8, in Iowa 29.9, and in South Dakota 76.8. In Maryland the units of government are 18.5 to each 1000 square miles of area, in New York 173.8, in Michigan 145.5, in Iowa 135.6, in South Dakota 64.3. Obviously such diversity reflects no principle but only accumulated tradition. A rational provision of local units based on current realities would greatly reduce the number. A British citizen lives, in most cases, under two layers of government only, the national and the city or borough, but the American citizen may live under (1) national, (2) state, (3) county, (4) township, (5) incorporated village, (6) school district, each empowered to borrow money and levy taxes. And sometimes a seventh layer, namely, one or more of those 5,950 special districts each governed by an elective board with taxing or assessing power, as in King County (Seattle), where there are 137 separate taxing districts for fire, water, sewer (98 of those), schools, hospital, airport, and drainage!

MODERN CONURBATIONS

Areawise we have cities and suburbs constituting a conurbation where the urban population expanding along automobile routes well beyond the reach of annexation will spread a population of, say, 200,000 over a maze of ancient and obsolete township and village boundaries, so that fifty feeble little governments are found serving a population that could to better advantage be served by one. Try to consolidate or abolish that extra forty-nine! Each of them has its coterie of officeholders, its traditional way of doing things, its local name and village personality! Such emotional factors are familiar blocks to simplification of the service. But the voters outside the central city are confronted with a tough task when, to get a trunk sewer or a high school, they must not only convince the officers of their local units but get simultaneous consent and cooperation from those of all the rest. Tasks which the nucleus city undertakes straightforwardly may require years to negotiate among the forty-nine suburbs. When Greater New York was formed, the greater city absorbed scores of reluctant cities, townships, villages, school boards, and special districts. But its creation had taken the lifetime of Andrew H. Green, the pioneer promoter of the idea. So elsewhere the reduction of the number of local units by annexation processes is laborious and belated.[3]

But that process of annexation cannot commonly reach out far enough to take in the ten-mile radius (300 square miles) so readily reached by the suburbanite's automobile, and another process comes into effect—attrition of little old local governments by transfer of functions like hospitals, roads, and other urban services to the counties, frail though the latter commonly are in powers and in capacity for new big tasks. When the attrition process goes far enough the little bailiwicks become little more than taxing, assessment, and accounting units, as in some parts of that fabulous conurbation of Los Angeles County.

Meanwhile new villages are being incorporated and other villages are becoming cities as the United States population figures grow. The net figure, however, shrank from 175,418 units of government in the 1930–33 count to 119,465 as of 1951.[4] Practically all the reduction was accounted for by a great net reduction in the number of school districts. That represents in part the abolition of little one-room schoolhouses in favor of central graded schools served by good roads and free buses.

Anderson's Program for One-Ninth as Many Governments

Applying common sense to the picture, undeterred by the difficulty of sweeping out the clutter of custom, William Anderson in 1942 proposed to have no separate school district governments whatsoever. The special districts, he believed, can with few excep-

[3] In England, too, there is complaint on this point. There the 12,602 local authorities (with about a quarter of our population), of which 11,100 are parish councils or parish meetings, could rationally and sensibly be cut or consolidated to 3000, according to articles in *The Municipal Journal*, London, May 25 and June 8, 1951.

[4] *Governments in the United States in 1951*. Bureau of the Census, Washington, D. C., 1952.

tions be merged into other local governments, and the same is possible for townships, except in New England where no counties in the usual sense are available to take over township functions. Finally, counties, reduced in number in some states, can take on the work done by many small rural organisms. Altogether Dr. Anderson imaginatively reduced our great array of local units of government (below the state level) down to 200 city-counties, 2100 rural and part-rural counties, 15,000 incorporated places, and 500 miscellaneous units—a total of 17,800 units, approximately one-ninth of the 1941 number or one-seventh of the 1951 number! [5] "The average state, instead of having nearly 3,500 local units, would have about 370." The top record has been 15,629 in Illinois!

CONSOLIDATIONS IMPROVE DEMOCRATIC CONTROL

Other factors being equal, it is obviously easier for 100,000 voters to control one county government than to control, say, a county government, a city government, four townships, and ten suburbs and villages. True democracy would gain ground, politician power would diminish by such progress toward unification and by such discarding of needless clutter. Efforts toward such simplification of the political scene will be resisted artfully by all who hold political power, with the allegation that every four-corner hamlet should have a tiny one-horse government of its own "close to the pee-pul," but the instinctive hostility of such gentry to consolidation programs reflects expert perception of a prospect of diminished importance for themselves thereunder and an unwelcome enlargement of the number of voters who will comprehend the whole simplified scene of politics.

The tying together of the now-scattered staff of individual governmental units and the tying together of groups of units by consolidations are commonly urged on grounds of efficiency, tax saving, and clarification of responsibility. But the deeper gain is in the superior democracy of such strengthened and simplified structures. Those advances move toward freedom—freedom from government

[5] *The Units of Government in the United States,* Public Administration Service, No. 83, Chicago, 1942 and 1949. Cf. also Chapter XXII.

by small cliques of politicians and reduction of conditions that frustrate democracy.

Therefore:

RULE THREE: GOVERNMENTS MUST BE WELL INTEGRATED

Ramshackle mechanisms and needlessly numerous units are difficult for even the active participants to control. Still more difficult is it for voters to control them. Intentionally or otherwise, they automatically frustrate the democratic process.

The voters on the street are in no position to compel teamwork if separately elected public servants take advantage of their separateness to quarrel and block. Neither are they usually in any position to determine which of the bickering officers has the rights of the issue. Controversies will always be, and should be, a feature of any live government anywhere but they should be resolvable by the simple taking of a vote so that decisions can be arrived at and action can begin.

Chapter VIII

OUR PECULIAR AMERICAN PARTIES

> I always voted at my party's call
> And never thought of thinking for myself at all
>
> —*H.M.S. Pinafore*

THE unique complexities of our governmental structures account for some unique and baffling features of our political parties.

There is much complaint about the lack of meaning and genuineness in the split between the Democratic and Republican parties. Academic thought on the subject gropes toward the idea of establishing in each party some sort of strong national governing committee to provide leadership and a defined, consistent ideology such as can be seen in British parties.

BRITISH PARTIES ARE MORE FAITHFUL TO PRINCIPLE

In Great Britain parties on either the parliamentary or the local levels are almost like American civic associations, voluntary and outside the law, and the party labels do not appear on ballots. The central party organizers pass their torches to successors of their own choosing and thus through the decades the party can hold its rudder true to principles. The rank-and-file members have no voting rights over selection of party candidates and are consulted only in the sense that the party management must cater successfully if it is to hold the allegiance of the party following. The party's nucleus in the London headquarters can recommend party candidates for distant parliamentary districts and can read deviationists, including whole local branches, out of the party. Accordingly British parties cluster around sets of principles and stay true to them for decades. The cleavage between parties is real and rests on basic differences in points of view. The party members in Parliament within reasonable limits think alike and vote alike. They do not really have to "do

71

just what their leaders tell 'em to" but being like-minded in general purpose they do, and without much strain. Consequently we see in British parties a genuineness and solidarity on principle which is badly missed in our major parties. There are central party officers and a staff, a committee system and some paraphernalia as well as a party treasury. And in each parliamentary district there is a local party committee with the duty of helping the central officers to select for that district an acceptable candidate for Parliament and of electing him. The candidate often is not a resident of the district he is to represent and indeed may enter it for the first time in his life when he appears to be introduced to the party's local officers and start his campaign. There is no way in which a party member may claim for himself the great advantages of the party label without the sanction of the central party committee in London. In other words, the party is effectively protected from invasion and capture by strangers to the original cause.

The party machine in England has little to do in comparison with an American party and is primarily a campaigning organization quiescent except at elections, when it musters a horde of volunteers to solicit votes and run meetings. Its year-round professional workers are, compared to ours, negligible in number or power. Victory rests on successful catering to public sentiment rather than on capacity to handle a big budget of annual business and to elaborate intensive organization in the wards.[1]

OUR PARTIES DUCK PRINCIPLES

Why can we not have such genuine homogeneous parties in the United States? Why are the Democratic and Republican parties so different from the Laborites and Conservatives? You can find prominent exponents of any principle in either party in Congress. Wendell Willkie, a Democrat in 1938, did not have to change his principles to become acceptable as candidate of the Republicans in 1940. General Eisenhower, without self-stultification, could have borne the banner of either party in 1952. There are greater differences as to public policy within each party than there are between the parties. Both parties have their hidebound reactionaries and

[1] Cf. Allen M. Potter, "British Party Organization, 1950," *Political Science Quarterly*, March, 1951.

their headlong radicals, and every shade of belief between the extremes.

What is a Republican anyway? He is one thing in Vermont and another in California! What is a Democrat? In New York the Democratic party platform for the state elections of 1950 pointedly omitted support of the Truman administration's Brannan plan, since New York agriculturists are largely dairymen hostile to any plan that would raise the prices of the grain for their cattle. And it omitted from its catalogue of commendation for the national administration's principal projects any mention of the controversial socialized medicine issue; indeed, one candidate for the gubernatorial nomination was considered too vulnerable because of his past official association with it! And if indeed some state Democratic platform specifically opposed a major project of the Democratic national administration, can it be conceived that there would be any attempt to rebuke or read out of the party those antagonistic local leaders and their rank-and-file supporters? Do the Democrats in the southern states who revolted in 1948 against the party's platform plank on civil rights for Negroes cease to be Democrats? And how little that momentary defection, or that of the Progressives from the Republican party in 1912, affected the long run of the history of the parties!

No, American parties reflect some crude class and occupational groupings, but principles are concepts which seep upward in both parties at the same time and reach fruition when widely accepted in both. This is a fact which steadies our politics and prevents sharp whipsawing of public policy. An unequivocal, bold stand on a controversial issue is a rare thing in American party platforms and leadership—it might alienate some votes! In American parties debatable principles of public policy are a nuisance to the managements. The latter would be well content to have no platforms at all except expressions of scorn for the claims and record of the opposite party and promises to achieve the same objectives more wisely. "Like railway car platforms, they are things to get in on, not to stand on." The conventions do not often split on platform planks but are concerned only to have them resound mightily with thunderous periods. I recall my dismay when the New York State committee of the Progressive party in 1915 considered whether to advocate the adoption by the voters of the new state constitution which was being submitted to referendum. I was given a thoughtful hearing and exhibited the simple fact that of six constitutional items in the Progressive platform five had been adopted or advanced in the pending constitution. But the prime question, I found, was how to discredit the output of that Republican-dominated convention. And so a progressive constitution was with Progressive help assailed and defeated!

In other words, principles are but thin façades on American parties and have little to do with the massive realities of the mere reach for power.

Our Parties Are Primarily Mechanisms

Our parties are mechanistic extensions of our constitutional structures. The latter fail to reach all the way to the people, so parties bridge the gap. Their necessity is related to the violations of the Three Rules of Democracy previously described. Parties could frankly abandon all pretense of being expressions of principles, could stop writing platforms, could stop making "the same promises as last time," and they, or at least their elaborate internal "machines," would still be essential to make most of our miserable complex ramshackle structures work at all.

Many Party Functions

Our political machines, resting on the support of blindly voting party members, perform many necessary functions and have a great deal to do—far more than the relatively trivial staffs and volunteers of a British party. Each must find and advance candidates to fill the elective offices chosen by partisan elections in six layers of government—national, state, judicial (in states where judges are elective), county and (where local elections are partisan) township, city or village, and school district. They will be embarrassed by the necessity of forecasting and catering to public opinion in respect to perhaps 10 per cent of their nominees and can exercise fairly complete discretion on the other 90 per cent. But candidates have to be found and presented in either case, and it is a gigantic task which cannot be handled by mass action, or inaction, of unorganized voters. Neither can it be competently done under the usual cloudy circumstances by candidates' advancing themselves and scrambling for votes. Some initiative must find and propose candidates.

The party machines must also solve the problem of mobilizing voters in unwieldy districts such as the states in state-wide elections. In a small city under tight setups conforming to the Three Rules, the charter may require the people to select a council of five members and, as described in Reading D, on "500 Non-Political Elections," the people, with simple local improvisations, can manage the task well enough while the local wings of the two national parties refrain completely from leadership or participation. But it can't happen that way if the constituency is the state of Pennsylvania!

Finally, we have the unwieldy district of the United States itself when voting for president. The attempt of the founding fathers to break that task down to workable units in the Electoral College having been aborted, we are left in dire need of a substitute and have found it in the mechanism of parties which contrive to bring together at quadrennial conventions a thousand-odd delegates covering every state, each backed by local organizations of sufficient importance to add up to great political power.

ONLY ROOM FOR TWO PARTIES

Given one such contraption, there is *ipso facto* room for one more to be the vehicle of those who dislike the first, just as the existence of the "ins" inspires the organization of "outs." Two organizations, but no more! For if the Progressives of 1912 had been able to establish a universal net of organization covering every county, capable of pursuing the Republicans whom they had outvoted, the Republican party would have been displaced and would have speedily withered up and we would have soon been back in a two-party duel. Indeed, it may be argued that no new party can ever hereafter get hopefully started on a national scale in the face of the inertia of the two massive establishments of political veterans. The country has gotten too big for such a maneuver to succeed although it is still possible in compact homogeneous England with its relatively trivial volume of elective offices to contest. The split-off of the southern Democrats in 1948, being only regional, was, of course, futile from the start so far as hope of ever becoming national in scale and successful in electing its presidential candidates was concerned. Another split running through all the states on some big issue might deliver to a new party a ready-made army of professionals, clubs, political veterans, and mechanicians, in which case the third strongest party when once identified as such would rapidly wither up and disappear, since neither professional politicians nor volunteer idealists can, under such circumstances, long keep up steam enough for the tasks of sustaining a strong national organization. The Progressives of 1912 probably represented the rank and file of Republicans more ardently and accurately than the Republican party managers did. But the latter had the organization adequate to handle the business of the six layers of government and the unwieldy national, state-wide, and metropolitan districts. Thus the party's organization rode out a storm of fresh thought!

So it appears that long ballots, ramshackle structures, and, in some districts, unwieldiness require a successful American party to be 90 per cent machine and, say, 10 per cent idealism.

If the Socialist Party Grew

One party in the American scene, however, is not subject to such characterization. The Socialist party is a group of idealists unified in a cause and uncorrupted by possession of power. Suppose it should show promising growth and begin to elect candidates!

Membership being open to all, it will forthwith enjoy an influx of newcomers, including some merely intent on sharing the power. The latter will dismay the idealists by their indifference to doctrine and their readiness to sacrifice it for victories; so the platforms become less obnoxiously explicit, and items alien to the original concept are put in as voter bait.

Pressure groups clamber aboard this vehicle and are eagerly welcomed and catered to. Management problems multiply, a party machine develops, and practical men take it over, utilizing the cause and the embarrassed idealists to mask their grab for power. Until at last the platforms become general and equivocal, the candidates nondescript, and people say, "What real difference is there now between the Socialists and the Republicans?"

Thus the party's mechanicians, taking full possession, would juggernaut the party's soul!

Such a cycle of degradation (long since completed in the major parties) has been seen twice in miniature in Greater New York's half-century, requiring, in small new reform parties, no more than four years to sink from honest idealism to narrow escapes from capture of key posts by self-seekers blatantly disdainful of party ideals.

CONTROL OF MINOR ELECTIVE OFFICES FOR PARTISAN ENDS

Immense and costly organization is necessary to qualify parties for success in the needlessly multitudinous tasks of American politics. Such organizations man and finance themselves largely out of the public purse. They do not steal anywhere near as much as they often could, but graft is always latent and is one of a party's perquisites. The most dependable support comes from the minor elective offices and their staffs, for the organization has unchallenged discretion amounting to appointive power over the minor offices. A new sheriff is to be elected, a matter of very slight interest to the voters in most bailiwicks but of very lively interest to the party managers and their aspiring hard-working satellites. So a docile party veteran gets the nomination, is elected unscrutinized by most voters, and appoints the deputy sheriffs from the party clubhouses in supine compliance with guidance from party headquarters. (As described in Reading C.)

Then comes the vaguer, almost legitimate factor of *influence*. To secure a large paving contract, the contractor, a stranger to the scene, looks around the town for a man of influence with the current administration, appoints him his agent, and pays for his services. The agent knows whom to see and calls them all by their nicknames, for his activity in local politics has contributed toward their election and they would be ingrates if they did not, other things being equal, throw the business his way or give him the lowdown on the pressures in city hall. The city's insurance business must be placed with somebody and the agent who gets it is careful not to seem lackadaisical in his attendance at party functions and his devotion to party duties, for if the rival party captures city hall, his livelihood is threatened. And then in every city and county there are firms of lawyers with a political member—or two, one in each party—and to such firms judges award lucrative trusteeships and important litigants pick them as counsel or associate counsel, not only because they are capable but because they are "in right" and can get the awed cooperation of courthouse clerks or a friendly private chat in judges' chambers.

Now if these rewards for political machine work were divided equally between the two necessary sets of politicians, the elective process might not be too much distorted. Indeed, an elective officer of New York County once issued plaintive publicity urging that party leaders and captains of both parties be paid for their political services by the city government directly instead of by indirection. But the favors are not equally distributed. These practically appointive powers over minor offices are utilized to fortify the party in its possession of power, to make the "ins" stronger and stronger against possible ouster by the "outs." Thereby the "ins" tie the pendulum of public opinion, distort and pervert the effect of elections; and the public pays for the entrenchments the "ins" thus construct to frustrate democracy and preserve their dominance.

Two-Party System Is Often a One-Party System

The idea that the "ins" will find their excesses curbed by a swing of the voters toward the "outs" is badly impaired by the ins' superior ability to man and perhaps finance themselves out of the public treasury. The two-party system thus is sometimes a bit mythical and the binopoly of control over minor elective officers and unwieldy district candidates becomes in fact a monopoly, and so much worse. New York's delegation to the House of Representatives (10 per cent of the House) fluctuates from time to time but of its forty-three districts, 1930 to 1948 inclusive, twenty stayed true to one party through ten successive elections and seven more fell from regularity only once. Among the states sixteen (one-third), with 30.4 per cent of the population, have stayed with one party through twenty years of senatorial elections and ten more have made only a single exception. We may assume that in those states other state-wide elections for governor and minor state offices are similarly under single-party dominance and that within each state half the legislative districts and counties run parallel with congressional districts in being under *one*-party systems. So in half the country the admirers of the two-party system must in logic switch their argument and find, if they can, ways to extol the virtues of the mysterious system whereby nominations almost equivalent to election are awarded by *one* party.

That dominant parties, whether in Democratic New York or Republican Philadelphia, ruling unchecked by fear of successful opposition, are wide open to entrance by self-servers is obvious. "The Democrats are the party to join in New York," said my cynical college classmate when I became a voter. And a dominant party is even more unfit to hand-pick obscure minor officers and to control nominations in unwieldy districts than one with a strong competitor.

Organizations in politics are in some fields essential to make our systems work at all. They are inevitable in the situations where they can help greatly toward victory. It is not their existence we should deplore, but only their unchecked possession of unscrutinized power.

REFORM OF PARTIES AWAITS COMPLIANCE WITH THE THREE RULES

So we arrive at the conclusion that reform of American political parties and their conversion to real parties clustered about principles, as in England, awaits the revision of the governmental structure by sweeping simplification toward compliance with the Three Rules. Thereby the machine, which now is 90 per cent of the party, would have so much less to do that it would lose its intraparty importance. The real leaders of opinion could then assert their proper right to steer party policy with less fear of being slapped down by the practical party heelers for stirring up controversial issues and taking sides.

Here ends our analysis of the mechanistic faults of the American political system. Not all those faults can be repaired but most of them can. And it is a hopeful augury that the faults are not moral, as editors sometimes assert, but mechanistic and responsive to mechanistic corrections.

Now we turn to narration of the programs of reform that are under way toward securing compliance with the Three Rules!

Part II

Progress Toward Compliance with the Three Rules

Ideals in politics are never realized but
the pursuit of them determines history.

—LORD ACTON

Chapter IX

THE SHORT-BALLOT CRUSADE, 1909–19

PRIOR to 1909 the excessive and unexampled number of elective offices in the American systems had been noted by Sir James Bryce and other political scientists. In the Brooklyn plan, where the strong-mayor feature first appeared, Seth Low and others had pointed out the necessity for integration and simplicity in municipal structures, and the National Municipal League had for some years, beginning in 1900, sponsored its first Model City Charter with a strong elective mayor and a council elected at large in rotation.

In 1903, casting my first vote as a college junior, I was, as previously related, taken aback to find myself unprepared on fifteen of the nineteen contests presented on my ballot and, for lack of other information, voted blindly for whatever names were marked "Republican." To my political hero of those days, the picturesque, dramatic district attorney of New York County, William Travers Jerome, I am indebted for a remark I heard him make at a banquet in 1905. He said, in effect, "It's all utter nonsense anyhow to elect officers like sheriffs and county clerks and coroners—those offices ought to be appointive and out of politics. The voters pay no attention to those obscure little offices and never will; the jobs are just so much pap for the politicians!" It was an offhand, unrecorded interjection in his speech but it ignited me; it appeared that neither I nor other voters were to be blamed for not mastering our ballots. It was the ballots that were faulty! The writers of state constitutions and city charters had made ballots too long!

THE SHORT-BALLOT PRINCIPLE

A few years later, in 1908, warmed by the receptions I got when I developed the idea in conversations, I wrote a little pocket-sized pamphlet entitled *The Short Ballot*, printed it privately, and circulated it to a hundred people known to be at home in such subjects,

CONDENSED STATEMENT OF THE SHORT-BALLOT PRINCIPLE

(In 1910 the first version was submitted to Woodrow Wilson as president of the National Short Ballot Organization for his approval; he elaborated it by adding the italicized phrases.)

The dangerously great power of politicians in our country is not due to any peculiar civic indifference of the people, but rests on the fact that we are living under a form of democracy that is so unworkable as to constitute in practice a pseudo-democracy. It is unworkable because:

First—It submits to popular election offices which are too unimportant to attract *or deserve* public attention, and

Second—It submits to popular election so many offices at one time that many of them are inevitably crowded out from proper public attention, *and*

Third—It submits to popular election so many offices at one time as to make the business of ticket making too intricate for popular participation, whereupon some sort of private political machine becomes an indispensable instrument in electoral action.

Many officials, therefore, are elected without adequate public scrutiny, and owe their selection not to the people but to the makers of the party ticket, who thus acquire an influence that is capable of great abuse.

The "short-ballot" principle is:

First—That only those offices should be elective which are important enough to attract *and deserve* public scrutiny.

Second—That very few offices should be filled by election at one time, so as to permit adequate and unconfused scrutiny of the candidates by the public, *and so as to facilitate the free and intelligent making of original tickets by any voter for himself unaided by political specialists.*

The application of this principle should be extended to all cities, counties, and states.

inviting comment. The returns were heartening; the idea was not new, of course, but was certainly neglected and underemphasized in the catalogue of reform. Woodrow Wilson was the most eminent of the early supporters and he became president of the little "National Short Ballot Organization" which we presently set up. My father, William Hamlin Childs, put up several thousand dollars a year to cover the deficits and I became the volunteer secretary in my spare time with a little staff and office located at 383 Fourth Avenue, New York, adjacent to the advertising agency where I worked.

"The Short Ballot" was published in *The Outlook* of July 17, 1909, and in successive revised editions has been the classic statement of the principle ever since.

The Short Ballot Organization

In 1909 progressivism in California, Oregon, and elsewhere was decrying the alliance between venal political machines and big business and proposing a string of new ideas—initiative, referendum and recall, proportional representation, preferential ballots, direct primaries, and the Galveston-Des Moines commission form of municipal government. Political inventions were in the air (in both senses of the phrase) and the municipal reformers who gathered once a year at the National Municipal League conventions viewed them warily. Most of the promoters of these ideas fondly promised too much and sometimes frankly disparaged all ideas but their own.

At the 1909 convention of the National Municipal League in Cincinnati I presented to political reformers and university professors of government the short-ballot principle. Charles W. Eliot, president of Harvard, then at the height of his reputation, was the principal guest of the convention that year and he pounced upon the idea, called it "absolutely the gist of political reform," and after a set speech on another subject at the banquet found an excuse to take the floor again unasked to call attention to the importance of the principle.

In our little Short Ballot office in 1910–14 my assistant, H. S. Gilbertson, and I diligently campaigned by mail. Broadcast mailings of *The Short Ballot* carried return postals whereby the recipient acknowledged his agreement with the principle and came on our rolls as a short-ballot advocate, with or without a contribution. We accumulated 15,000 such advocates, serviced them with news of our activities thereafter, and in a few spots put them into touch with leaders in their own states who attempted to do something. Local groups as described hereafter went to work to shorten state ballots in New Hampshire, Kentucky, Ohio, Illinois, Iowa, Missouri, New York, Wisconsin, and Oregon, formulating bills and constitutional amendments, with scholarly supporting pamphlets in some cases. In Illinois they helped defeat an attempt to lengthen the already long ballots by making the civil service commission and the state warehouse commission elective.

In 1910 a charter revision committee in San Francisco, after receiving our material, submitted a revision of the charter with lengthened terms of elective officers and elections in rotation so as to bring the local ballot down to six places which made it also practical to make the local election nonpartisan. It was adopted in November.

RESPONSE IN CALIFORNIA AND OREGON

1910 saw the triumph of the Progressives in California and the election of Hiram Johnson as governor with a mandate to put the Southern Pacific Railroad out of state politics. Our pamphleteering in 1910 must have struck the leaders at the right moment, for the principle was in the platform of the Lincoln-Roosevelt League in the Republican primary, was featured in the campaign speeches for the nomination, and became the first specific plank in the Republican platform.

Governor Johnson came to New York in December, 1910, and visited our office unannounced. All of us were out to lunch! But an alert office boy did what he could, gave him everything we had, and he devoted one-sixth of his message to the legislature to the subject a few weeks later with verbatim quotations from our pamphlets. Johnson, moderately, urged prevention of the submission of more than twelve candidates on any voter's ballot. The central committees of the captured party drafted bills to cut off the tail of the state ticket, to facilitate adoption of the commission plan for cities, and to provide for short ballots in counties. Chester H. Rowell, president of the Lincoln-Roosevelt League, reported this development to us in January, 1911, in response to a letter suggesting formation of a California Short Ballot Organization, and added, "So you see the present prospects are that the purposes of a short ballot organization in California will have been accomplished before such an organization could be formed. However, if there should still remain anything else to do after the legislature adjourns in March, we should by all means take up the question of such an organization then. The early approach of a realization of the ideas of The Short Ballot Organization in California is very largely due to your work. . . ."

A bill to take the statutory office of state printer off the California ballot was passed, and amendments to the constitution to remove the superintendent of public instruction and clerk of the supreme court from the ballot were submitted to the electorate and subsequently adopted. But the rest of the short-ballot program got no further.

A home rule county government law was passed expressly providing that counties might frame their own charters and that judges, sheriffs, justices, county clerks, treasurers, recorders, license collectors, tax collectors, public administrators, coroners, surveyors, district attorneys, auditors, assessors, and superintendents of schools, hitherto elective, could in such charters be either elective or appointive. Several counties moved promptly toward simplification and in 1912 Los Angeles County swept away ten minor elective offices leaving on the elective list only the supervisors, sheriff, assessor, and district attorney.

In 1909 in Oregon William S. U'Ren's Peoples Power League took on the short-ballot principles at sight and Mr. U'Ren, visiting New York, lamented to me that he had not heard of the idea sooner. With his usual boldness he launched a fresh but complex program that would have brought Oregon ballots down to eight or less. He filed an initiative petition in 1909 and again in 1911 to cut off the tail of the state ticket except the auditor, to make sheriffs and district attorneys appointive, to provide a single-house legislature and a county manager plan for all the counties. "But," as he explained to me on a visit east, "each time we added a plank to the platform, some people got off." Later events showed that his crusades were waning in their power and no progress on this issue was achieved under his leadership.

Pennsylvania, in 1909, by a series of amendments with which our efforts had nothing to do, got rid of a freak constitutional requirement that the three election officers in each urban precinct must be elective. There were 1170 of them in Philadelphia—the most minuscule of all American elective officers, numerous beyond any remote possibility of individual public scrutiny by any urban electorate. They were, of course, hand-picked—including sometimes names of nonexistent persons duly elected and impersonated when the time came to serve—and there were in consequence sometimes 70,000 phantom voters supporting the dominant party.

GOVERNOR HUGHES AND GOVERNOR WILSON

New York's great governor, Charles Evans Hughes, picked up the short-ballot idea at sight and put it into his annual message in 1910, as related in the next chapter.

Woodrow Wilson, when he became governor of New Jersey in 1911, did not drop his interest or title in the Short Ballot Organization—indeed, he let us use his name until his death—but, as it happened, he could do little for the cause in New Jersey. That state's constitution could be amended only at five-year intervals and the next chance did not come until 1914. Since the state ticket had no tail, the path toward a short ballot in New Jersey consists in making legislators elective from single-member districts instead of at large by counties, two (one state senator and one assemblyman) for each voter to elect instead of as many as twelve. Governor Fort had fought vainly for this in 1909 and Wilson put in a word for it before he left the governorship.

LIP SERVICE IN PARTY PLATFORMS

In 1912, when forty governors and legislatures were elected, short-ballot planks appeared in the platforms of all three parties in Ohio and Illinois, in the Progressive platforms in Nebraska, New York, Minnesota, and Pennsylvania, and in the Democratic platform in Utah. It all seemed like a quick and favoring gale of astonishingly prompt response. Alas, it was all lip service; even in states where all three parties endorsed the idea the bills were pocketed in legislative committees.

Likewise in vain were the messages of eleven governors in January, 1913. The short ballot was urged by the governors of Michigan, Colorado, North Dakota, Iowa, Washington, Illinois, and Wyoming in line with the earlier efforts by Governor Hughes in New York and Hiram Johnson in California.

Fourteen governors wrote short-ballot paragraphs in their messages in 1915 and ten did it in 1917, but without legislative result anywhere.

COMMISSION PLAN IN CITIES

In respect to city government we made ourselves the central authority on the spread and the experience of the commission plan, which, for all its faults, did offer short ballots and, by breaking the cake of custom, taught America that a miniature duplicate of the federal government was not the only conceivable basis for organization of a municipality. For charter revision commissions we accumulated abstracts of most of the commission-plan charters and published them in *Beard's Loose-Leaf Digest of Short Ballot Charters* in 1911. Our *Story of the Commission Plan* pamphlet was sold in bulk quantities for use in local campaigns. Every charter commission needed that material—it was available nowhere else—and when, soon after, in Lockport, New York, in 1910, and in Sumter, South Carolina, in 1912, the council-manager plan became objectively reportable, as related in Chapter XV, we were in a strategic position to give it prominence as an improvement. We called it the commission-manager plan to tie it to the commission-plan movement which was moving fast.

EFFORTS ON THE COUNTY LEVEL

We also broke ground in the hard pan of county government. In 1914 we held three little "Conferences on County Government" at the City Club. The attendances were under twenty-five, but the papers presented were serious and competent. The proceedings as solemnly published in pamphlet form did not betray the smallness of the turnout and became a useful part of the scanty literature of the subject. One assistant district attorney of New York County, J. DuVivier, dealt vividly with the condition of the eleven shabby political elective coroners in New York City, leading the City Club to demand an investigation by Mayor Mitchel's commissioner of accounts, Leonard Wallstein. His report scorched the elective coroners out of existence; a bill passed in the legislature in the 1915 session set up a qualified medical examiner selected from the classified service after civil service examination, who went to work in January, 1918, as related in Chapter XXIII. We also set up a Good Government Association of New York State which, quite hopelessly at that time, sponsored a bill in the 1916 legislature providing an optional county-manager system for upstate counties on lines which, much later, did become law.

Gilbertson wrote and we published the first book devoted exclusively to the subject.[1]

END OF THE SHORT BALLOT ORGANIZATION, 1919

In 1917 we entered the First World War. It seemed a poor time for propaganda on our subjects and I took a leave of absence from business and went into the War Department for service which continued until the war ended in 1918. The war and the disintegration of the Progressive party after the 1916 election broke the triumphant stride of all the movements and fond inventions designed to end political bossism, "invisible government," and undue corporate influences in politics. After a year or two of handling the modest amount of momentum business that came to the National Short Ballot Organization I was glad to combine it into the National Municipal League, which moved from Philadelphia to New York, adopted our more active dissemination practices, and went on under the fresh leadership of young Harold W. Dodds.

Fuller details of the progress in 1909–17 and thereafter are in the chapters on the various fields which follow.

Be it remembered gratefully here that the organization's letterhead exhibited the imposing support of Woodrow Wilson, president, Winston Churchill (the New Hampshire novelist and reformer), Horace E. Deming, a political scientist, Ben B. Lindsay of Denver, John Mitchell, the leader of the coal miners, William S. U'Ren, the initiative and referendum pioneer of Oregon, William Allen White of Emporia, and Clinton Rogers Woodruff of the National Municipal League as vice-presidents, and an advisory board which, under simple bylaws written by Wilson, was the governing body consisting of himself and me plus Lawrence F. Abbot, editor of *The Outlook* magazine, Henry Jones Ford of the Princeton fac-

[1] H. S. Gilbertson, *The County, The Dark Continent of American Politics*, 1917. Out of print.

ulty, and Norman Hapgood, the crusading editor of *Collier's Weekly*. A junior board in New York met occasionally to check my initiatives; it comprised Robert S. Binkerd, then secretary of the City Club, Walter T. Arndt, then secretary of the Citizens Union, and Arthur C. Ludington, a widely beloved young scholar of reform, selflessly active in local reform efforts. It was Ludington who recruited Woodrow Wilson to our group and I was deeply indebted to him when, in 1911, he went through the manuscript for my book *Short Ballot Principles* [2] with a fine-tooth comb and screened out many a half-cooked assumption.

Out of the whole group only Binkerd lives today to share these memories.

In the separate New York State Short Ballot Organization (1909–19) the governing committee consisted of George W. Alger, Edgar Dawson, Horace E. Deming, Merrill E. Gates, Jr., Charles P. Howland, George Haven Putnam, Elihu Root, Jr., and Henry L. Stimson. Mr. Stimson's biography [3] relates how valiantly he carried the ball for us in the state constitutional convention of 1915.

[2] Houghton Mifflin Co., Boston, 1911. Out of print.
[3] McGeorge Bundy, *On Active Service*, Harper & Brothers, New York, 1951.

Chapter X

PROGRESS IN STATE ADMINISTRATION

NEW JERSEY elects its governor but no other state officers, the successor being the president of the senate. But Jersey ballots are long nevertheless, for legislators are chosen at large by counties —twelve in populous Essex and nine in Hudson. The governor's appointments require consent of the senate but his appointive power is otherwise complete, covering the judiciary, the attorney general, and the county prosecutors, thus following to the end the system of the federal government. Governor Fort in 1909, Woodrow Wilson in 1912, and Governor Fielder in 1914 vainly advocated shortening the ballot by providing single-member districts for the legislature.

Tennessee elects only the governor, his successor being the Speaker of the senate, but the legislature appoints the secretary of state. In Maine the governor is the only elective administrator but he is encompassed by an elective council of seven members, who obscurely share his powers of appointment, and the legislature picks the secretary of state and the treasurer. Likewise in New Hampshire, where the council has five elective members and the legislature picks the secretary of state, treasurer, and commissary general.

Elsewhere the state tickets carry tails of minor isolated elective officers—lieutenant governor, secretary of state, state treasurer, attorney general, state auditor, superintendent of schools, and so forth. These officers are usually frozen as elective into ancient state constitutions, unreachable by legislation and remote from public scrutiny.

To trim off these tails would accomplish the dual purpose of shortening ballots and advancing the integration of the badly divided state administrations.

New York's Partial Success and the Hughes Commission

Charles E. Hughes, then the brilliant governor of New York, led off by putting a demand for the short ballot into his annual message in January, 1910, calling for cutting off the tail of the state ticket and making appointive the five minor state officers—the comptroller (then a large office), secretary of state, state treasurer, attorney general, and state engineer and surveyor.

An amendment in the New York legislature passed one house in 1914. It would have cut off the entire tail of the state ticket below the lieutenant governor. The issue split the 1915 constitutional convention of New York, where Elihu Root, Henry L. Stimson, "Al" Smith, George W. Wickersham, and other notables fought through an amendment cutting off the elective secretary of state, state treasurer, and state engineer and surveyor, unwillingly leaving the attorney general and a comptroller, with powers greatly reduced to pre- and post-audit, on the elective list. But the excellent constitution submitted by that convention was defeated at the polls.

Ultimately, in 1925, effective in 1927, the short-ballot measure was finally adopted as a separate amendment, the terms of the four remaining elective state offices being two years, afterward increased to four. The amendment was not self executing, and extensive legislation was left to be done to rearrange the 180 state agencies into an orderly cabinet. So in 1925 "Al" Smith as governor, faithful to the purpose of the amendment, indicated his intention to create a special commission to plan the reorganization. Whereupon, overnight, two political small-fry legislative officers, alarmed for the future status of the jobholders in the departments, including those scheduled for transfer to the appointive list, hastily stole a march on the governor and announced appointment by themselves of a large and undistinguished commission to perform that task. Further, they indicated one docile party character as the logical person for the commission to elect to its chairmanship. Governor Smith induced the legislative leaders to let him add a minority of fifteen members of his choosing to their forty-five and selected Charles E. Hughes, George W. Wickersham, Henry L. Stimson, and others whose eminence was calculated to offset their lack of numbers. (He also appointed me.) Hughes' agreement to accept the chairmanship if elected put an end to the covert attempt to steer the effort up Salt Creek. Hughes was elected chairman and the selection of sub-committees, the piloting of discussions, and the sponsoring of the results came into the hands of the most capable man in the state. Then, to the further dismay of the foes of such progress, the commission, instead of reporting a general plan which could have been the object of procrastinating lip service and sly dismantling in the process of conversion into law, proceeded to draft a bill for the whole bold project. With Hughes' sponsorship and "Al" Smith's support, a thorough reorganization [1] went through intact.

It has withstood the weather of twenty years thus far and the state has enjoyed expert and nonpolitical departmental administration under governors of both parties. All the 180 agencies of the state were grouped appropriately into a limited number of departments which technicians of the highest rank were afterward readily recruited to supervise. The benefit to the state administration was immediate. Continuous petty tampering with administrative bureaus by the legislature diminished when they were no longer isolated and defenseless; so did the direct importunities of administrative bureau employees in the legislative lobbies. Budgeting requests began to come through in good order from responsible major department heads, and interference in personnel matters by the legislative appropriations committees was blocked off. Once the plan was installed, the obstructive theories about "too much power to the governor" evaporated and were never heard of again. The voters, who had for a century been voting for secretary of state, state treasurer, and state engineer and surveyor, never seemed aware of the disappearance of those offices from the ballots. The next constitutional convention, in 1938, took the situation as a matter of course and left it untouched. In the state conventions which, under New York's election law, nominate party candidates for the four state-wide offices the shortening of the list improved the atmosphere. There were fewer minor offices to trade in and the two that remained elective were more visible and harder to assign to party hacks.

Testimony as to the internal effectiveness of the Hughes reorgan-

---

[1] Report of the Commission on State Reorganization, New York, 1926.

ization of New York's state government was furnished fifteen years after its adoption, by Governor Franklin D. Roosevelt.[2] Incidentally, he confirmed after experience the desirability of making the attorney general appointive as in the federal and in the usual municipal systems.

A highly competent observer of the state's political scene was the late J. W. Wadsworth. He was Speaker of the assembly in Governor Hughes' time and once left the chair to speak unavailingly on behalf of the short-ballot amendment. He was afterward U.S. senator and a representative in Congress. In 1949 he wrote me:

No, I have never heard a word of complaint against the shortening of our state ballot since that day. It was accepted by the people, generally, as being sensible and I am not aware of any effort to change it since then. The lessening of the number of state candidates to be nominated by a state convention has removed from the convention atmosphere a lot of pulling and hauling, trading back and forth and jockeying for the support of racial and religious groups. The modern convention does its work in a cleaner atmosphere, politically. It spends more of its time seeking out the best men for the fewer number of offices.

In 1950 Governor Dewey, addressing fellow governors at White Sulphur Springs at the end of his second term, testified from his experience in favor of limiting the state-wide elections to governor and lieutenant governor, which limitation in New York would mean making the elective attorney general and comptroller appointive.

THE OHIO EFFORT

Ohio in 1912 had a constitutional convention. William Howard Taft and Theodore Roosevelt, invited to address it, spoke for the short ballot effectively, and the press widely supported the idea. The amendment proposed to transfer to the appointive list the secretary of state, attorney general, state treasurer, auditor, and dairy and food commissioner. It was defeated fifty-seven to forty-seven. But all three parties adopted short-ballot planks at the subsequent November election, and partial success was achieved by removal from the ballots, by legislative action, of the public works commissioner, dairy and food commissioner, and commissioner of common

[2] *National Municipal Review,* April, 1930.

schools. The next year the legislature submitted an amendment to make the attorney general, state treasurer, auditor, and secretary of state appointive. There ensued a lively state-wide debate in which the three incumbents, the attorney general, the auditor, and the treasurer, toured the state with lurid rhetoric and homely hokum. These offices had, before 1851, been appointive—by the legislature. Nobody was proposing to revive any such setup, but that experience had been bad and was used to bedevil the new proposal. No more than twelve appointments would have been added to the exempt list under the governor, but the opposition painted a picture of dictatorship. The amendment won in the urban counties, Cuyahoga (Cleveland), Hamilton (Cincinnati), and Lucas (Toledo), by narrow majorities but lost in the rural districts. Total vote was 233,153 to 447,493.

An amendment to take county officers out of the constitution so that new forms of county government could be presented by legislation also lost, 213,865 to 436,739. It appeared again, however, and was adopted at the polls in 1933. (But, as related later, no counties up to 1952 have been successful in trying to proceed thereunder.)

Indiana and Elsewhere

Indiana in 1919 removed from its ballots the state geologist and the state statistician (the final incumbent of the latter office was a stonemason) and transferred from the elective auditor to the governor the control of the commissioners of banking and of insurance. But it defeated at the polls an amendment that same year to remove from the elective list the superintendent of public instruction, clerk of the supreme court, and clerk of the appellate courts.

Michigan's senate in 1913 passed a bill to trim the list of elective state offices, but the bill got no further.

In 1915 Oregon made its elective state engineer appointive by the governor and in 1919 made two elective district water superintendents likewise appointive, ultimately, in 1923, combining the latter.

Illinois's Advisory Referendum

In Illinois in 1912 a petition with 114,000 signatures put on the ballot the advisory question, "Shall the next general assembly create a legislative commission to investigate the most practical means of shortening the cumbersome election ballot and report to the 49th general assembly its recommendations?" It was carried 508,780 to 165,270 as hereafter related, and was fortified by endorsement in the Republican, Democratic, and Progressive party platforms. But no action followed, then or since.

And there the frontal attack for shorter state ballots petered out!

Chapter XI

PROGRESS IN STATE ADMINISTRATION (CONTINUED): THE STATE REORGANIZATION MOVEMENT

THE Bureau of Municipal Research,[1] launched in 1906 in New York City, opened up a new method of attack on governmental methods. It has been followed by scores of other such institutes in other cities, all dedicated to improving departmental organization, administration, and costs in the structures of municipalities and states below the elective offices. It pressed toward sound budgets and orderly financial methods and in its sweep came to the need for integration of structure for efficiency's sake. In states, following an incomplete (and still incomplete) pioneer reorganization of the state system of departments under Governor Lowden of Illinois (1917), there was a long sequence of studies and reforms to streamline disorderly uncoordinated growths of appointive offices.[2] In the studies and in various state constitutional conventions, the logic of putting all the minor state offices into an orderly cabinet system under the governor was repeatedly recognized and urgently proposed, but merely as a measure of internal good order.

For some years I hoped that the short-ballot principle would quietly find its way into adoption as a logical part of such reorganizations and without the necessity of drumming up support for the short ballot as a separate contentious feature. But, in every case except New York and Virginia, where the accomplishment is incomplete, the interest of the political machines in retaining their direct access to the minor offices has provided intense and stubborn resistance fortified by shallow and superficially plausible rhetoric against "giving such great power to the governor" (it would usually

---

[1] Now the Institute of Public Administration, New York City.

[2] A. E. Buck, *The Reorganization of State Governments*, Columbia University Press, New York, 1938.

add no more than 5 per cent to his existing staff and appropriations)
or "taking away from the people the power to select their own secretary of state" (as if they had ever really had the power!).

In this narrative we will neglect the stories of useful regrouping
of scatterations of offices already appointive and stick to our concern with reduction of the list of obscure and needlessly elective
posts whose position on the elective list flouts our Rules One and
Three.

Roll Call of the State Reorganization Efforts re the Short Ballot to 1952

Alabama in 1932 had a Brookings Institution report which recommended consolidating ninety-two agencies into nineteen departments, all under the governor, except an auditor, to be chosen by
the legislature. It included cutting off the tail of the state ticket and
reducing the legislature to one house. None of it became law except
some good reallocation of financial functions.

In 1950 at the request of the Legislative Council, the local Legislative Reference Service reported a project for abolishing thirty-
three agencies, largely obsolete, and reducing major agencies from
ninety-nine to forty-two. It proposed (vainly) that the elective
secretary of state be abolished and that the elective attorney general, commissioner of agriculture and industries, and state treasurer
be made appointive by the governor.

Arizona in 1933 developed a plan to collect sixty agencies into
eleven departments under the governor, eliminating the tail of the
ticket except the attorney general and the superintendent of public
instruction, who were to remain elective, and the auditor, to be
chosen by the legislature. The bills failed to pass.

In 1950 the state's "little Hoover" committee, called Special Legislative Committee on State Operations, aided by Griffenhagen and
Associates, recommended cutting off the elective secretary of state,
state auditor, state treasurer, superintendent of public instruction,
and state mine inspector as part of a plan of orderly departments,
leaving elective only the governor and attorney general, whose
terms would be extended from two to four years. Legislators were
also to have four-year instead of two-year terms.

Of this program the 1950 legislature passed and submitted amend-

CONSTITUTIONAL AND STATUTORY ELECTIVE ADMINISTRATIVE OFFICIALS

(From *Reorganizing State Governments*, 1950 Council of State Governments)

	Governor	Lt. Governor	Secretary of State	Attorney General	Treasurer	Auditor	Controller	Education	Agriculture	Labor	Insurance	Mines	Land	University Regents	Board of Education	Public Utilities Comm.	Executive Council	Miscellaneous	Total Agencies	Total Officials
Alabama	O	O	O	O	O	O		O	C[a]							S3*		Tax Commission—S3	9	11
Arizona	O		O	O	O	O		O				O				C3			9	12
Arkansas	O	O	O	O	O	O													7	7
California	O	O	O	O	O		C	O										Board of Equalization—S4	8	11
Colorado	O	O	O	O	O	O		O						C6					8	13
Connecticut	O	O	O	O	O		C		O				S						6	6
Delaware	O			O	O	O		O			O					S3			7	7
Florida	O		O	O	O		C	O	O	O						C5		Collector of Oyster Revenue—S	8	10
Georgia	O	O	O	O	O	O		O	O										10	14
Idaho	O	O	O	O	O	O		O				S		S9					8	8
Illinois	O	O	O	O	O	O		O											8	16
Indiana	O	O	O	S	O	O		O					O						7	7
Iowa	O	O	O	O	O	O		S	S							S3		Printer—C	9	11
Kansas	O	O	O	O	O	O		O	C[b]		S								9	9
Kentucky	O	O	O	O	O	O		O					O			C3			10	12
Louisiana	O	O	O	O	O	O	C	O	C[c]				O		C8	C3			11	20
Maine	O		CL	CL	CL	SL			SL								CL7	Highway Commissioner—S	7	13
Maryland	O			O	CL												C8	Board of Agriculture—C6	4	4
Massachusetts	O	O	O	O	O	O													7	14
Michigan	O	O	O	O	O	O	C	O					O	C8	C3				12	26
Minnesota	O	O	O	O	O	O					S		S			S3		Tax Collector—S	7	9
Mississippi	O	O	O	O	O	O		O								S3		Highway Commission—S3	13	17
Missouri	O	O	O	O	O	O			S[d]										6	6
Montana	O	O	O	O	O	O		O				S				S3			8	10
Nebraska	O	O	O	O	O	O	C	O						C6		C3		Surveyor General—C Printer—S	9	16
Nevada	O	O	O	O	O			O						C5	S5			Fish & Game Commission—S17	13	37
New Hampshire	O		CL		CL	CL											C5	Commissary General—CL	5	9
New Jersey	O					CL													2	2

State	Governor	Lt. Governor	Secretary of State	Attorney General	Treasurer	Auditor	Controller	Education	Agriculture	Labor	Insurance	Mines	Land	University Regents	Board of Education	Public Utilities Comm.	Executive Council	Miscellaneous	Total Agencies	Total Officials
New Mexico	C	C	C	C	C	C		C					C			C3			9	11
New York	C	C		C				C						CL	CL9				5	13
North Carolina	C	C	C	C	C	C		C	C	C	C			CL 100				Board of Public Welfare—CL7; Tax Commissioner—C	12	117
North Dakota	C		C	C	C	C		C	C		C					C3			11	13
Ohio	C	C	C	C	C	C		C	C	C	C					C3			6	6
Oklahoma	C	C	C	C	C	C		C	C	C	C	C5						Commissioner of Charities & Corrections—C; Examiner & Inspector—C	14	20
Oregon	C	C		S		C		S		S									6	6
Pennsylvania	C	C																Secy. of Internal Affairs—C	6	5
Rhode Island	C	C	C	C	C		C		S		S					S3			5	5
South Carolina	C	C	C	C	C	S	C	C								S3			12	12
South Dakota	C		C	C	C	C	SL	S C	S				C					Adjutant & Inspector General—C; Librarian—S	10	12
Tennessee	C	C	CL	CL	CL	C	CL												5	7
Texas	C	C		CC	CCC	CC CL	C	C					C			C3			9	11
Utah	C	C	C	C	C	C			S				C						6	6
Vermont	C		C	C	C														6	6
Virginia	C							C	C		S		C			CL3			5	7
Washington	C	C	C	C	C	C		C					C						9	9
West Virginia	C		C	C	C	C		C	C										7	7
Wisconsin	C	C	C	C	C			C											6	6
Wyoming	C		C		C	C		C			S								5	5

Symbols: C—Constitutional   L—Elected by Legislature   S—Statutory
* Where used, numbers indicate number of officials.
a Commissioner of Agriculture & Industries.
b Commissioner of Agriculture, Labor, & Statistics.
c Commissioner of Agriculture & Immigration.
d Commissioner of Agriculture & Commerce.
e Commissioner of Agriculture & Labor.
f Secretary of State, & Auditor.

Source: U. S. Department of Commerce, Bureau of the Census, *Elective Offices of State and County Governments* (Washington: Government Printing Office, 1946); modified in accordance with the most recent information available to Council of State Governments.

ments extending the terms of the elective state offices and legislators to four years and extending the terms of nine county officers to four years if the corresponding state- and legislative-proposed extensions of term were approved by the people. But the proposal failed at the polls in September. The tail of the state ticket—ten offices—was left intact.

In 1951 amendments were passed, for submission at the polls in November, 1952, to eliminate the elective state treasurer and incorporate his functions into an appointive department of finance.

Arkansas in 1930 considered a report by the Institute of Public Administration proposing trimming the tail of the state ticket to elective lieutenant governor and attorney general for four-year terms and providing post-audit by an auditor chosen by the legislature. The program did not pass the legislature.

Colorado in 1933 consolidated thirty-three statutory agencies into six, headed respectively by the governor, the elective state treasurer, state auditor, attorney general, secretary of state, and superintendent of instruction, and submitted to the people constitutional amendments to make the treasurer, attorney general, secretary of state, and superintendent of instruction appointive by the governor, leaving only the auditor elective. This program was lost at the polls.

Connecticut in 1937 counted 157 more or less independent agencies in its state government, and a commission report advocated a bill to group them into twelve departments. The legislature decimated the bill into little ones and only two of the groupings were created.

In 1950 another commission, bipartisan and ably staffed but linked in the minds of legislators with the Democratic governor, brought in "The Report," which included bold recommendations to remove from the elective list the comptroller, treasurer, attorney general, and secretary of state and to abolish the elective county sheriffs, justices of the peace, town courts, and probate judges. Fourteen departments under heads appointed, without senate confirmation, by the governor were proposed to group "a bewildering patchwork" of nearly 200 boards and other agencies. The program in ten bills was put before a special session of the legislature—which adjourned without action.

Delaware in 1918 engaged the Institute of Public Administration to survey the state and the three county administrations. It recommended combining 117 existing agencies into nine with sole power in the governor to appoint and remove their heads, and proposed abolishing the office of lieutenant governor and trimming from the elective list the attorney general, insurance commissioner, state treasurer, and auditor of accounts. The program was sidetracked by the legislature to another commission, which reported a few bits of it favorably but without significant result.

In 1950 a Commission on Reorganization found ninety-seven agencies, "separate, permanent, and in many instances quite independent" in the executive branch, including the elective auditor, treasurer, attorney general, and insurance commissioner. The report prepared by Griffenhagen and Associates included the following eloquent comment on the democratic implications:

The governor sits in the driver's seat but the wheels do not always turn in response to his driving. The clutch slips, the brakes do not hold, the steering gear is defective and the motor sputters discouragingly. . . .

There is little reason to have to prove that the governor cannot exercise effective control under the present form of administration. It is rather obvious. All sorts of barriers have been raised to prevent it. With considerable ingenuity some of the barriers have been disguised behind such seemingly worth while objectives as the following:

Taking activities out of politics
Providing continuity of policy
Broadening the base of interests
Providing representation for varied interests
Making the state government responsive

Most of these efforts actually have the effect of removing the actual operation of state agencies farther and farther from the people. They encourage irresponsibility, bureaucracy, extravagance, and autocratic government. Seldom do they accomplish for long the high sounding stated objectives.

Some of the devices that have been used to remove control from the governor are as follows:

Long, overlapping terms of board members
Ex-officio memberships on boards and commissions
Self-perpetuating board memberships
Term appointments

  Assignment of administrative responsibilities to boards instead of
   single agencies
  Multiplicity of separate autonomous agencies
  Assignment of executive functions to judicial agencies and officials
  All of these devices are inimical to the basic concepts of democratic
and republican government. They cancel the effect of representation in
government.

  If Delaware is to have responsible government responsive to the will
of the people, it must eliminate these obstacles to effective control of the
executive branch of the governor.

The report proposed grouping administrative agencies into fifteen
departments under the governor but left on the elective list the four
separate elective department heads "since constitutional amendments would be required" although the elective treasurer was
scheduled to lose some functions to a new department of revenue
under the governor and the auditor to be reduced to post-audit
functions.

Georgia in 1932 adopted a reorganization act which reduced
ninety-odd agencies to nineteen but it did not molest the sacrosanct
minor elective state offices, and these, the secretary of state, comptroller general, attorney general, the commissioner of agriculture,
the five members of the public service commission, state treasurer,
and the three prison commissioners, were left with their revised
powers in their traditional separateness.

In 1945 a new constitution was adopted. It included some advances but it added two elective offices to the state list, the only
such instance in forty years.

Idaho in 1919 consolidated fifty offices and boards into nine under
the governor but left elective the statutory inspector of mines and
the constitutional tail—secretary of state, state auditor, treasurer,
attorney general, and superintendent of public instruction. In 1921
the governor pressed for a constitutional amendment to remove all
these from the ballots but was unable to get it through the legislature.

In 1950 a Legislative Committee for Reorganization proposed reducing the tail of the elective state ticket to state auditor, the governor to appoint all the others, namely, secretary of state, auditor,

treasurer, attorney general, and superintendent of public instruction. No action resulted in the 1950 session.

Illinois in 1911 had an Illinois Short Ballot Organization at the Chicago City Club which published a proposal for cutting off the tail of the state ticket. Ballots had grown from eight elective officers for each voter to choose in the state, judicial district, and county in the 1818 constitution to twenty in the 1948 constitution, twenty-five in the 1870 constitution, and finally as high as forty-nine. The Illinois group, as previously mentioned, succeeded in inspiring submission of a "public policy" referendum, advising creation of an official commission to prepare a "short-ballot" proposal. It was carried by 508,780 votes to 165,270. But the legislature disregarded the advice.

Illinois's pioneer state reorganization of 1917 under Governor Lowden, effective in 1919, condensed a hundred administrative agencies into nine but left on the ballot the old constitutional offices —attorney general, auditor, secretary of state, treasurer, superintendent of public instruction, and nine statutory trustees of the University of Illinois.

In 1920 Illinois held a constitutional convention preceded by a scholarly preparation of printed information on all the leading reforms. The short-ballot idea was ably set forth and documented, and the issue divided the convention without, however, making serious headway; none of the elective offices on the tail of the state ticket were made appointive but it was proposed to make an array of elective court clerks appointive by their respective courts, to make appellate judges appointive, and to permit the legislature to make the elective county superintendents of schools appointive. Simplification of county governments was also facilitated. But the new constitution failed at the polls and the 1870 constitution survives.

The "little Hoover" commission of 1950–51 disclosed a story of great increases in the personnel and activities of the departmental structure under the governor. The nine departments and the dozen other agencies of Lowden's day had grown to thirteen and fifty-nine respectively and again needed rearrangement. Passage of the "gateway" amendment in 1950, reducing the absurd prior difficulties of amending the constitution, encouraged the commission to revive the idea of cutting off some of the six minor elective state officers, pointing out the tensions resulting from the multi-headed character of the structure.

In actual operation in Illinois, the election of these officers has resulted in division of responsibility and sometimes in fragmentation of functions. Distribution of functions between those offices which are the responsibility of the governor and those offices headed by elected officers has too often been based largely upon considerations of relative political strength. Considerations of this kind have caused unsound allocations of operating responsibilities—often manifested by the division of a single governmental function between one of the governor's departments and a unit under one of the other elective officers.

There also results a lack of standardization as among state agencies with regard to procurement and personnel methods. Centralized purchasing procedures and expenditure controls which are operative with respect to the agencies under the control of the governor are (with the exception of printing) not applicable to the offices headed by elected officers. In the main, provisions of the civil service and salary standardization statutes are also applicable only to the agencies responsible to the governor.[3]

In other words, the obscure elective officers have more successfully stood off the application of the merit system and orderly methods.

Iowa in 1933 employed the Brookings Institution for a survey. The survey recommendations included making the secretary of state appointive but left the treasurer and auditor elective, the latter being restricted to post-audit. Two governors thereafter tried in vain to get legislative attention to the recommendations.

In 1950 a legislative Reorganization Commission, reviewing the 1933 proposals and the further growth of illogical additions to the administrative structure, recommended a series of single-headed departments under the governor and removal of administrative responsibilities from boards but left the constitutional offices outside the system and, contrary to the drift in other "little Hoover" commissions, actually proposed to add some items to their powers.

Kentucky in 1934 grouped over a hundred agencies into sixteen

[3] Report of Commission to Study State Government, Springfield, Ill., Part IV, chap. 6, 1951.

departments and seven independent agencies, but only eleven of the departments were put partly or wholly under the governor; the other five were left with the five elective constitutional officers on the tail of the ticket in their usual isolation from the rest of the structure. A 1936 reorganization improved the structure but left the five elective department heads independent, as well as an elective auditor and railroad commission.

In December, 1951, an official Committee on Functions and Resources of State Government recommended appointment of all the hitherto elective administrative state officers below the lieutenant governor, except the auditor of public accounts, who was to be selected by the legislature.

Louisiana's constitution of 1921 named the usual list of minor state elective officials but provided that the legislature could consolidate the auditor, register of the land office, commissioner of conservation, and commissioner of agriculture and immigration, only the secretary of state and treasurer being frozen in. But they were all, except the commissioner of conservation, still separately elective thirty years later.

Massachusetts in 1919 regrouped its activities into twenty departments but left four of them in the hands of the four elective constitutional officers, secretary, treasurer and receiver general, auditor, and attorney general.

Michigan created a commission whose report in 1921 proposed reducing the state elective list to governor and auditor, the auditor to be successor to the governor in case of vacancy. The elective secretary of state, treasurer, commissioner of the state land office, auditor, general highway commissioner, superintendent of public instruction, and attorney general were to be merged into one or another of ten departments under the governor. The proposal got nowhere and in 1921 a gentler measure elevated the six elective offices to form with the governor a powerful administrative board.

In 1935 the governor proposed amendments to make all except the lieutenant governor and auditor appointive by the governor and to cut in half the size of the two legislative houses, but the legislature did not support the measures. In 1938 a commission made the same recommendation without result.

In 1950 a "little Hoover" commission began work, finding that the state agencies had again grown in number and diversity. Its report in November, 1951, undertook to rationalize an unusually complex structure of 114 state agencies including twenty-five elective administrative offices and board members (not all elected at one time, however). It recommended making the elective auditor general appointive by the legislature, for post-audit and performance audits, making the elective attorney general appointive by the governor, and making two elective educational executives appointive by their appropriate boards. It provided the first official inquiry in history into the question of how little the voters know about minor elective state offices (Reading B) and stated, "The most powerful reason why such offices should not be filled by election is the simple fact that the public knows too little about them and has too little basis to exercise a qualified judgment." But, although it had demonstrated that no more than 4 per cent of the voters knew the name of the state treasurer, etc., the staff faltered in following its own logic and left on the proposed elective list the state highway commissioner, secretary of state, state treasurer, and two boards—agriculture and the university regents. Lengthening of terms from two years to four was proposed.

Minnesota in 1925 regrouped its agencies into ten departments but left the constitutionally elective auditor, secretary of state, treasurer, and attorney general to circle in their own orbits as before. The bill survived obstinate efforts in the senate to amend it drastically to give the minor elective officials more power and to make some of the other departments independent of the governor.

In 1951 a "little Hoover" commission reported a logical proposal for seventeen single-headed departments appointive by the governor without senate confirmation, calling for constitutional amendments to remove from their independent elective status the secretary of state, auditor (to be chosen by the legislature), treasurer, attorney general, and clerk of the supreme court (to be appointed by the court); also plans in the education department for putting elective county superintendents of education under appointment by the county commissions with consent of the state commissioner of education to insure professional qualifications. One dubious exception to a logical structure involved election of the state board of education by the legislature.

Missouri in 1945 adopted a new constitution which reduced a scatteration of state agencies to "not more than fourteen" departments. The elective state superintendent of education was made appointive by an appointive board, but the auditor, secretary of state, and treasurer were continued elective although with loss of some of their duties to the governor's departments; the attorney general likewise withstood efforts at integration.

Mississippi's "little Hoover" committee in December, 1950, with a touch of charm reported after consultation with the numerous bureaus:

Without exception the heads of the bureaus and commissions and all persons thus interviewed replied as follows:

"I think this is one of the very best things that has ever been done in the State of Mississippi and I have long been of the opinion that this work should have been accomplished in the past. However, my department is of a type, character and kind that cannot be consolidated with any other agency, as its duties and functions are unique, and a reduction in the personnel or a transfer of any of the duties of this department would work a hardship and prevent certain citizens from receiving benefits to which they are entitled."

It proposed to reduce 100 agencies with their 14,000 employees to fifteen departments and eleven other agencies, to reduce the heads from 442 persons to 129, to reduce the seventeen elective administrative officials to nine, and to reduce the number of appointees reporting to the governor from 263 to 111. It described the political condition of the minor elective offices in one-party Mississippi thus: "Secondary executive positions, when elective, benefit chiefly the patronage interests of the contending political factions, enabling candidates for the more important office to bid for the support of blocs of voters supporting one or the other of the lesser officials or candidates."

Two dissenting committee members denounced the prospect of "dictatorship," "relieving the people of their right to elect their own public officials," and "taking the government from the hands of the people."

Nebraska in 1919 and 1920 regrouped the activities under the governor but the plan did not engulf any of the independent elective officers and boards. Although incomplete, it brought such economies that the governor called a special session in 1922 to reduce the state tax rate by one-third. Nevertheless the next governor assailed the code as "undemocratic." The finance department under the governor, by enforcing fiscal control, irritated the independent officers, two of whom, indeed—the auditor and the tax commissioner —somewhat overlapped it, and in 1929 the legislature dismembered the department.

In 1950 its Legislative Council discussed shortening the state ballot but referred it to the proposed constitutional convention.

Nevada in 1924 engaged the Institute of Public Administration to plan a reorganization. The Institute recommended tying seventy-eight agencies into nine departments and provision of a single-house legislature. Nothing significant was passed by the legislature nor did the discovery in 1927 that the elective controller and treasurer had used over $500,000 of state money for their personal speculative purposes sway the legislature from continuing its defense of the independent status of those offices.

In 1948 the Legislative Council Bureau made a survey report recommending a shorter ballot, without result.

New Mexico created in 1920 a commission appointed by the governor to study taxation and retrenchment. It recommended a short-ballot constitutional amendment providing that only the governor and lieutenant governor be left elective, the other elective state officers, secretary of state, auditor, treasurer, attorney general, superintendent of public instruction, and commissioner of public lands, to be added to the governor's appointive list. Four-year instead of two-year terms were provided. The legislature did not move in the 1921 session or in 1927, when the effort was pressed again.

New York's story of trimming three minor elective state offices from the ballot has been told in the preceding chapter.

North Carolina was presented, under the leadership of the governor, with a reorganization plan in 1923. It proposed making seven statutory elective state officers appointive by the governor but left unchanged another seven whose separateness was embedded in the constitution.

In 1930 a survey by Brookings Institution recommended consolidation of over ninety agencies, including all the elective offices, except the auditor, into thirteen departments under the governor. A few of the statutory departments were reorganized by the legislature thereafter, including removal from the ballots of the corporation commission.

Ohio, after its 1912–13 episode (Chapter X), considered a reorganization plan in 1919, prepared by a joint legislative committee, which would have given the governor a four-year instead of two-year term and vested in him appointment of all the state officers except the lieutenant governor and the auditor. In 1921 the governor, having campaigned successfully on the issue, secured enactment of the parts of it involving statutory offices, which were grouped into eight departments. But the elective constitutional offices, secretary of state, treasurer, attorney general, and auditor, still encumber Ohio's ballots, the terms of governor and the others are still two years, except the auditor who serves four years, and long lists of legislators elected at large by counties confront the voters in the larger cities.

Oregon in 1919, after William S. U'Ren's Peoples Power League had subsided, had an official commission which reported a plan to consolidate the administration, including the minor elective state officers, into ten departments, but efforts to pass bills that year and in 1923 failed. In 1927 an attempt to group the statutory offices only failed. In 1929 an amendment to reduce the elective list to governor, secretary of state, and treasurer was submitted and lost at the 1930 election. In 1937 a fourth attempt at regrouping without touching the elective minor offices was defeated.

In 1951 a "little Hoover" Legislative Interim Committee in its final report deplored the diffusion of executive responsibility through the scatteration of 125 state agencies including the six elective state executives.

Pennsylvania in 1923 adopted a plan that consolidated 105 administrative agencies into fourteen departments and three commissions, but the auditor general, treasurer, and secretary of internal affairs were left elective with some increase of powers.

Rhode Island in 1935 grouped its activities into eleven departments, three of them, however, under the constitutionally elective secretary of state, attorney general, and general treasurer, the others being under single heads appointed by the governor with confirmation by the senate.

Tennessee, as previously mentioned, has no state-wide elective offices except the governor (his successor being the Speaker of the state senate) and the three members of the statutory railway and utilities commission, but the administration is not completely centralized since the secretary of state, treasurer, and comptroller are chosen by the joint vote of the legislative houses, and the attorney general is chosen by the supreme court.

In 1921, forty-nine statutory offices and boards were consolidated into eight, but the commission, being elective, was left unconnected although some functions of the other independent officers were transferred to the command of the governor.

In 1932 appointment of the department heads was made subject to confirmation by the senate with resulting complications which led to repeal of the provision two years later. In 1937 further reorganization transferred functions from the comptroller to positions under the governor and left the comptroller as a post-auditor. But the statutory railway and utilities commission of three members remains elective.

South Carolina in 1948 created a Reorganization Commission but specifically prohibited it from touching the constitutional elective offices.

Texas in 1929 was urged by the governor to trim four offices from the state elective list leaving lieutenant governor and attorney general, as part of a consolidation of administrative agencies. The legislature did not budge then but created a commission which in 1933 brought in a report prepared by Griffenhagen and Associates grouping 130 agencies into nineteen; the head of one was to be the elective attorney general, but the elective treasurer, comptroller, and commissioner of public lands were to be put under the governor. The secretary of state was already constitutionally appointive by the governor. A post-auditor was proposed, responsible to the legislature. The project failed in the legislatures of 1933, 1935, and 1937.

Utah in 1935 developed an official project for centralization under the governor, but the plan left the minor elective officers elective with only an attempt to corral them into an executive council where they would meet with the appointive heads of other departments. The 1937 legislature took no action.

Vermont in 1923 created seven departments under the governor out of a scatteration of agencies but did not touch the elective treasurer, secretary of state, and auditor of accounts.

Virginia's Governor Harry F. Byrd in 1928 secured removal of four constitutional officers from the state's elective list, namely, secretary of state, state treasurer, superintendent of public instruction, and commissioner of agriculture. There had been nearly 100 bureaus, boards, and departments, many of which were independent of each other and of the governor as well. The governor had been permitted to appoint the heads of only twenty of the fifty-seven administrative commissions and departments and five were appointed by the legislature. Reorganization brought this scatteration of authorities into twelve departments appointive by the governor, leaving only governor, lieutenant governor, and attorney general on the state ticket. The amendment required trial of appointment of the other formerly elective administrative officers for one term, after which the legislature was left free to restore them to the elective list at any time.

There were predictions that this short-ballot amendment, having been adopted by a narrow margin, would soon be reversed by the legislature. Opponents of Governor Byrd used the standard hokum to assail it, but in the next Democratic state primary for governor (1929) ex-Senator G. Walter Mapp, who strongly opposed the short ballot, trailed by 75,000 votes behind Professor John Garland Pollard, who favored it and the rest of the Byrd program. At the general election for governor Pollard was opposed by an anti-Smith Republican coalition candidate, who devoted much time and energy in his speeches to denunciation of the short ballot and lost by the almost unprecedented majority of 70,000 votes.

By the time the 1932 elections to the assembly came around the short ballot had ceased to figure as a usable issue and the results indicated an overwhelming majority of both houses opposed to repeal.[4]

[4] George W. Spicer, "The Short Ballot Safe in Virginia," *National Municipal Review,* September, 1932.

One bill for repeal, introduced in 1932, died in committee, and Governor Byrd, later U.S. senator, stated his recollection that there had been no other such bills introduced up to 1951.

Washington in 1921 consolidated seventy statutory agencies into ten under the governor without, however, disturbing the unconnected elective state officers—secretary of state, treasurer, auditor, attorney general, superintendent of public instruction, insurance commissioner, and commissioner of public lands—except to include them in a system of administrative committees. A later reorganization in 1935 likewise was balked by the difficulties of including the constitutional minor elective offices.

West Virginia in 1933 called a special session of the legislature to consider a reorganization program which would have taken from the elective list the secretary of state, superintendent of free schools, auditor, treasurer, and commissioner of agriculture, leaving only the attorney general elective. The legislature refused to submit the amendments.

Wyoming in 1933 created a committee of three senators and three representatives which engaged Griffenhagen and Associates to prepare a reorganization program, and a special session of the legislature was convened to receive it. The report proposed replacing elective judges with judges appointed by the governor after nomination by a judicial advisory council, reducing the legislature to a single house of nine to twelve members elected at large by proportional representation, the governor to be either elected or chosen by the house from among its own members, the administrative staff to be headed by a manager called state administrator chosen for indefinite tenure and removable by the legislature. Nothing resulted.

Hawaii in its 1950 tentative constitutional convention, starting on plain paper with no vested elective minor offices to upset, followed avowedly the Model State Constitution and proposed creation of no such disconnected elective offices.

Obviously such tangled administrative charts as that of Delaware bedevil the democratic process in their own way by obscuring responsibility and snagging the efforts of governors and legislatures to progress. They entrench bureaucracies against their lawful elected superiors and exhaust the energies of well-intentioned governors, thereby, too, baffling the people. Straightening out the organization charts into rational military order, under a governor equipped and empowered to manage, diminishes the capacity of the bureaucrats to resist all change including changes consciously desired by the voters.

LITTLE PROGRESS TOWARD THE SHORT BALLOT VIA REORGANIZATIONS

This chronicle of the failure of such reorganizations to push through to logical completion is not to be construed as disparagement of their abundant accomplishments in the internals of state governments; it merely means that we are stopping at the capitol door and sticking to our outdoor field of democratics.

So the reorganizers, encountering the minor constitutional state officers, have almost always thus far compromised with or been defeated by latent or active political opposition. But they have sometimes gained a little ground by transferring functions to the governor's establishment and leaving the elective state officers with diminished powers and patronage.

Thus after forty years the short ballot has made little progress, for either democracy's sake or efficiency's sake, in *state* governments. Frozen into state constitutions, which usually are amended rarely and with difficulty when vested political self-interest is at stake, the tails of the state tickets remain intact, eluding not only the voter scrutiny necessary to protect them at elections from direct control by party managers but even the voter scrutiny required to procure their abolition as administrative islands.

Overcoming constitutional barriers requires more sustained effort and widespread conviction than can be mustered for so seemingly academic and dull an issue. The opponents need not be numerous to be able to snag progress somewhere along the difficult road of constitutional revision.

TAILS OF THE STATE TICKETS DIMINISHED IN RELATIVE IMPORTANCE

Meanwhile the administrative establishments of governors have grown and grown; new departments under appointive heads have appeared and developed into high importance. New projects and functions are rarely handed to the failing hands of the minor elective officers, and the latter shrink in relative importance with smaller and smaller percentages of the patronage and funds within their withering grasp.

Thus Illinois, which under Governor Lowden in 1917 was the first to consolidate its scattered state administration, left untouched the sacrosanct tail of the ticket—the elective auditor, secretary of state, attorney general, superintendent of public instruction, and treasurer —and in 1950 the Commission to Study State Government found the tail offices still there doing about the same things.[5] The percentage of the state's budget under the five minor elective officers, however, which (excluding the School Fund) was 7.8 per cent in 1919, had dwindled to 3.4 per cent in 1949.[6]

Which, of course, is good as far as it goes.

All disinterested observers and all the professional analysts who make governmental surveys agree that the only administrative office that should be independent of the governor is that of state auditor for post-audit only. This officer can be elected by the legislature and can be used also for investigative service by legislative committees. It is not by nature a suitable office for submission at the polls.

But the point which this book makes is amazingly neglected in state reorganization reports—the point that only a trifling percentage of the voters apply any scrutiny to the "tail" offices or can even name the incumbents or candidates, with the effect of leaving their selection "unsight unseen" in the hands of self-serving party managers!

[5] Commission to Study State Government, Springfield, Ill., December, 1950.
[6] From data kindly tabulated for me by the Illinois Legislative Council staff.

Chapter XII

PROGRESS IN STATE LEGISLATURES

IN ALL the states since early days legislatures have been divided into two houses. There was some semblance of reason for this division while property qualifications survived to provide in some states a different constituency for each house. The example of the federal government was never apposite. Differences exist in some states between methods of districting for the two houses but are indefensible and merely set up vested privileges in some districts which thus obtain disproportionate representation that ought to be corrected (see the section on mal-apportionment in Chapter XXVIII). Moreover, most of the houses are unnecessarily large.

LEGISLATURES VIOLATE TWO OF THE RULES

The dual structure violates Rule One and Rule Three: The powers, immense in total, are so far divided that membership in a legislature becomes a small obscured job, attracting little voter scrutiny at the polls. Performance in office is obscured by the scatteration of responsibility and the ease with which bills can be and are defeated or emasculated in shadowed committees or by purposeful boggling over minor conflicts between the houses. A third house—the interhouse conference committee for composing differences when bills pass both houses but with differences of detail—sometimes becomes a further pocket of obscurity. The notion that each house will catch and block bad bills coming from the other has been found not to be demonstrable in realistic count-ups. The procedures of American legislatures defy effective public scrutiny and control and cannot be corrected by mere correction in their rules. Indeed, improvements in other governmental areas are leaving legislatures as the most backward, incompetent, and machine-ruled of our institutions. They are filled with small fry, ranging from nice young lawyers supplementing incomes from incipient practices to party hacks who

117

diligently do the bidding of invisible masters, and a few devoted senior habitués who know the business and make a small ill-paid profession of the service. The turnover is high, bringing in for one term, or two, a great biennial influx of green members. Bills which have no enemies pass too easily and frequently; bills which incur the hostility of the party machines and their friends have hard sledding no matter how the public storms.

LEGISLATURES CAN IGNORE PUBLIC OPINION

Legislators who evade obedience to popular opinion easily dodge the rare attempts at political punishment at the next election.[1] The governor may carry the state for an issue; then comes the skepticism as to whether he can get it through the legislature. For the very voters who admired the governor's purpose are likely to have elected at the same moment legislators who will do their covert best to baffle and distort his projects, particularly if those projects threaten the powers of the machines which hand-picked them. Indeed, the people find it difficult to keep from contradicting themselves at the polls when electing legislators—who are not visible in the meaning of Rule One. In Pennsylvania, for example, they voted a constitutional municipal home rule referendum by a majority of 132,490 in 1922, but the legislature did not pass implementing legislation and had not done so up to 1951. In Idaho in 1923 the people at referendum voted a constitutional amendment to permit initiation of amendments by petition, but it was not self executing and the legislature has stood off all efforts to implement it.

More recently both political party platforms in Maryland pledged support for the proposed constitutional convention. The vote for having one passed in November, 1950, 200,439 to 56,998. But three months later the house of delegates, with many members who faced fairer apportionment as one result of the convention, refused, sixty-four to fifty-six, to implement the popular verdict!

Another spectacle of the same sort appeared in 1951 in Rhode Island. For years civic organizations and an efficient local press stormed at the legislators for municipal home rule, sometimes with

[1] Cf. Hallie Farmer, *The Legislative Process in Alabama*, Bureau of Public Administration, University of Alabama, University, Ala., 1949,

the support of favorable local referenda, while the legislators, many of whom held additional jobs in city halls, yawned and maintained there was no real demand for it. But when a two-day constitutional convention, called suddenly for a brief, technical task on another subject, was induced to submit also a self-executing home rule amendment, the latter was promptly carried by a vote of 48,429 to 7983!

Efforts Toward Simplification

The fault is fundamental, and curable only by the drastic yet sensible step of following Nebraska and substituting for obfuscation and confusion the orderly procedures of a single small house worthy of the attendance of high-grade and able members of congressional caliber. The combination of far more power and dignity per member with the intrinsic debatability of their highly interesting tasks can lift the members into visibility (Rule One) and reduce the scatteration of power (Rule Three).

Seven of the nine Canadian provinces switched from bicameral to single-house legislatures decades ago, beginning with Ontario in 1867. There the upper houses, however, had been appointed for life or long terms by the lower house or otherwise.

There was considerable interest in single-house legislatures here as one phase of short-ballot progress in the Progressive party era, 1909–19:

1912. U'Ren and his Peoples Power League in Oregon proposed a single house of sixty members, losing by 71,183 to 31,020. In 1914 a similar proposal with the added backing of the state Grange and the Oregon Federation of Labor lost, 62,376 to 123,429.

1913. Governor George H. Hodges of Kansas ardently pressed for a very small house of eight to sixteen members on a nonpartisan ballot, without result.

1914. Oklahoma submitted an amendment for one house of eighty members and it was defeated, 71,742 to 94,686.

Governor Eberhardt of Minnesota also unavailingly proposed it that year.

1915. Governor George W. Hunt of Arizona urged a single house of seven to fifteen members and, failing to secure submission of his measure by the legislature, supported an initiative, which was lost, 11,631 to 22,286.

In Washington Governor Ernest Lister in his 1915 and 1917 messages urged a single house of twenty-five members.

1917. Governor Peter Norbeck of South Dakota urged a single house, did it again in 1925, followed by Governor W. J. Bulow who asked for it in 1927, without result.

How Nebraska Got Its Single-House Legislature

In Nebraska, however, the idea persisted. In 1915 a joint legislative committee advocated submission by initiative of an amendment for a single house and supported its proposal with this sound and terse statement of the case:

1. Representative government by the people should be direct and responsible. One body can more directly represent the public will of a democratic people than two or more.

2. Cities all over the civilized world having a larger population and more diverse interests than Nebraska are governed by one body, and the tendency is to make that body smaller with more direct responsibility upon each member than hitherto.

3. The arguments for a two-house legislature may be summarized under three heads:

a. The need of proper representation for different orders or classes of citizens in respect to wealth, education, or social position. The answer to this is that the spirit of American institutions is to abolish class distinctions in government and to diffuse education and wealth letting social position take care of itself.

b. Another argument is that two houses are required in order that they may be a check upon each other and prevent the enactment of unwise legislation. In practice it has been found that the so-called "check" between the two houses results in trades and absence of the real responsibility which should be felt by representatives of the people. Nothing is more common than for one house to pass a bill and the members who voted for it to urge the other house to defeat it, or for a little group of members in one house to hold up legislation from the other house until they extort from it what they demand.

c. The third point urged for two houses is in order to prevent hasty legislation by requiring more time and machinery for the enactment of a law, thus securing deliberation and reflection. Deliberation and reflection do not now mark the work of a two-house legislature, which passes most of its acts in the last ten days of the session. A smaller body with a more direct responsibility upon each member arising therefrom will tend to greater deliberation and reflection than the present system.

Mr. J. N. Norton, chairman of that committee, was defeated in his effort to pass a resolution for a house of sixty members in 1917. In 1919 he succeeded in getting a constitutional convention called, became a member of it, and fought for the project to a tie vote. In 1923 an initiative petition for a single house was circulated but never completed. In 1924 the Farmers Cooperative and Educational Union, with a membership of 35,000 in Nebraska, resolved in a convention with 1000 present to urge a single house of 100 members. Legislative bills failed in 1925 and again in 1933.

Senning reports [2] that the appearance of the National Municipal League's Model State Constitution in 1920, with its provision for a one-house legislature, was widely publicized in Nebraska and was influential. An article by Senator George W. Norris, which appeared in the New York *Times* of January 28, 1923, was, he says, also reprinted and quoted extensively.

In 1933 the people of the state had accumulated irritation with the way progressive schemes for ameliorating the problems of the depression got lost in "the dual network of procedural intricacies" of the legislature, and the Democratic party landslide had brought to the capitol an almost complete change of membership without improvement in the performance. A citizens' Model Legislative Committee, including J. N. Norton again and led by Senator Norris, went to work to secure agreement on a specific amendment for a single house. Senator Norris favored a house of twenty-one members and a nonpartisan ballot. The size ultimately was left in the amendment to be determined between thirty and fifty by the 1935 legislature, which also was authorized to divide the state into single-member districts. Nonpartisan elections were specified and aggregate salaries were limited to $37,500.

Senator Norris stumped the state for four weeks denouncing the mazes of legislative procedure and the conference committee—"the

[2] John P. Senning, *The One House Legislature*, McGraw-Hill Book Co., New York, 1937.

third house"—wherein six members often controlled the most important matters. Evidence was adduced that the theory that one house caught the errors of the other was mythical. Labor and the Grange were in support. In vitriolic opposition a Representative Government Defense Association, including active members of both parties, called the proposal un-American, centralized, and depriving the people of 75 per cent of their representatives. The press was almost all contemptuous and hostile.

Proponents and opponents both were surprised at the vote— 286,086 for, 193,152 against. The amendment lost in only seventy-three out of 2029 precincts!

The *United States News* (November 19, 1934) found that press comment throughout the nation was 66 per cent favorable to the innovation.

In twenty-one legislatures amendments toward the same end turned up in 1935.

Professor Senning, employed as adviser by the committees of both houses, describes in his book the tangled debates and the procedures of the 1935 legislature in carrying out its mandate to redistrict. Committee members disagreed, committees disagreed with each other, the houses disagreed, and everything was done over several times. Ultimately a sensible arrangement of forty-three districts was enacted and the first single-house legislature took its seats in 1937.

SUCCESS IN NEBRASKA SINCE 1937

Opposition to the single-house idea vanished after the referendum, and the 1935 legislature as a whole did not attempt to bedevil it by its implementing bill. No sentiment for repeal thereafter reached the stage of organizing.

The new single house was already provided with a chairman, the lieutenant governor, and a clerk. A legislative council and reference staff was provided to assist in investigations and bill drafting. Candidates for membership in the legislature gained somewhat in prominence in the election campaigns and were voted for by a high percentage—80–90 per cent of those voting for governor—despite their less conspicuous place on the separated nonpartisan section of the ballots. There is a high percentage of reelection of incumbents. In Reading E, Dr. Richard C. Spencer exhibits the relative good order and freedom from the typical hurly-burly with which business is conducted and the relative ease with which members themselves can know what is going on. The number of bills introduced is half what it used to be and half of those that pass are disposed of in the first half of the session. Legislation is freer from errors of form. Final sessions have always been orderly and uncrowded with business. Press and people watch the open and simple proceedings without the traditional sense of bewilderment and mystification.

In the 1950 election nine of the forty-three legislative districts were uncontested. An amendment to enlarge the house was defeated, 71,173 to 129,677.

NEAR-ADOPTION IN MISSOURI, 1945

In 1945 in Missouri an initiative proposal for a single-house legislature, sponsored by civic groups, came to a vote on November 7 just after the constitutional convention finished its work for submission the following February. The convention had rejected the single-house idea and defeated plans for making suitable adjustments in the event of the passage of the initiative. To avert conflict and confusion, the backers of the initiative then tried to withdraw their proposal from the ballot and sent out 5000 letters trying to beat it at the polls. But the orphaned and unsupported proposal showed startling vitality, losing by only 5 per cent margin—364,608 votes to 401,716!

In 1945 a poll conducted by the Minneapolis *Star-Journal* showed 38 per cent favored and 24 per cent opposed (38 per cent undecided) the suggestion that the Minnesota legislature of sixty-seven senators and 131 representatives be reduced to a single chamber of fifty.

In 1948 the Ohio Association of Cities, made up of municipal officials, astonished itself by voting unanimously in favor of reducing the Ohio legislature to a single house of seventy members.

There are thus some interesting indications that, in the thirteen states where constitutional amendments can be submitted by initiative petition, the getting of more single-house legislatures is not as hard a job as might be supposed!

Chapter XIII

PROGRESS IN STATE JUDICIARIES

> I was elected in 1916 because Woodrow Wilson kept us
> out of war. I was defeated in 1920 because Woodrow
> Wilson did not keep us out of war. In both elections, not
> more than five percent of the voters knew that I was on
> the ticket.
>
> —FRED L. WILLIAMS, a judge of
> the Supreme Court of Missouri

IN the federal system all the judges are appointed by the president with the consent of the Senate. The Senate's scrutiny of candidates for the U.S. Supreme Court is sober and genuine and concerned with the importance of the post. In the case of district judges, courtesy of the Senate, whereby all senators follow the wishes of the senators from the state where the new appointee is to serve, appears as a mischievous factor and may result in an unwholesome interchange of function whereby one or two senators select and the president confirms. A long run of Democratic presidents results in a long run of mostly Democratic judges—214 out of 231 in the years 1932–48. But no one, least of all the bar, ever suggests a switch to a practice of electing those judges.

In the states where judges are appointive by the governor with confirmation by the state senate or executive council, there is room for similar confusion of responsibility. The potential obscuration is worse in the states where judges are elected by the legislature.

There remain the thirty-eight [1] states where all or most of the judges are elective on state-wide and district bases and there the selection is generally deep in politics. Where the elections are partisan, the degree to which the party managers defer to public taste will depend on the visibility of the office. Nomination by the management of one party will be enough to assure election in about

[1] "State Court Systems," Revised, Council of State Governments, Chicago, September 1951.

half the cases. In a strongly Democratic district Republican aspirants might as well not try, and within the dominant party the candidates will be confined to persons long friendly and cooperative with the party leaders. The respect which Americans have for judges is an immense protection to the office and inspires caution in party managers to avoid being caught soiling ermine. But there is much in the condition of our elective state judiciaries—witness the New York City story in Chapter IV—that deserves to be blown open and would be if it were not so futile to try the complaint before the court of public opinion—when that court has so much else to do!

NONPARTISAN JUDICIAL ELECTIONS

As a measure designed to reduce the influence of party managers in selecting elective judges, some states have moved to *nonpartisan* judicial elections—see the arrangement on the Cuyahoga Ohio ballots in Chapter II. No clue is given there as to whether a judicial candidate is a Republican or a Democrat and the voter is, to some advantage of the merits, left to vote for either candidate for each judgeship without sense of apostasy to his party or even to the management thereof. But still remains the question of whether, in the dusty cloud of contests on that day, the typical voter had, as to those offices, any opinion to express. A provident voter may carry to the polls a pocket list for his own guidance based on a Citizens League "Voter's Directory" or a Bar Association list of recommendations, but most voters are not as provident as that and may follow trivial indications such as Irish names rather than Polish. In any case a considerable percentage will find themselves without an opinion and in this case without a party label and will wisely refrain from voting at all—a common result as shown by a sharp falling off in the vote on the nonpartisan judicial ballots compared with the partisan ones at the same election. Rule One is violated—the office in that environment and by its intrinsic nature fails to attract adequate public scrutiny.

Thus in nonpartisan elections and in the equivalent rare circumstances (outside the South) of a well-attended intraparty primary election, discarding the self-serving leadership of the party managers leaves a situation where self-seekers with circus methods and scant merit may advance their dubious claims and benefit by a fitful gleam of limelight amid the murk.

The noble discontent of the bar with the kind of judges thrown up (a) by party conventions, (b) by direct partisan primaries and partisan elections, and (c) by nonpartisan primary and run-off elections was recited in 1950 by the president of the American Judicature Society (Reading G).

Kales' Contribution

In 1912, a year after my *Short Ballot Principles* was published, Albert M. Kales, an important attorney of Chicago, came to me, eager to develop a way to apply the principle of the short ballot to the selection of judges. I cheered him on and he wrote a book, *Unpopular Government* (1913), and went to work in the American Bar Association and in the American Judicature Society, then newly formed and dedicated to improvement of judicial procedures and structures. The National Municipal League thereafter left efforts for the application of the short-ballot principle in the elective judiciary states to the American Judicature Society and the American Bar Association to work at. Shrinking apparently from the difficulties of a direct assault on the elective state systems and of urging a switch to the federal method of appointment, Mr. Kales and others devised what is now known as "the Missouri plan." Its adoption in principle in California in 1934 and in full in Missouri in 1940 constitutes the only progress thus far toward lifting state and local judges out of the jungles of the elective process.

Mr. Kales' proposal was that an elected chief justice appoint the other state judges from a list of names submitted by a nonpartisan nominating body, the appointees to go before the voters after a trial period of service and be voted on as to their retention in office for a full term.

California's Semi-Appointive Judges, 1934

In 1934, leaders of the bar in California, responding to complaints of the quality of the bench, worked up interest in Kales' idea and submitted an amendment by initiative. The state chamber of commerce offered a slightly different rival proposal, which was adopted by the voters; it reversed the proposed procedure, providing the more familiar arrangement of nomination by the governor subject to confirmation by the commission, which consists of the elective chief justice, the (elective) attorney general, and the (elective) presiding justice of the district court of appeal. Adoption of a parallel setup for district courts, optional in the districts, was facilitated, but up to 1952 no district has taken up the opportunity.

The American Bar Association in 1937 adopted the Kales program and its constituent state bar associations and members in states with elective judiciaries have made numerous efforts to enlist support for the idea.

Amendments of this nature failed at the polls in Ohio and in Michigan in 1938.

ADOPTION IN MISSOURI, 1940

In 1940, leaders of the bar in Missouri secured adoption of "the Missouri plan" (as the Kales ABA proposal is now called) whereby, as vacancies come along in the supreme court, the courts of appeal, and the circuit courts of St. Louis and Kansas City, the governor fills them from a list of names submitted by a nominating commission consisting (for supreme and appellate court judges) of the chief justice, three lawyers elected by the bar, and three laymen appointed by the governor, the latter six being chosen in rotation for six-year terms. After an appointee has been on the bench a year, the question comes up on a separate ballot: "Shall Judge ——— be retained in office? Yes   No."

The answer of the people has been a perfunctory yes in all cases up to 1951 in California and in all but one case—a Pendergast holdover—in Missouri. In California the governor's selections were disappointingly political and partisan for some years, but certainly no more so than the fruits of the prior obscure elective process; then in 1946 Governor Earl Warren, elected by the nomination of both parties, sharply improved the standard, to the widespread approval of the bar. In Missouri every Republican governor has up to 1952 picked Republicans from the list and every Democratic governor has picked Democrats, except in one of the twenty-one cases when the three eligibles were all of the opposite party, but the quality has improved. The Missouri voters in their yes votes for retention have disregarded the party complexion of incumbents and, in the midst of a Democratic drift, Republican judges have been renewed in office and vice versa. Long terms of service by undebated extensions of terms of incumbents have produced the complaint that the offices do not get passed around enough and that appointment becomes equivalent to tenure till the retirement age, in marked contrast to a meaningless turnover of judges previously.

SATISFACTION IN MISSOURI

Missouri opinion supports its plan. The adoption in 1940 was by 90,000 majority. Opponents got it resubmitted in 1942 and encountered a 180,000 majority. They tried to oust it at the constitutional convention of 1945, but it was left unchanged except for an extension to an additional court, and the new constitution was adopted by 150,000 majority.

In both California and Missouri the plans have been adopted only in the unwieldy districts—the state-wide, the appellate division, and the two Missouri metropolitan districts—not in rural districts.

The Missouri judges who come within the scheme enjoy a high degree of long-term security like federal judges, and the people have yielded nothing—they had perfunctorily assented to the election of judges named on a long partisan ballot before; thereafter they assented perfunctorily to selections submitted by the governor. But let it not be imagined that the voters review the performances of judicial candidates during their first trial year or their previous term and arrive at decisions of their own as to whether the incumbents should continue on the bench! The chance to vote yes or no is simply a chance to express an opinion when they have no opinion to express. The Missouri and California plans make that condition of the elective process less damaging than it was before.

ADOPTION IN BIRMINGHAM

In 1950 the Alabama State Bar secured passage of a referendum providing that judges of the circuit court of one district, Birmingham, hitherto elective, be filled by appointment of the governor from a list of three nominations submitted by a judicial commission of two lawyers, two laymen, and a judge, without subsequent submission to the voters.

In September, 1951, New Mexico voted on an amendment on the Missouri model, but it was defeated.

In the Model State Constitution, the National Municipal League follows the original Kales idea: appointment of judges vested in an elective chief justice, selecting from candidates screened by a council of lawyers, judges, and laymen chosen by the governor, the appointees to serve for four years and the question of further retention for eight years more to be submitted at the polls.

A STATUTORY PLAN PROJECTED IN NEW YORK

The City Club and the Citizens Union of New York City have kept alive a plan submitted first to the constitutional convention of 1915 by the New York Short Ballot Organization to replace the elective supreme court and court of appeals. It was introduced by Henry L. Stimson. It requires the governor to recommend a candidate for each vacancy, after which time is left for making nonpartisan counter-nominations by petition, the governor's designees to be indicated by the words "Recommended by the governor" on the voting machine. All this could be done by legislation in New York or made optional in supreme court districts. A further step would be to have no election if no counter-nomination be offered. If the governor made nonpolitical "recommendations," recognizing merit in both parties, judiciary elections might become perfunctory or be omitted most of the time and highly illuminated in exceptional cases where his recommendations were assailed. As compared with the Missouri plan, where the governors' selectees are so uniformly of his own party, the governor would face the certainty that if he made all his recommendations from his own party, the other party would routinely put up opponents by petition; he would have reason to recognize merit in both parties.

The basic fact that consistently listless inattention by the voters awaits, and almost always will await, the submission of judges to balloting is recognized and the American Bar Association and the American Judicature Society have broken through in two states with good results!

Chapter XIV

PROGRESS IN MUNICIPAL GOVERNMENTS

Our municipal governments are honeycombed—simply
honeycombed—with honesty.

—DON MARQUIS

MUNICIPALITIES are created by state legislation and have
often been treated as conquered provinces, particularly when
the legislatures were dominated by the rural vote. Legislatures,
however, have often granted new and diverse optional charters to
individual cities or to classes of cities, and cities in many states have
broken free from such remote control still further by securing
amendments providing constitutional home rule, enabling them to
draft and adopt new forms of government by themselves. Accordingly, in municipalities fewer legal obstacles to experimentation
and advance are presented than in the case of the refractory state
constitutions.

So from the forty-year chronicle of failure to advance the Three
Rules at the state level we turn to the impressive array of victories
in the cities.

In the 1800–50 period American cities were governed by single
councils. Separately elected mayors developed and became well
established in the 1825–50 period. In meaningless imitation of the
state governments some cities, but never a majority, indeed had
councils of two houses, Select Council and Common Council, sometimes dubbed select rogues and common rogues; Philadelphia
started that trend in 1796. There were in 1951 still twelve such cities
left, all but two in New England.[1] But the bicameral councils were
well on their way out and when the present century began the pre-

[1] Augusta and Waterville, Me.; Everett, Malden, Northampton, Springfield,
Mass.; Central Falls, Pawtucket, Woonsocket, R. I.; Danbury, Conn.; Atlanta,
Ga.; and New York City.

vailing pattern provided a weak or strong mayor and a one-house
council.

THE STRONG-MAYOR PLAN, 1880

"Weak-mayor" setups linger in some cities as a relic of older days.
They leave the mayor rather helpless and give the council and its
committees contact with and oversight of municipal departments;
often they give parts of the administrative establishment to independent boards—"Board of Public Works," "Park Board," even
"Police Board." St. Louis in 1838 was perhaps the first to give the
mayor appointive power over department heads, but within two
years four of such officers were transferred from the appointive to
the elective list; two more were transferred in 1843 and another
five in 1853. Chicago, beginning with a weak mayor in 1837, added
eleven separate elective officers in 1851, two more in 1857, and an
elective police board in 1862. Such false notions of democratic organization were characteristic of the Jacksonian theories of that era
and we are still paying dearly for them in many local governments
from coast to coast.

In 1880 came the Brooklyn plan with a strong mayor and this
time it stuck and became widely admired. In 1898 the principle
appeared in the consolidation charter of Greater New York, whose
mayor has ever since enjoyed complete power to appoint department heads to serve at his pleasure without confirmation by the
Board of Aldermen, which, as the subsequent history of that mediocre body now reveals, would have been disastrous.

Although the mayor's powers thus cover departments whose personnel is nowadays over 150,000 and whose expenditures are over
$1,000,000,000 a year, nobody has ever demanded division or shar-
ing of that concentration of authority. New York has had more
kinds of mayors in the years since 1898 than the charter draftsmen
could have imagined, but a cold air has always blown in with that
clear-cut conspicuous responsibility.

Nevertheless it is hazardous to vest so much unchecked discretion
in a single man! There is the precedent of the presidency, of course,
but it is hazardous there too. No other nation except the autocracies
gives as much authority to frail wisdom and fallible perception of
single persons.

MAYOR-COUNCIL FORM

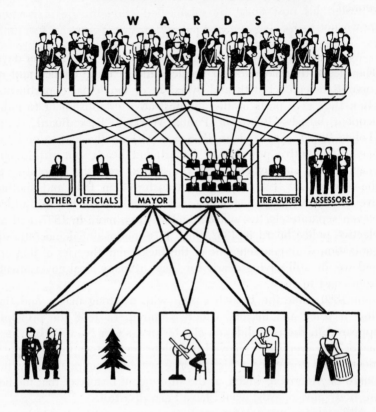

National Municipal League

But confirmation of appointments is a poor way to check the executive since it involves a confusion of responsibility and an interchange of power. The evils of confirmation by the U.S. Senate are of long standing in Washington. By senatorial courtesy the Senate respects the wishes of the senators from the state in which a proposed presidential appointee is to serve. The president, therefore, is due for a rebuff if he ventures to submit to the Senate a nomination unacceptable to those two senators or their state's delegation in the other house. So when I offered a new job to a commissioner of immigration at Ellis Island some years ago, I found that his decision to resign his post must, by established etiquette, be first made known not to his departmental superior but to a senator, and until the senator was ready with a candidate for the vacancy and so reported, the imminency of the vacancy must be kept confidential. Then the senator, having located a successor, submitted the latter's name on the heels of the resignation and it was the president who "confirmed" the choice. Efforts of the Hoover Commission to abolish confirmation of postmasters as a gross political interference with departmental morale and discipline were met with the defense that, in a run of a thousand submissions, every one had been confirmed; which proved only that presidents had thus habitually succumbed to what a congressional committee in 1951 called the "patronage rights" of legislators.

The 1952 scandals among the regional internal revenue collectors also reflect the recklessness with which legislators can thus control appointments without taking visible responsibility for the results.

So (to get back to mayors) confirmation of appointments by the municipal legislative body went out of fashion as a result of parallel experiences. Unification of administrations under the mayor was seen as necessary, and independent boards gave way to single-headed departments and appointive power without confirmation became a tenet of the National Municipal League's first Model City Charter issued in 1899. Chicago, Detroit, Los Angeles, Cleveland, Boston, Pittsburgh (cf. Chapter XIX) all gave their mayors bold grants of power and abolished other elective administrative officers and boards, leaving on the ballots none in Boston and Cleveland and only one or two in the other cities named. In such cities the mayor may be fairly described as constituting 80 per cent of the government.

In smaller cities where the total powers of mayors were less impressive because those cities have smaller staffs, the same drift from weak-mayor to strong-mayor forms has brought cities into better compliance with Rules One and Three.

But the strong-mayor government is two headed. The mayors and councils are frequently at loggerheads. Councils claim the mayors have money enough to get the desired results while mayors protest that the department services are crippled—issues on which the only appeal is to the man in the street, who cannot possibly pass judgment on them.

The feasibility of carrying compliance with Rule Three to its ultimate ideal of lodging all powers in a single body is demonstrated in the 63,000 elective school boards and the 1100 council-manager cities and towns, under which, incidentally, there is no problem of one-man power, as demonstrated hereafter.

The Commission Plan, 1903

In 1900 a tidal wave and hurricane swept over the low levels of Galveston, Texas, wrecked the city, and left its 40,000 people temporarily homeless. The existing government had been in default on its bonds, had $200,000 of floating debt, and was paying its bills with scrip IOU's. It was adjudged incompetent to cope with the emergency and to accomplish with sufficient celerity and skill the vast undertakings the situation required. So by hasty legislation the local government was suspended and the governor appointed a commission—hence the subsequent name—of five capable citizens as an emergency government. As compared with the prior debating-society procedures of messages from the mayor to council, drafting of ordinances, reference to committees, reports of committees, first reading, final passage, veto, perhaps, by the mayor, repassage over the veto, and performance by a possibly unwilling mayor, the speed, honesty, and effectiveness of the compact little huddle of commissioners astonished the town. Galveston climbed out of the debris, jacked up its houses, pumped in sand to raise the ground level, built a great sea wall, and operated the familiar services with a refreshing efficiency. And, withal, reduced the tax rate and the debt!

Nobody wanted to go back to the two-headed mayor-and-council plan but neither was it conceivable that government by a commission appointed by the governor could go on forever. So a new charter was drafted in 1903 providing for a commission of five, three appointed by the governor and two locally elected. After this was in effect a court action invalidated it on the ground that, the emergency being over, the appointment of the three commissioners was no longer constitutionally permissible. So by legislation dated March 30, 1903, all five commissioners were made elective and the

COMMISSION FORM

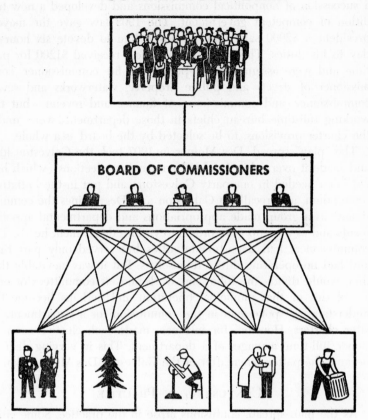

BOARD OF COMMISSIONERS

National Municipal League

existing personnel including the governor's appointees were elected a few weeks later.

Thus began the historic episode known as the movement for the "commission plan." It was, however, an accident, not a plan. The court decision which forced it to become a regular elective structure was unexpected and to many Galveston citizens alarming. But at the first election and the second and third, able citizens were found willing to run for the five important positions. The offices were

highly visible and the district was wieldy. Galveston put into office
a succession of nonpolitical commissions and developed a new tradition of competent government. The 1903 law gave the mayor-
president a $2000 salary and required him to devote six hours a
day to his duties. The four commissioners received $1200 for part
time and were assigned titles—police and fire commissioner, commissioner of streets and public property, waterworks and sewer
commissioner, and commissioner of finance and revenue—but the
working full-time bureau chiefs in those departments were, under
the charter provisions, to be selected by the board as a whole.

The "plan" spread. Des Moines in 1907 took the Galveston idea
and made it over a bit. It added nonpartisan elections (which had
not been needed in one-party Galveston) and put in the initiative,
referendum, and recall. In Galveston and Des Moines the commissioners as a group made appropriations and departmental appointments and as a group gave orders to various department heads. The
commissioners had departmental titles but served only part time
and had no operating duties themselves. But it was inevitable that
they would divide the follow-up work and, as committees of one,
patrol this or that municipal operation and perhaps become the
understanding spokesman in the commission for a department. So
later charters, Houston, for instance, made each elective commissioner full-time manager of a department. This in varying degrees
became the pattern thereafter of the Galveston-Des Moines plan.

Confusions in Practice

As the plan spread, confusions arose in the practice. Some cities
left the commission with the duty of assigning the departments to
commission members, which procedure was awkward if three members all wanted the direction of the public works department or if
no member wanted to be director of the law department or was
fitted for the job. Sometimes the chairman was elected by the commission with the title of mayor and empowered to distribute the
departments to his fellow members and keep one for himself. And,
finally, some cities followed Houston and divided the city administration into five departments and provided for separate election to
each of the department headships; thus there might be four candi-

dates for the position of head of the safety department (fire and police), two for the welfare department, and so on. That made each commissioner the responsible proprietor of his department in the public mind and in his own, and commission meetings became in effect a conference of departmental superintendents.

The theory that the commission as a whole controlled its members in their departmental activities became neglected—the commission could not discipline a recalcitrant member. In Montclair, New Jersey, for example, one commissioner spent his year's appropriations within three months and came around to get an emergency appropriation from his confreres for operation of his department for the remainder of the year. And when each commissioner had his pet department, logrolling for appropriations was a logical result. "You attend to your own department and quit criticizing mine" or "I'll vote for your appropriation if you'll vote for mine" —with nobody taking responsibility for the whole bill. Or where the commissioners were by the provisions of the charter elected to specific departments, they were found to have been elected as representatives of the west side or of labor or of Catholics rather than for any technical preparedness for supervising a modern municipal department. Commonly the budget would not stand five adequate salaries for the part-time or full-time service demanded, and able candidates could not be recruited since the duties involved the distasteful processes of self-advancement, the hurly-burly of campaigning, and sacrifice of private careers by reason of time and energy devoted to learning the techniques of departmental operation and becoming effective before giving way to another transient amateur at the next election. Sometimes three commissioners would combine to starve the appropriations or cut down the authority of the other two, as in Jersey City in 1951, where a minority was left with no staff or appropriations. Departmental permanent personnel learned how to stand off the amateurish efforts of new commissioners to correct abuses or install new policies. It never could make sense for five departmental supervisors to make up their respective budget requests and then meet as a group to pass on each other's demands!

Des Moines eventually found itself being governed by shabby political routineers who, despite obsolete low salaries, were content to serve successive terms as a career. Some cities, San Diego, for instance, went through periods when they seemed to have five quarreling governmentettes.

But the commission plan did appear for a time as a new broom. A single vote stopped talk and let action begin. The spirit of a board of directors replaced the heavy procedures of legislative machinery, which was right, for modern city governments are 90-odd per cent administrative rather than ordinance-making.

With its unified powers and short ballot the Galveston-Des Moines commission plan spread and the National Short Ballot Organization did some pamphleteering for it in 1910 and 1911.

SPREAD OF THE COMMISSION PLAN

Our press releases and successive pamphlets of that period counted the commission-governed cities as follows:

> December 31, 1910—108
> December 31, 1911—183
> December 31, 1912—222
> December 31, 1913—316
> September 30, 1914—346
> September 30, 1915—465

The figures are the Short Ballot office's counts. After September, 1914, it stopped keeping the tally, which in all cases was based on the input of news clippings and was undoubtedly incomplete anyway in respect to villages. The 1915 figure of 465 is from the annual report of the secretary of the National Municipal League and may not have been supported by a full list. These counts undoubtedly missed many of the little places below 5000 population. Neither the states, the federal census nor the *American Year Book* (published 1910–19 and 1925 to the present) kept a list, and just when the peak of the commission plan movement was reached is not knowable. The most exhaustive study of the history of the commission plan in subsequent years was a University of Iowa monograph by Tso-Shuen Chang, Ph.D., in 1918 but its 200 pages provide no list of the cities under that plan and refer to the total as "over 400."

DECLINE OF THE COMMISSION PLAN

In 1916 Salem, Massachusetts, became the first city to abandon the plan, followed by Denver, Colorado, and Huntsville, Alabama. In several succeeding years there were more adoptions than abandonments in the news items of the *National Municipal Review*, but the *Review* was not keeping a count and neither did anybody else, for the commission-manager plan became the new wonder and the subject of our periodic tallies.

In 1923 L. T. Beman [2] published a list of 301 cities of *over* 5000 population under the commission plan and stated that the plan was in effect in 200 or 300 places *under* 5000. There never have been lists of forms of government in towns of 5000 or less. As of the same year, Mr. Stutz, secretary of the City Managers' Association, counted 303 (20.6 per cent of 1467 cities of over 5000 population), fifty-three others having abandoned the plan; he commented that practically all adoptions had been before 1914.[3]

When the comparable commission list finally emerges from neglect, the number of commission-governed cities turns up first in the *Municipal Year Book* of 1940 with a drop to 307 (17 per cent) out of 1807 communities of 5000 population or more and 390 (15.3 per cent) out of 2525 in 1951. In the decade ending 1952 there were only three adoptions—Vancouver, Washington, 1945,[4] Bessemer, Alabama, 1947, and Aurora, Illinois, 1950. The plan is clearly on the way out, and Pennsylvania's forty-seven uniform third-class cities, Illinois's seventy, and New Jersey's fifty-nine commission cities are the largest remaining state groups. The Pennsylvania Federation of Labor and the Chamber of Commerce fight annually for the right to switch to the council-manager plan, and a 1951 law has released the Illinois cities to switch to it. Abandonments and advances to the council-manager plan in New Jersey have long been retarded by the presence of defects in the available optional council-manager law, defects which were happily removed in 1950 by the Faulkner

[2] L. T. Beman, *Current Problems in Municipal Government*, H. W. Wilson Co., New York, 1923.

[3] *National Municipal Review*, January, 1924.

[4] Changed to council-manager plan, 1952.

Commission's revision of the law designed to put skids under the commission plan in that state.

Thus inadequately chronicled, the commission-government movement becomes a passing episode in American history. Des Moines itself abandoned the plan in 1949.

The prime contribution of the commission plan to history was the cracking of the assumption that the mayor-and-council plan was the only conceivable structure for a municipality. New forms could, it appeared, be invented. Experimentation was feasible. That removed from the legal and the public minds the major obstacle to consideration of the council-manager plan when that came along in 1911.

Chapter XV

PROGRESS IN MUNICIPAL GOVERNMENTS (CONTINUED): THE COMING OF THE COUNCIL-MANAGER PLAN

The government of the cities is the one conspicuous failure of the American democracy.

—Sir James Bryce, *American Commonwealth,* 1894

[But is providing America's brightest democratic achievements today.]

HERE we come with our Three Rules to a scene of heartening victory in the last forty years!

Indeed, in 1952, 658 of the 2525 United States cities of 5000 population or over have come under the council-manager plan, the Model City Charter of the National Municipal League, designed in compliance with the Three Rules. (Outline in Part IV.) That's over 26 per cent and in the groups above 25,000 the figure is 34.8 per cent. In communities below 5000 population a similar number raises the total to over 1083 including thirty-six in Canada. Twenty-three million people live under the plan. Its rate of spread in this decade seems destined to make it the favorite form in the United States by 1960.

The plan provides for election of a small board of directors, called the council, in which all the powers of the city are vested—no other elective officers—and its members are of high and equal importance. The smallness of the board—commonly five members—makes each membership important. If more than five members are desired, the number can be seven or nine, but to keep the ballot short the terms are in that case rotated.

Election is at large in 73.7 per cent of the cities so as not to compartmentalize the scrutiny of the voters and the press or perpetuate

COUNCIL-MANAGER FORM

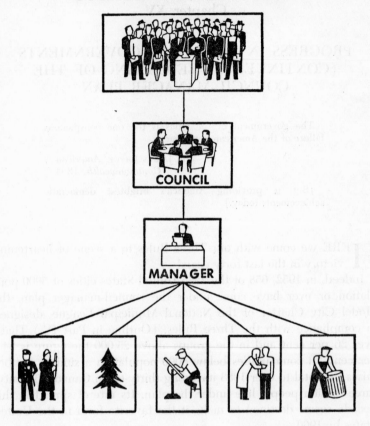

National Municipal League

the ancient evils of the ward systems. All of that provides compliance with Rule One—the short-ballot principle. Except in metropolitan cities, Rule Two re wieldy constituencies is not encountered. And Rule Three—integration—is completely respected since the single council holds in one place all the reins of power and cannot pass the buck to any other agency. The internal structure under the council is well integrated too, for the council in turn hires and fires the city manager who appoints and controls the heads of all operating departments. Nonpartisan elections are used in 84.6 per cent of these cities and Reading D, "500 Non-Political Elections," shows only two cases where the local wings of the national political parties figured in the municipal elections under this plan.

It has all come about since 1911 and brings us experience now of about 16,000 city-years of conformity with the Three Rules.

Although I am dubbed nowadays "the father of the council-manager plan" and hold in consequence a treasured honorary membership in the International City Managers' Association as a result of its inquiries into the beginnings of the profession, the principle is hardly novel enough to be patentable. Indeed, its structure is exactly that of over 80 per cent of our school boards, where the voters elect a small board which hires a professional superintendent who hires and directs the rest of the staff. Accordingly its existence in the 63,000 independent school districts with taxing powers is in itself enough to make it the commonest form of government among the 112,420 units.

THE FIRST CITY MANAGER, 1908

In 1908 Staunton, Virginia, had had imposed upon it by state law a requirement that it must have a bicameral council, a ridiculously cumbersome structure in a small city. The procedures tired out the participants. So there was created by ordinance the post of general manager, and Charles E. Ashburner was appointed thereto with power to manage the departments except those of police and fire. He reported to the mayor and the two councils. Taken as a whole, the form of government was nothing to admire or copy. But the choice of Mr. Ashburner was a fortunate one and, in a period when novelties in governmental forms excited quick and friendly curiosity, his achievements won national publicity. A tablet in the Staunton city hall honors him correctly enough as the first city manager in the United States. Staunton's municipal letterhead bears the phrase "Birthplace of the City Manager Form of Government," which is incorrect. The correct claim would be "First City to Have a City Manager." In the International City Managers' Association's roster of cities that have the council-manager plan, Staunton is assigned the 1908 date, the earliest in the list, but actually it did not adopt the *plan* and was never listed until 1920, when it replaced its mayor and two councils with a single strong council.

In 1909 and 1910 as volunteer secretary of the National Short Ballot Organization I eagerly gathered and reissued news of the successes of the commission plan with emphasis on its short-ballot feature. It existed then in about 100 cities and towns. The National Municipal League was not stirred from its strong-mayor Model Charter by either the appearance of the commission plan or the success of Mr. Ashburner in Staunton.

CONCEPTION OF THE COMMISSION-MANAGER PLAN, 1910

One day in 1910, reading a labored editorial which undertook to show that the commission plan was like a board of directors of a corporation, I said to myself, "No, there would have to be a manager put under that board to make it resemble a corporation!" The New York State Short Ballot Organization, of which I was also the secretary, was at that time drafting legislation for shortening ballots at state and local levels. We had in hand the draft of a constitutional amendment for cutting off the tail of the state ticket and it seemed logical to get up also an optional bill to enable the upstate second- and third-class cities to adopt the commission plan. This involved an extensive task of draftsmanship and for this I engaged the services of a Columbia postgraduate student, H. S. Gilbertson. Setting him on his way I told him to provide that the commission should select a city manager and handle its administrative or operating functions through him. Gilbertson was a little startled and asked if this was not a departure from the precedents of the commission plan. This I admitted but I wanted it put in nevertheless to submit to our board as a possible improvement. He drafted it, but when some months later, in anticipation of the approaching legislative session, I called a meeting to consider our program, my board unexpectedly resolved not to attempt anything on the local level but to stick to the single item of trying to cut off the tail of the state ticket. There lay the bulky manuscript of Gilbertson's draft and I was abruptly shut off from even reporting that I had gone so far as to have it prepared!

However, since the New York State Short Ballot Organization

board was made up of New York City residents anyway, it was an illogical sponsor for a bill affecting only upstate cities. So when our newspaper clipping service brought in an item showing that the Lockport Board of Trade had created a committee to look into the commission plan, I offered them our ready-made draft, explaining that, being optional and state-wide, it might get further than a bill for Lockport alone and that it contained, as the latest wrinkle, an advanced feature providing for a "controlled executive." The name for the latter, "city manager," was picked from a list of all the alternatives I could think of—municipal manager, municipal executive, municipal secretary (to emphasize his subordination to the council), civic manager, executive secretary, administrative chief, chief administrator, etc. Precedent was provided in Staunton's "general manager." "City manager" fitted handily with the idea of calling the total form "the commission-manager plan" since it seemed important tactically to get it introduced on the moving cart of the commission-plan movement headed not in opposition but in the same direction and desirable as only a variation.

THE LOCKPORT BILL, 1911

The Lockport Board of Trade at any rate was not disturbed by the element of novelty in the bill; it sponsored it and arranged its introduction at Albany. Our office was issuing releases to the press on every pretext it could dream up and it was easy to put into circulation "the interesting new Lockport Plan." We printed up the text of the bill with approving comments and the pamphlet went out from the Lockport Board of Trade to the press. Woodrow Wilson, touring the West, picked up the new Lockport idea and mentioned it approvingly in one of his speeches before he learned that it had come from the office of the National Short Ballot Organization, which he headed.

All through 1911 we did all we could with press releases to keep alive the quick interest which the Lockport idea aroused in newspaper editors. There were more newspapers then and fewer releases. One glad day in 1912, when I came from my advertising business to the adjacent Short Ballot office, Gilbertson, then assistant secretary, had placed on top of the incoming mail a telegram from the

Chamber of Commerce of Sumter (pop. 8109) reporting that the South Carolina legislature had passed a bill submitting our plan to local referendum as an alternative to the regular commission plan. First blood! Weeks later came news of its adoption, on June 12, three to one; the first commission was elected the same year and the plan took effect in January, 1913.

SUMTER AND OTHER CITIES, 1912–14

In our publicity we dropped Lockport—it had enjoyed its year of fame but the legislature ignored the bill—and began calling it "the Sumter plan." With cooperation from the Sumter Chamber of Com-

---

October 14, 1912

The city of Sumter hereby announces that applications will be received from now till December the first for the office of City Manager of Sumter.

This is a rapidly growing manufacturing city of 10,000 population, and the applicant should be competent to oversee public works, such as paving, lighting, water supply, etc.

An engineer of standing and ability would be preferred.

State salary desired and previous experience in municipal work. The City Manager will hold office as long as he gives satisfaction to the commission. He will have complete administrative control of the city, subject to the approval of the board of three elected commissioners.

There will be no politics in the job; the work will be purely that of an expert.

Local citizenship is not necessary, although a knowledge of local conditions and traditions will of course be taken into consideration.

A splendid opportunity for the right man to make a record in a new and coming profession, as this is the first time that a permanent charter position of this sort has been created in the United States.

At the request of the City Commissioners these applications will be filed with the Chamber of Commerce of Sumter, A. V. Snell, Secretary.

The first council-manager city's proclamation inviting applications for the managership set a good precedent!

merce we prepared a pamphlet which was mailed to a thousand newspapers from Sumter with the imprint of the Sumter Chamber.

In 1912, soon after the election of the first Sumter commission of three, we sent down a proposed proclamation inviting applications for the managership. The commissioners changed the wording somewhat and allowed us to issue it for them, with the Sumter postmark, to our press list. It stirred a grand bubbling of editorials and brought them 150 applications. It was a major contribution to the ensuing movement that the commission hired its first manager, Malcolm McLean Worthington, from out of town. He took charge in Sumter on January 7, 1913.

In North Carolina, Hickory (pop. 3716) adopted a partly verbatim copy of the Lockport text in April, 1913, and was followed by Morganton, North Carolina (pop. then 2713), the same year.

In Dayton (pop. then 116,577) a charter commission headed by the picturesque John H. Patterson, the genius of the National Cash Register Company, was elected May 20, 1913, to take advantage of the Ohio home rule amendment of 1912. It presented and won adoption of the commission-manager plan, as it now began to be called, on August 12, 1913, which went into effect January 1, 1914. Springfield, Ohio (pop. then 46,921), chimed in the same year on August 26. In Douglas, Arizona, Youngstown and Elyria, Ohio, similar charters failed of adoption but they succeeded in Whittier, California (pop. then 4550), LaGrande, Oregon (pop. 4843), Amarillo, Texas (pop. 9951), Cadillac, Michigan (pop. 8375), Manistee, Michigan (pop. 12,381), Phoenix, Arizona (pop. 11,134), all in 1913.

So by the end of 1913 the plan was on the map in eleven cities—off in two years like a bunch of firecrackers! Indeed, in December, 1914, there were enough city managers to meet in Springfield, eight in attendance out of seventeen, to form the City Managers' Association.

DAYTON AND CITY MANAGER WAITE

Dayton, for many years the biggest city under the plan, was highly conscious of the publicity value of its leadership. Its new commission—this title is still in use there as the name for the council —offered the managership to Goethals, the great engineer who was just completing the Panama Canal. He declined but the incident made fine copy. Then Henry M. Waite, a one-time city engineer of Cincinnati during Mayor Hunt's brief reform administration there, was engaged as city manager and proved a magnificent choice. He was a truly noble man by any way of counting—warm, generous, natural, human, and transcendently able. There have been no city managers since that quite matched him. He went off to the war after four years but his administrative personnel and clean-cut methods were a fine and permanent legacy. He not only saved taxes but he rehabilitated the drunks in the workhouse and brought good music to Dayton. A steady output of exhilarating stories of achievement came out of Dayton. They were not press-agent inventions, either. They stirred up the press and brought in delegations from remote states and cities to see for themselves and go home and copy. The delegates found no chance to scoff at Waite! The quality of his pioneer managership in the first sizable city became the foundation and inspiration of the new profession. For his fellow managers for a decade, he set the pace! For the new movement, his appearance at that strategic spot was rare good fortune.

The political history of Dayton for the following generation is told in Reading H. It is also told, up to 1938, in the Stone-Price-Stone survey.[1]

Politics went out the window when Dayton's first city manager blew in and, after a single sputter, the local wings of the political parties ceased to function in municipal elections, either visibly or covertly. A self-renewing group of responsible and respected citizens finds and sponsors candidates, and its leadership suffices to prevent scatteration of the good-government vote. It has always seen its nominees in a majority on the commission, and its efforts have commonly consisted only of deciding whom to sponsor, seeing that petitions are gotten up in proper order, and spending $4000 more or less in newspaper advertisements. After election the citizens' committee puts away its lists and disbands until next time. The task is simplified a bit by the fact that the five commissioners are elected for four-year terms, in rotation, three, or two, every two years.

[1] *City Manager Government in Seven Cities*, Public Administration Service, Chicago, 1940.

When things go well, as they seem to have done in Dayton, the reelection of incumbents as long as they can be induced to run seems to be rather easy.

The stories of achievements, of new vigor and quality of administration after adoption of the council-manager plan are so numerous and similar that city managers at their conventions have long since

---

SANTA MONICA FINDS GOLD

Santa Monica, California (pop. 53,000), proved in one year with the council-manager plan that the battered taxpayer is not the only source of needed revenue. City Manager Randall M. Dorton reported in June 1948 that income had been boosted $147,000 by items like these: Leasing to Douglas Aircraft Company at $6,000 a year a strip of land for which the company had been paying $1 a year; leasing five acres of airport property to another operator at $8,710 annually; persuading the county to raise its appropriation for lifeguards from $15,000 to $27,000, and to double its $3,000 rental for City Hall space. By consolidating the public works and engineering departments the new administration saved $80,000. The transportation department budget was cut $30,000 by installing a bus-washing machine and by rearranging schedules. Voters liked these changes so well that they gave overwhelming approval to four bond issues totaling $2,975,000.

TEANECK'S MODEL GOVERNMENT

Teaneck, New Jersey (pop. 25,000), is a model community. Its municipal services are topnotch. Its training school for firemen is so good that many other New Jersey communities send their fire officials to it. Its police force has held crime so low that a national magazine ran an article headed, "There Is No Crime in Teaneck."

Things were not ideal in 1930 when the manager plan was adopted. The bonded debt was $5,000,000, or $301 per capita, and services were deplorable. There was not an acre of parkland. By 1948 City Manager Paul A. Volcker had cut the debt to $1,800,000, or $57 per capita, and the town had acquired 95 acres of parks. Furthermore, taxes had been reduced.

—From *Story of the Council-Manager Plan*,
National Municipal League, 1952

CAMBRIDGE CLIMBS OUT

Cambridge, Massachusetts (pop. 110,000), has had the manager plan with both council and school committee elected by proportional representation since January 1, 1942. That date ended a dreary era of inefficiency, graft and low civic morale. Almost overnight the taxpayers and civil servants, who had been alarmed by the combination of rising taxes, falling valuations and bad politics, found a new confidence in themselves and their city.

A policy of no firings or pay cuts reassured public employees. Reclassification of the civil service and an end to unnecessary hiring (especially before elections) brought personnel costs under control. To meet higher living costs the city granted an average pay increase of $500 even though taxes went down. The tax rate dropped 23% in the first six years. Yet the $10,000,000 bonded debt was cut about two-thirds during the same period.

Centralized purchasing saved many thousands. The city had been buying, for example, 100,000 pills a year at a retail price of 60 cents a dozen. The new administration got the wholesale rate of 18 cents a dozen, saving $3,500.

Spectacular savings were made by using city crews instead of favored contractors for snow removal, refuse collection and street repairs. While Boston's garbage collection costs were trebling, Cambridge bought 18 trucks and reduced expenses. The contract prices of $1.25 to $2.50 a square yard for resurfacing streets were slashed to 60 cents.

Some of the money saved was plowed back into the field of service. Recreation facilities were expanded. The health department and city hospital were modernized. The library book budget was tripled. The police department was modernized.

A Boston editor asked, "Is Cambridge out of this world?" He answered himself: "The success of its government is due to nothing more magical than honesty, efficiency and competence. But the curiousest part, as Alice would say, of this wonderland where you get both lower taxes and higher municipal salaries is that among the prime beneficiaries are those who originally regarded the plan with the most skeptical eye, the city employees."

—From *Story of the Council-Manager Plan*,
National Municipal League, 1952

abandoned the practice of telling them or listening to them. Such stories are told from time to time when reform administrations replace political dynasties under any form of government; their real distinction under the council-manager plan is the way good government persists through long series of elections.

But while most of the stories can be told for several years before the National Municipal League has to abandon them and print a fresh, up-to-date batch, one story must be preserved here as tops— the dramatic tale of Knoxville, Tennessee, under Louis Brownlow, the first city manager there. He budgeted his first year's operations for $500,000 less than the previous political administration's and before the end of the first year declared a kind of dividend by handing back to the taxpayers checks for 10 per cent of the levy! [2]

Model City Charter Revised, 1915

In 1915 the National Municipal League rewrote its Model Charter to bring it into accord with the commission-manager plan and it became the orthodox ideal of the municipal reformers. The name commission—and commission-manager plan—persists in early charters but it was, of course, a misnomer after the Galveston commission ceased to be an *ad hoc* appointive agency of the Texas governor. In later years the City Managers' Association and the League switched to the present name, "council-manager."

Spread of the Plan Without Alteration

As the council-manager plan spread, the charters kept with astonishing fidelity to the true principles defined in the League's Model Council-Manager Charter. The model itself has been restudied and reissued to take into account the ever accumulating experience without altering the main concept. The alterations have been in the useful collateral provisions on such subjects as election procedures, franchises, condemnation of land, which the model includes as necessary to charter completeness. Some provisions get widely copied verbatim, notably one originally written into the text by A. Lawrence Lowell, then president of Harvard and a member of the League's 1915 Committee on the Model Charter; it reads:

[2] *National Municipal Review,* November, 1924.

"Except for the purpose of inquiry, the council and its members shall deal with the administrative service solely through the city manager and neither the council nor any member thereof shall give orders to any subordinates of the city manager, either publicly or privately." (Article II, Sec. 11, Model City Charter, 1948 edition.)

Home rule amendments to state constitutions spread as cities developed more impatience with remote control and uniform laws regulating the pattern of municipal governments. Cities obtained the right to draft and amend their own charters by procedures independent of the legislature and, if desired, independent also of the vested interest in the *status quo* represented by the officeholders in their city halls. States also facilitated the spread of both the commission plan and the council-manager plan by passing optional laws providing several ready-made forms of government—Plan A, Plan B, etc.—which could be submitted to the voters in individual cities by ordinance or initiative petition without the delays involved in writing a special charter.

THE SOCIAL SCIENCE RESEARCH COUNCIL'S SURVEY, 1940

An important event in the progression of the council-manager plan is the extensive field investigation that was made into its workings in 1937–40 by a team sent out by the Social Science Research Council. This Stone-Price-Stone survey required two years and resulted in a three-volume report [3] covering fifty sample cities. There, in abundant circumstantial detail, is proof galore of bright progress, so much proof indeed that the voluminous texts could never get extensive circulation. The stories of the individual cities are available in separate pamphlets, and the seventeen fifty-page narratives of individual cities are precious vignettes of American local politics at its happiest. Since that publication, the burden of proof as to the contentment of the people who live under the plan is on the opponents.

Although the field work underlying the Stone-Price-Stone survey

[3] Stone, Price, and Stone, I. *City Manager Government in the U.S., A Review after 25 years;* II. *City Manager Government in Seven Cities;* III. *City Manager Government in Nine Cities.* A project of the Social Science Research Council published by Public Administration Service, 1313 East 60th Street, Chicago, 1940.

is dated 1938–39 it remains the best and most impartial account of how the council-manager plan works, and its analyses of various aspects of the experience are more authoritative than any other. I doubt if its able young authors would find much to retract if they went back over the same ground now. Their fifty samples at the time included half the cities of over 100,000 which had the plan and a third of those over 25,000. Realizing that good government in diverse constituencies is not measurable validly by comparisons of tax rates or any other such oversimple criteria, they made in each city comparisons of administrative methods before and after adoption of the plan: Did they move nearer to modern standards of management—budgetary controls, for instance, to prevent overdrafts and unforeseen floating debts? On each count of the appraisal they were able to cite several example cities to exhibit the character and benefits of the improvement in method. Although, of course, evidence was sometimes mixed or contradictory, the conclusions were uniformly favorable to the plan and so are quoted extensively below as still valid and consistent with the steady inflow of similar information which has accumulated in the office of the National Municipal League in the subsequent 1939–52 period.

The authors found that municipal politics in America is marked by extreme diversity, ranging from cities of mutually distrustful factions and population groups dominated by self-serving political gangs to serene homogeneous communities conscious of no political strain, well governed by devoted public servants despite their preposterously ramshackle old organization charts. Their classification of their samples into machine-ridden, faction-ridden, and community-governed was in itself a contribution to thought on the subject and, at the same time, an explanation of why some cities of the first groups continued, under the council-manager plan, to be scenes of political turbulence and contention with shorter tenure of managers, whereas the comfortable third class jogged along serenely with long-service managers whose advent had involved no implied criticism of the prior city officials or of their supporters. In the first two classes the elective officers in the city hall were commonly ousted at the first election under the plan by the same forces which had forced adoption of the new charter; in the third class adoption came without much heat and frequently at the instance of the elective officers themselves looking for expertness greater than their own, personal relief from detailed duties, or improvement of an annoyingly complex and antiquated system. The latter phenomenon in growing suburbs is increasingly common in recent years. Adoption of the plan is thus not necessarily a drastic reform or revolution in local politics.

We pick out and quote the conclusions at some length to give them a new lease of life since the report is now out of print, necessarily skipping the voluminous supporting proofs, for which we must refer you to the reference library copies of the survey itself:

Machine-ridden cities. About *half* the cities in this study adopted the city-manager plan only after a bitter political fight between two groups: one composed of leaders of business and reform organizations and the other composed of leaders of political organizations maintained by systematic patronage and special privilege.

Faction-ridden cities. No political organization that made use of continuous, systematic spoils or patronage existed in *fourteen cities* studied. In these, city manager charters were advocated by community leaders and civic organizations in order to get more public-spirited citizens on the council and to provide a single, professional chief executive. The movement was, therefore, for the purpose of improving both the politics and the administration of the government.

Community-governed cities. In other cities members of the city council, wishing to improve the methods by which it directed municipal affairs, took the initiative in promoting the adoption of the city manager plan.

In some of the cities, especially in the larger ones, the most important community leaders had habitually shunned municipal politics, and their decision to advocate a new form of government aroused the antagonism of those who had been the traditional political leaders. In such cities this conflict between the businessmen and the politicians distorted the attitudes of the community toward the nature of the city manager plan, for the new form of government and the city manager himself were popularly identified with the businessmen and their motives.

In other cities, more often the smaller ones, the adoption of the city manager plan involved no such factional struggle, because it did not involve the displacement of one set of political leaders by another. The city manager plan, therefore, came into existence in these cities as a form of government that every political group could accept without loss of face, and the city manager himself was not identified in advance as the agent of one faction in a political struggle.

. . . .

In the fifty cities studied not more than a handful of skilled administrators had appeared over a long period of years. There was rarely one man clothed with full administrative authority. Councilmen did not have administrative authority; it was not part of their jobs to run the business side of a city government. Mayors were often designated as the executive heads of the government, but they were seldom elected for their administrative ability, were hardly ever given authority over all parts of the government, and were usually faced with the perplexing problem of dividing their time and energy between their private business and the city's business. More important, administration seldom claimed any of the mayor's substantial interest. . . . In many cities there was no record of any mayor with an interest and competence in administration.

. . . .

Commissioners in cities having the commission plan had nearly always competed with one another, and seldom was one strong enough or forceful enough to be commander-in-chief of the administrative parts of the city government.

. . . .

The new position of city manager provided an unprecedented opportunity to administer services efficiently. It was an important position—the highest administrative post in the municipal government. The manager was given authority over most departments and over most employees. His was a full-time job, usually at a much higher salary than had ever before been paid by the city to a purely administrative officer. He was not hampered in administration, as mayors and other elective officers had been, by a lack of authority over work for which they were responsible.

. . . .

Perhaps the strongest support for the position the city managers took in regarding themselves as professional men lay in their attitude and in their conduct. Many city managers thought of themselves as professional executives devoting themselves to a job which required technical skill and a high sense of moral obligation. Many felt that they were selected as managers because they possessed special qualifications for the position and that political and private connections played no part in their appointment. With a large majority of managers, the job was the thing. Because city managers generally lived up to the ideals which they had set for themselves through the International City Managers' Association, they were quite widely recognized as professional men. They were in a position similar to that of the superintendent of schools, whose job like-wise required special qualifications and imposed certain ethical standards.

It was feared in the early years of the city manager plan that councils elected by political parties or factions might appoint a partisan manager without qualifications to the position of city manager. This fear was not borne out, for councils usually appointed managers without partisan or factional affiliations.

The experience of the cities studied showed that the adoption of the manager form of government made it possible to arrange the divisions into a smoothly running organization, to adopt those methods which large-scale industrial enterprises had found successful, to eliminate vexing delays and to direct the entire city government at one objective—that of giving services to the citizens in accordance with the policies adopted by their representatives in the council. The managers were made respon-sible for setting up and directing an organization which would achieve this objective, and within the limitations of their own ability, the char-acter of the council, and the nature of the community, broadly speaking they accomplished the task.

The ideals of the city manager movement were instantly accepted in cities that were ready for them and distorted or abused wherever they were in conflict with local political traditions. But nearly everywhere they added to the prestige of city government, lessened its preoccupa-tion with trivial details or factional interests, and increased its ability to render service to the public.

In one respect I found the survey disappointing. It neglected the phenomena of the election campaigns. The diminution of impor-tance of political machines, improvement in the quality of elective councils, the greater independence of elective councils from political pressures, and the alteration in the atmosphere of the elective process could, I believe, have been far more fully spotted and docu-mented. For the council-manager plan was an experiment, now long past the testing period, in *democratics;* the subsequent progress in *administrative* performance below the level of the elective offices reflects improvement in the elective process and the choice of better councils.

Chapter XVI

PROGRESS IN MUNICIPAL GOVERNMENTS (CONTINUED): COUNCIL-MANAGER EXPERIENCE IN THREE LARGE CITIES

THE adoption of the council-manager plan in Cleveland (adopted 1921; in effect January 1, 1924) was for a time an important landmark in the plan's progress because of the size of the city—800,000 at that time.

CLEVELAND AND A. R. HATTON

The drafting and adoption of the plan was almost the feat of a single man, Dr. A. R. Hatton, charter-drafting expert of the National Municipal League and, at that time, also a professor at Western Reserve University. As member of the charter commission when an unprogressive program was brought in by a subcommittee, he assailed it so disconcertingly that he was invited to draft a better one. He came back with the outline of a council-manager plan adjusted for a large city. He provided a city council of twenty-five members (which in retrospect now seems quite a bit too large) and solved the problem of the unwieldy district by dividing the city into quadrants—two long straight streets which crossed at the center of the city provided the boundaries. From each of the four districts thus created, councilmen were elected by proportional representation,[1] the number of councilmen—five, six, seven, and seven—from each district being adjusted in relation to the size of the district population. A quota of about 4000 thus became enough to elect, and a candidate could seek his supporters anywhere within his spacious quadrant. Nonpartisan elections diminished the ability of the party machines to marshal voters in the party's name; voters could mark a first choice, second choice, etc., as they pleased, without a sense of apostasy to their traditional party. The council thus chosen was

[1] Explained in Chapter XXVI.

authorized to pick a chairman from its own number and to hire and direct a city manager.

The Republican boss of Cleveland did not oppose the project. Hatton, a happy warrior, campaigned for his charter in a series of public debates with the unconscious aid of an opponent who did not seem to know that Hatton steadily won the audiences. Then when the charter had been adopted and the time for nominations for council came round, Hatton hired a student to circulate his nomination petition and began accepting invitations to show himself and speak at various gatherings. He wrote his own public statements for the press. He did not gather a campaign or sponsoring committee. He made no expenditure beyond the $46.79 which the footwork for his petition cost. Without aid or blessing from either of the political camps, he was elected by the second largest vote in the city. Three other members were elected that year in similar independence. But there was no strong organized effort in Cleveland as there has always been under the same plan in Cincinnati, to assemble a list of citizen-sponsored nonpolitical candidates of superior caliber and public spirit and procure their election.

Both political parties put forward candidates and helped elect them, although party sponsorship was unofficial and some candidates who got endorsement believed they could have elected themselves without it. But the bulk of the members of the first council were party hacks with no sense of purpose and docile to orders from political headquarters. Eighteen of them had been members of the prior far less important council and, despite the charter, persisted in seeking access to patronage. Some of them practiced law before departmental boards or helped purveyors to make sales to the city. Their habit of serving as errand boys for constituents interested them more than major measures such as correcting unsound pension systems or making a long-term program of public improvements. Patronage at the outset was divided between the parties by the city manager on a sixty-forty basis. The council's power to appoint the three civil service commissioners was used to turn it into a tool of the Republican machine.

The council chose for city manager at $25,000 salary an able and flamboyant promoter. Finding little help or hindrance in that mediocre council, he fell into the way of making policy and running out ahead with a lively sense of headlines, and the council neglected to use its powers to keep him under restraint. At one point he published a huge project for straightening out the river which wound through the middle of the town and left the council to learn of it through the newspapers!

At the second election two years later, in 1925, Professor Hatton repeated his exploit of getting elected to council without organized help and found at his side another minority of independent members.

Within the council an interlocking group of four or five found it possible to use the party whip and produce enough votes to prevail, and neither the membership of the council nor this condition altered much after the second and third biennial elections. The old council's tradition of trading in petty favors continued in the new; to members and to much of the public that was what council membership meant despite its vastly enhanced authority.

The Republican machine, which had been tolerant of the new scheme at first, soon turned against it.

In 1925 came the first attack. The council was at any rate the best that Cleveland had had in years and the manager was dramatic, able, and popular. So the attack took the form of a petition and referendum to abandon proportional representation elections for the council. P.R. had permitted Hatton and others to run as independents, muster a quota of 3000–4000 votes among 40,000 registered voters in a quadrant of the city and—shocking!—get elected and reelected. Party managers found elections somewhat unpredictable, and leaders in both parties sought to reestablish partisan elections and thirty-three ward-elected councilmen. Both sides were surprised by the outcome of the 25 per cent turnout at a special August election, 20,353 to 20,918 against the change.[2]

Meanwhile administration was greatly improved. In 1926 as compared with 1920 the city cleaned 40 per cent more streets 35 per cent more frequently for $100,000 less. The revenue from garbage by-products went up from $118,900 to $299,000, and the cost per ton for collection and disposal was cut from $14.50 to $7.41. Cleve-

---

[2] Norman Shaw, "Cleveland's P.R. Election," *National Municipal Review*, October, 1925.

land went to the top in public health work. And so forth; the period was rated by the local Citizens League as the best in the municipality's history.[3]

The irrepressible disposition of City Manager Hopkins to initiate and sponsor policy led him into controversy and in November, 1927, the second assault upon the charter swirled largely about the question of retaining him. Ex-Governor Harry L. Davis, who had been three times mayor, led off with aid from the local Republican leader, and two other groups also put forward proposals for substitute setups by initiative petition. And the Citizens League sponsored another measure providing for a charter commission where the issues could be examined in orderly fashion. The charter, however, was apparently merely one factor in a struggle between factions for political control of the Republican party. The Davis amendment lost, 73,732 to 80,148, and the other measures lost by much larger majorities.[4]

In January, 1928, a revised Davis amendment was filed by petition. The charter supporters were tired, except the League of Women Voters, which does not tire and which ended up by carrying almost the whole task. But the Davis side, after defeat, had lost its drive too and on April 24 the vote was 44,122 for retaining the charter and 40,890 for the Davis proposal.

In 1929 a vigorous new district attorney under no obligations to the Republican party took office. He got thirty-six indictments in county election frauds and opened up neglected scandals in the activities of certain city councilmen. A councilman was convicted of accepting a $200 bribe. Another councilman pleaded guilty to the charge of profiting in a sale of land to the city. Two others were indicted, one for soliciting and accepting a $500 bribe for using his influence to reverse a denial of a building permit, but they were not convicted.

The situation supported another assault on the charter by Davis

[3] "Five Years of City Manager Government in Cleveland." A report of the Citizens League, Mayo Fesler, director. Republished in *National Municipal Review*, March, 1929.

[4] Randolph O. Huus, "The Attack on Cleveland's Council-Manager Charter," *National Municipal Review*, February, 1928.

and others proposing an elective mayor and a council of thirty-three from wards. The prospects seemed dark but resistance was organized; house-to-house canvassing was undertaken by the women and the Davis hokum could not stir up the original heat. The charter was retained by 3044 majority.[5]

In November, the council member scandals being still in memory and refreshed by some new exposures of the machine's men elsewhere, Cleveland elected a greatly improved council in which the Republican boss for the first time lost control. Thirteen, instead of the usual sixteen (out of twenty-five), were rated as regular and had the support of the party organization, but three of the thirteen had independent leanings and two had the endorsement of the nonpartisan Progressive Government Committee. The other twelve included eleven nominal Democrats and a Republican. The improvement reflected the first impressive effort to develop a nonpartisan citizen organization to enlist and support superior candidates like the successful Charter party in Cincinnati.

On January 13, 1930, however, City Manager W. R. Hopkins, after six years' service, was suspended by a vote of fourteen to eleven. The fourteen included twelve Republicans, Hopkins, to his credit, having long since gone out of favor with the Republican machine. He demanded a statement of the charges and was served with vague and general statements, the first of which was "usurping the policy-determining powers of the council and failing to work in harmony with that body," an issue of which the council was, of course, free to hold its own view although its policy-determining powers had been too rarely asserted. Daniel E. Morgan, a lawyer of excellent repute, past president of the City Club and of the Citizens League, was selected as Hopkins' successor. He began by asking the mayor to do all the speechmaking and the council reformed its rules in a freshened spirit.

In a careful and thorough review in June, 1931, the Citizens League made a second elaborate analysis of the Cleveland govern-

[5] Mayo Fesler, "Cleveland Again Defeats Attack on City Manager Charter," *National Municipal Review*, October, 1929.

[6] "Greater Cleveland," Citizens League, Cleveland, Ohio, June 4, 1931.

ment [6] covering two and one-half years of experience beyond that of the five years described in its earlier report. It reported:

> While the council of the last two years has been far from an ideal legislative body, there has been a definite improvement in its personnel, in its procedure and also in legislation. . . . There is in our opinion . . . a much healthier atmosphere at the city hall than at any time in the last twelve or fifteen years, especially in the relationship between the legislature and administrative departments of city government. . . . When the comparative continuity of the service in Cleveland under the manager plan is compared with the total lack of continuity under changing mayors prior to 1924, the conclusion cannot be reasonably avoided that Cleveland on the whole has been enjoying comparatively good government. . . . But whatever may be said of the defects of city manager administration during the past seven years, and there are many, we believe it cannot be gainsaid that there has been more continuity in policy and administration, and a greater degree of economy and efficiency under the city manager plan than under any similar recent period of governmental history in Cleveland. Furthermore, the last two years have shown many improvements over the preceding five.

Soon after that report another petition was filed for shift to an elective mayor and a council elected one from each of thirty wards. Ex-Manager Hopkins appeared as a candidate for council and the Democratic county prosecutor started a carefully timed attack on the administration of the police. The League of Women Voters, the Citizens League, the Chamber of Commerce, the Republican organization, and the three leading newspapers were arrayed on behalf of the charter against the Democratic party but in the shock of the depression the battle-weary volunteers could not be mustered for doorbell ringing as numerously as in previous defensive actions. The amendment carried on November 3, 1931, by a vote of 61,267 to 51,970 out of a total registration of 248,788, 164,516 of whom went to the polls. Of the 155,942 who voted for councilmen, 31 per cent failed to vote on the amendment.

The fourth council, retiring December, 1931, was praised by press and by the Citizens League as the best yet.

The fifth council elected climaxed a steady improvement in the character of that body and in the diminution of its partisan spirit; fifteen of the twenty-five members were on the Citizens League's

"Preferred List" and three more were rated as "qualified." By a rough-and-tumble process it had gradually emerged from the original partisan control and could have provided a firmer foundation for cooperation with a nonpartisan manager. But the victory came too late!

Two months later the city manager, Mr. Morgan, ran for mayor, survived the primary, and was defeated by the Democratic prosecutor. Thirty-three gerrymandered single-member wards of obvious inequity replaced the mathematical precision of the P.R. system in subsequent elections.

Cleveland's charter, in providing a council of twenty-five members, violated Rule One in that the office of councilman was not important enough. To be sure, the voter had only the task of marking a first choice, and preferably a second and third choice, for a councilman from his quadrant of the city, but the division of the council's powers into twenty-five bits made each bit seem trivial to the voter and, even worse, trivial to the type of potential candidate who could have made great councils. Efforts in three of the four quadrants at the first election to enlist high-grade citizens to run for the office failed badly. The traditions of the prior councils in Cleveland had been shabby and uninspired, and neither voters nor candidates seem to have grasped the fact that the new council was to be the supreme board of directors with many, many times the power and opportunity of the old one. Nor did the good citizens succeed in developing a strong local nonpartisan nominating and campaigning association like that which in Cincinnati with a council of nine has brought out candidates of vision and courage and re-elected them and their like for a generation.

Four years later, in 1935, Cleveland indicated repentance, for a *county* charter commission in Cleveland's county, Cuyahoga, submitted proposals for an elective county council of nine elected by P.R. and a county manager who would appoint all other department heads except a controller chosen by council. By that time there was widespread criticism of the Cleveland government under the 1931 mayor-and-council plan, and the referendum on the proposed county charter carried in the city of Cleveland by 18,000 and in the county as a whole, failing, however, to carry also some of the outlying units whose separate assent was necessary.

CINCINNATI'S REDEMPTION

Cincinnati (500,510 pop. in 1950) was in 1925 a shabby, run-down, corrupt municipality controlled from New York by a Republican boss and operator of burlesque theaters. The people were voting down every bond issue because the money seemed likely to be diverted to political ends. A valiant insurrection of citizens by a vote of 92,510 to 41,105 secured adoption of the council-manager plan with a council of nine elected at large by proportional representation. This conformed to all Three Rules. Then, organized as the Charter party with some unofficial aid from the Democrats, they elected six of their candidates, a majority, including some of the ablest men in town to whom the $5000 salary was a low rate of pay for the generous share of their time which they gave to the city. Cincinnati, which had admittedly been the worst-governed city in the country, began, not without reason, to call itself the best governed. The managers were men of top capacity—Colonel C. O. Sherrill from Washington, Clarence A. Dykstra from Los Angeles (afterwards president of the University of Wisconsin), and Wilbur R. Kellogg, a local successful businessman, ex-superintendent of the great Cincinnati railroad passenger terminal.

But the Republican machine remained a threat. Nourished on national, state, and county patronage, it turned up as a bloc in every election and installed a minority of councilmen of improved character and independence. The score in successive elections ran thus: 1925, six Charterites (out of nine seats); 1927, six; 1929, six; 1931, five; 1935, four plus an independent; 1937, ditto; 1939, ditto; 1941, four; 1943, four; 1945, four; 1947, five; 1949, five; 1951, four.

In the periods when the Republican machine had a majority the spirit of the routineer prevailed and municipal policy lost freshness and vigor, but the prior manager continued to serve undisturbed, too secure in the respect of the town to fear ouster for political reasons.

Efforts were made in 1935 to convert the county (Hamilton) to the council-manager plan and thus put an end to the use of the county pay roll by the dominant machine as a base of supplies, but the citadel of patronage was successfully defended and continues to afford a dark contrast to the bright history being made at the city hall. As the largest city under the council-manager plan for twenty-five years (except while Cleveland had it), Cincinnati refutes the doctrine that forms of government make no difference; the same people install good councils in city hall and the usual political job lot in the county courthouse; the same voters know what they are doing when voting for city council and are all but unaware of even the names of the candidates they vote for for the scatteration of little county offices.

KANSAS CITY CLIMBS OUT

Kansas City (1950 pop. 453,290) adopted the council-manager plan in 1926 and is the second largest city under the plan. The city's powers are vested in a council of nine, five including the mayor elected at large and four from districts, on nonpartisan ballots. In Boss Pendergast's time, 1926–40, it was the black sheep among the council-manager cities with a local docile party hack as city manager, who turned to party headquarters for his appointees and maintained on the pay rolls hundreds of district henchmen drawing municipal salaries for party services. The ineffectiveness of local efforts to shake off Pendergast was explained when 60,000 ghost voters were finally cleaned out of the registration—there had been in two wards more voters than population, babies and children included. This situation ended when Pendergast went to jail; in 1940, with an honest count, high-grade candidates were elected to council and the successful manager of Saginaw, Michigan, was hired and has served with high distinction through four elections since.

In recent years the friends of the charter have provided an element of trusted, selfless civic leadership averting scatteration of the good-government vote. Kansas City has good government; the Binaggio and other police scandals reflect only on the condition of the state government, which controls the police of both Kansas City and St. Louis.

Chapter XVII

PROGRESS IN MUNICIPAL GOVERNMENTS (CONTINUED): THE MODERN PROFESSION OF CITY MANAGERSHIP

The new municipal executive, the city manager, represents in conception and operation, one of the most daring creations of American skill.

—Report of the Urbanism Committee
to the National Resources Commission, 1939

THE profession of city managership was, of course, nonexistent in 1913 and for twenty years thereafter. But from the beginning in Sumter and Dayton, effective local obstruction rarely arose to prevent bringing in nonresidents for the managership. Cities now almost always appoint their first manager from outside. A rising percentage of the total annual list of appointments to managerships has been from out of town, as follows: 1939, 38 per cent; 1943, 32 per cent; 1944, 33 per cent; 1945, 48 per cent; 1946, 57 per cent; 1947, 60 per cent; 1948, 63 per cent; 1949, 64 per cent; 1950, 76 per cent; 1951, 74 per cent. In 1939, 23 per cent of appointees whose prior experience was available had been managers or assistants to managers in other cities; in 1951 the comparable figure was 55 per cent.

The fact that 74 per cent of city managers are chosen from out of town has become one of the proofs of the nonpolitical character of these governments since it has meant conferring on an outsider the best-paying job in the gift of the council. Promotions of well-regarded city managers to larger cities came within a few years after the start; the basis of professionalism and of long careers in city managership was thus established without obstruction or challenge.

PROMOTIONS AND CAREERS

On December 31, 1950, 73 per cent of the 953 managers were still serving in their first city, 16 per cent were serving in their second city, 6 per cent in their third, and 3 per cent in their fourth. There have been thirteen managers who have served five or more cities. Fourteen per cent had been managers for fifteen years or more.

The average tenure of the 115 managers who died or left managerships in 1949 was five years, four months; the corresponding figure for the 120 who died or left in 1951 omits those who were less than two years in the service, producing for the others an average tenure of 9.7 years. The average length of time the 942 city managers in the United States had been thus far in their respective posts on March 1, 1950, was four years, eight months. One manager, the durable Mr. H. L. Woolhiser of Winnetka, Illinois, was manager of his suburban community from 1917 till his death in 1951. Fifty managers have been cited by the city managers as having served as such in one city or another a total of twenty-five years or more. The lengthening of average tenure as time goes on is partly offset by additions of new cities where the accumulated tenure, of course, is zero or one year, retarding the rise of the average.

These statistics and the complete list of cities and villages under the plan are issued each June by the International City Managers' Association.[1] The council-manager cities of over 100,000 population as of December 31, 1951, are Cincinnati, Toledo, and Dayton, Ohio; Dallas, Fort Worth, Austin, Corpus Christi, and San Antonio, Texas; Kansas City, Missouri; Oakland, Berkeley, Long Beach, San Diego, Pasadena, and Sacramento, California; Cambridge and Worcester, Massachusetts; Charlotte, North Carolina; Des Moines, Iowa; Flint and Grand Rapids, Michigan; Hartford, Connecticut; Miami, Florida; Norfolk and Richmond, Virginia; Oklahoma City, Oklahoma; Phoenix, Arizona; Wichita, Kansas; Rochester and Yonkers, New York.

[1] "Recent Council-Manager Developments and Directory," 1313 E. 60th St., Chicago 37, Ill.

THE CITY MANAGERS' ASSOCIATION

The city managers who met each other first in Springfield, Ohio, in 1914 (eight out of seventeen in attendance) have continued to meet in annual conventions. The membership was for a long time, of course, too small to sustain an association secretariat, but in 1930 funds for research were found and one of the city managers, Clarence E. Ridley, was established as secretary in Chicago with enough money to launch the International City Managers' Association as it now exists. Its monthly magazine, *Public Management*, is small but deals authoritatively with city management problems as they come to the desks of managers. The conventions are serious working sessions with none of the extraneous attractions that divert so many such affairs and with no effort to get publicity. Salesmen of municipal supplies are not admitted and the sessions are for managers only. One of the days is given to the conference of managers from cities of each population class; another day the managers group around subjects. The self-discipline and earnestness of the managers make these conventions hard-working and productive of useful comparisons. Necessarily, the spread of the plan for a long time brought calls for more new managers than could be produced from the practice of the art; the successful managers have had prompt invitations to larger cities and promotion has sometimes been rapid, with $25,000–$30,000 salaries at the top.

GROWING LITERATURE OF MUNICIPAL ADMINISTRATION

The Public Administration Service, alongside the City Managers' Association in Chicago, builds up for the managers a live library of specialized pamphlet information on topics of municipal administration. The association has devised correspondence courses in eight of the principal departmental techniques for the city managers and their department heads (set up formally now as the Institute for Training in Municipal Administration) and managers and departmental officers subscribe, fill out their lesson papers, and are required to adduce in their replies their own experience, whereby the practical field experience finds its way back for the correction of the courses. An impressive Municipal Information Service has been built up; if as many as three managers make the same inquiry in a month, a mimeographed report on the subject is gotten up, subject to incessant correction and renewal, in readiness for further demands. So what managers do not know they have extraordinary facilities for finding out! Their disposition to learn is far beyond that of the wholesale grocer who takes for a term or two the office of mayor. What a manager learns becomes a part of his professional equipment.

The managers nowadays include hundreds who qualify as professionals by virtue of length of time and definite success in the service. The larger cities find and hire these men while the small cities usually have to create their own. About a third of the managers have assistants or interns who are getting training to qualify for management.

Councils today have in smaller cities an abundant pool of tested city managers to choose from; the ninety-seven council-manager cities of the 25,000–50,000 population class, for instance, can draw upon 250 managers of cities of 10,000–25,000; in every case except that of the small villages the class next below is always relatively large. The International City Managers' Association has published the procedure adopted by the first Park Forest, Illinois, council in seeking a manager as the ideal way to go about it.[2] The association cannot discriminate among its members and goes no further than to publish each month the list of cities seeking managers. The process of finding qualified candidates for a new managership usually begins soon after the council is elected without awaiting the beginning of its term of office and is commonly accomplished within a few weeks without difficulty.

PROBLEMS OF THE MANAGER'S FUNCTION

The managers cannot be reduced to a type—a look around their convention shows that. Men of many types of personality seem to have succeeded in the game. Brownlow, who declared the Knoxville dividend, looks and talks in very different terms from Cookingham of Kansas City or Harrell of San Antonio. Some have the affability

[2] "How to Recruit a City Manager," by Dennis O'Harrow, Village President of Park Forest, in *Public Management*, journal of the International City Managers' Association, November, 1950.

and skill with people of a politician and others are impersonal engineers. College and postgraduate degrees are common here as elsewhere, and engineering training, saving a small city the separate salary for a city engineer, was often helpful for entrance into the profession. Sometimes managers break under the annoyances of a cityful of people who inconsiderately harry them for petty matters. Usually they have learned a great deal of patience and a practice of not talking too freely. They can't always do the right thing because of inability to convince their councils or their public, for they soon learn that they are there to administer, not to govern.

Some cities have changed managers far too frequently, sometimes, but not often, after almost every election. A number have never hired a city manager from out of town; others have never had any but outsiders. Quite commonly a city, after hiring its first manager from out of town, will find his successor among his department heads.

Managers incessantly exhort each other at conventions to keep clear of local politics despite temptations to get into controversy. They do become sometimes the most effective spokesmen for a policy after they have cleared the policy with the council and may thereafter go down with the council in an election. Initiative by the managers in their dealings with the council is usually desired and welcome. The council members coming from private affairs to a biweekly meeting expect to find the agenda well prepared and the manager asking permission to initiate various projects or expenditures and ready to expound and defend his requests. When a policy has been adopted, he is not infrequently the best available man to explain it to the taxpayers' association or the Rotary luncheon. But he usually takes care not to overdramatize himself or to become more conspicuous than the mayor-chairman of the council. To head off petty interference by council members he is commonly protected by the charter provision quoted on page 152 and by the intent of the charter but must sometimes struggle to treat all members of the council alike and keep any one councilman from developing the prerogatives of an insider or possessor of earlier information. The councils commonly and properly have no committees and no specialized points of contact with administration except, as intended, by way of the whole council openly meeting with the manager.

The idea is that the council is to act always as a whole and stick to policy and that the manager is not to govern but to administer. Charters describe that differentiation as best they can and the wording gets invoked from time to time to protect the prerogatives of either. But policy, as an experienced administrator observed, is "anything on which I must consult my superior." The proposed purchase of a fire engine in a village may become a major question of policy involving a hump in the tax rate whereas in Kansas City it is a routine item in the purchasing officer's budget. In one small city, enforcement of the dog-tag ordinance ran up against a resolute old society lady who publicly defied it so far as her precious lap dog was concerned, and a trivial matter became high public drama, and hence policy, as well as a month-long headache to the city manager and the council. But a major virtue of the council-manager relationship is that it is a strong flexible joint, adjustable to all conceivable situations by the fact that the council controls; there is nothing in a tussle to require an opinion from the corporation council or an appeal to a court. Hence in villages councils stew over issues that a city council never hears of, and the border line of authority varies also with the personalities involved and leads to a highly desirable variation from town to town and from year to year.

"Herding" the Councils

At the first city managers' convention a lanky Oklahoman inquired for advice from the others on how to "herd" his councilmen. The others chuckled with recognition of the problem and the problem has reappeared in one guise or another on the agendas of the annual conventions ever since. For there are councilmen who, if they could, would have a finger in every appointment and promotion or dance around every sizable purchase order; others who make themselves champions of some ward or of some group of constituents seeking special favor. When the councilmen have been active in the prior form of government, they may know a good deal about the departments and be reluctant to let go of their former authority. The manager of a New Jersey suburb in 1950 encountered this variation. The former councilmen reappeared in the new council and went on as before, taking many months to pick the first manager. They finally installed an able one but short-circuited his authority over the municipal employees, giving direct orders to the staff as before and leaving the manager to learn thereof as best he could. After exhausting his tact, he finally resigned, explaining briefly to a mass meeting that the council had made his job untenable. The difficulty seemed to be that the councilmen fancied themselves as amateur departmental overseers and could not bear to delegate the work and become a board of directors.

Such troubles might have been reduced if the councils had been called boards of directors in the charters, as recently in Manchester, Connecticut. The new title might have helped the people of Cleveland to realize that the new council was to be one of much higher power and charged with a new importance, and to look for a more imposing type of representative. But the continuance of the name "councilman" carried over in the public mind the connotation of a ward errand boy and the voters went on electing small fry who could not stand up to Cleveland's dynamic city manager or take up the control which the charter handed to them.

But with either too strong or too weak a council the plan can and does work, although with a varied position of equilibrium.

AN IRIDESCENT DREAM FOR YOUTHS

There has developed among young men a lively interest in becoming city managers, an interest which contrasts with the common indifference of college students toward other public officeholding as a career. A number of colleges have provided courses designed to prepare men not specifically for managerships (since such jobs, except in little Maine hamlets, are not for inexperienced boys fresh from school) but for municipal administration generally. Such graduates sometimes become "interns" under city managers—one-third of the managers have such staff helpers. The line of promotion goes on to departmental line duties and thence to managership of a small city by the time the man is thirty or thirty-five.

In July, 1915, I wrote in the *National Municipal Review* the first summary of evidence as to "How the City Manager Plan Is Getting Along." I ended it romantically with this:

My final note is most significant of all. It concerns a letter received a while ago from a California school boy. He admits that he has not stood any too high in his studies, but he has decided that he could do great good to thousands of people as the manager of some city (of course a small one at first) and can I please tell him what to read and where to study as a preparation? Forsooth! Municipal administration in America an iridescent dream for youths!

Long afterward, in 1949, I sat by while a newspaper reporter interviewed a manager, asking, "How did you happen to get into the city manager profession?" "I read about it in school," he said, "and it seemed to me like a fascinating kind of position. So I took the college courses that might be helpful and after graduation hunted up a job in a municipal department and stayed in municipal work until I landed the managership of a Michigan village, then a larger one and then my first city, Saginaw, Michigan. After some years there, I moved on to my present job—the managership of Kansas City." Thus, figuratively speaking, I met that school boy!

Chapter XVIII

PROGRESS IN MUNICIPAL GOVERNMENTS (CONTINUED): CURRENT STATE OF THE COUNCIL-MANAGER MOVEMENT

THE spread of the council-manager plan in the cities and villages of the United States and Canada since 1912 runs thus:

1912	1	1930	388
1915	49	1940	521
1920	157	1950	1013[1]

As each accession diminishes the mayor-council or the commission form list, the council-manager plan at recent rate of growth seems destined to become the prevailing form in the United States by 1960. About half of the United States council-manager communities (omitting those in Canada) are below 5000 population and include hamlets of a few hundred people. Every city of Virginia of over 10,000 population has the plan and all but one of the cities of 5,000–10,000—sixty-three altogether, counting villages below 5000 and four counties. Maine with 110 leads the states. California has ninety-six, Texas ninety-one, Michigan eighty-four, and Florida fifty-six. Every state is represented except Arkansas, Indiana, Louisiana, and Rhode Island.

OBSTRUCTIONS TO FURTHER SPREAD

The spread of the plan would have been even faster if the cities desiring to adopt it had not in many states encountered hostile legislatures.

In Illinois no city over 5000, as distinguished from villages, was permitted to adopt council-manager government until a vigorous concerted civic effort broke through at last in 1951. In Indiana the legislature, responding to pressure from city halls, has kept it out of

---

[1] As of August, 1952, 1116–1101 cities and 15 counties.

the state altogether although Indianapolis once voted for it. A man described as boss of the Pennsylvania senate in 1951 flouted the representations of the State Chamber of Commerce and the Pennsylvania Federation of Labor, vowing defiantly that he would never permit passage of an optional bill permitting the forty-seven third-class cities of that state to switch from the commission plan to the council-manager plan.

46 ABANDONMENTS

As of December 31, 1951, forty-six council-manager cities, out of more than 1000 (then), had abandoned the plan by vote of the people, excluding eight more which voted it out and voted it back in again. Some others, including Knoxville, where Manager Brownlow paid his famous dividend, had it snatched away without local consent by the legislature, and in others, mostly little communities, councils left the office unfilled. A few cities disappeared from the list by reason of being annexed to bigger neighbors. Of the forty-six first mentioned thirty are over 5000 population and may be related to the 658 of that size remaining, or a defection of 4.6 per cent. But the 2525 cities now of that size (1950 census) practically all had the mayor-and-council plan in 1900 and that plan has lost 390 to the commission plan and 658 to the council-manager plan in the half-century, a total defection of 40 per cent. The commission plan from its high point has lost about 40 per cent among cities now of 5000 population. Or, using gross figures for cities and towns of all sizes, the mayor-and-council plan has suffered about 800 abandonments, the commission plan 200, and the council-manager plan forty-six by local vote and a few additional by other methods.

Professor Arthur W. Bromage has described thirty-six abandonments of the council-manager plan by vote of the people in a National Municipal League pamphlet.[2] The stories he collected show no pattern except the common persistence of an opposition group of politicians ready to utilize any crisis or dispute to throw out a plan of government whose adoption they had bitterly opposed. In some cases, local friends of the plan were clearly caught napping

[2] *Manager Plan Abandonments,* National Municipal League, New York, 3rd ed., 1949.

by covert opposition in a light vote. Sometimes defects in charters—
variations from the Model Charter—led to disorder in administration; Bromage picks Denton, Texas, Akron, Ohio, Santa Barbara,
California, and Stevens Point, Wisconsin, as examples. In three
cities in Florida the plan went down in the local collapse of land
speculation. The reasons used against the continuation of the plan
were commonly insincere camouflage for the efforts of displaced
politicians to resume power. In two cities where citizens awoke too
late they proceeded to elect the city manager as mayor.

Patterns of Local Campaigns for Adoption

Local campaigns for adoption are going on somewhere all the
time. Visitors, letters, and clipping services bring in the news of
them daily to the office of the National Municipal League in New
York. The League has always made itself the central source of
information on the movement and handles likewise the inquiries referred by the city managers and their association office; the individual managers sometimes accept invitations to show themselves
in other cities and describe their own towns' experience at a Rotary
Club luncheon, but they keep out of campaigns. The City Managers'
Association wisely avoids promoting the spread of the plan and likewise ducks the inquiries of councils for advice as to which are its
most outstanding members available for appointment.

The campaigns for adoption of the council-manager plan are
sometimes started by mayors and councils seeking relief from detail
or feeling the need of professional advice and full-time follow-up
in administration. Such initiation is commonest in cities of swift
growth where new and urgent problems crowd the council calen-
dars. In other instances, citizens are motivated by a desire to have
the best for their town and not let neighboring cities claim greater
alertness for progress. Public officials or some of them are induced
to assent or to put up no resistance and the adoption may go
through without heat. More often, however, public officers in city
hall resent any proposal for change, construing it as an implied or
explicit reflection on the existing management or as an attempt by
the outs to get into power. When the proposal includes a shift from
partisan to nonpartisan elections, the ghosts of Lincoln and Jeffer-
son are invoked. If the chamber of commerce inspires the effort,

labor is likely to reject a belated invitation to join in and may rally to the support of municipal employees who fear a change of supervisors, although on the other hand organized labor has sometimes furnished the leadership for initiating the plan and has elected a majority of the council subsequently. In Brunswick, Maine, the municipal employees bought a quarter-page in the newspaper to oppose the plan; a year later they took a page to retract and praise the new conditions. In Bayonne, New Jersey, where Boss Hague's high tax rate was forcing industry away, CIO members formed a United Workers Organization and in 1948 carried a referendum for adoption of the manager plan by 2000. (The yes vote, unfortunately, was less than the 30 per cent of the total cast for president then required by the New Jersey law.) The League of Women Voters always supports the project and frequently does 80 per cent of the work and gets 20 per cent of the credit.

The commonest pattern begins with dissatisfaction with conditions and traditions at city hall. A casting about for remedies suggests modernizing the charter. A group of people active in civics rather than politics sends for pamphlets and lines up some key personalities. A speaker is brought in, some publicity is secured in the local paper, and presently petitions are in circulation for submitting the plan to referendum. The sponsors get up printed matter, radio talks, and press releases. Neighborhood meetings in private houses build up the word-of-mouth discussion. Doorbells are rung and pamphlets handed in: "Whatever you decide, be sure to vote!" The opposition in city hall sneers at these amateurs and thereby pours kerosene on the kindlings and the contest warms up. Some of the most influential people are strangely silent—they have to do business with both sides, you know! (The campaign in Richmond, Virginia, described in Reading I, is typical.)

The Squawks of Politicians

But although the pattern of promotion is varied, the arguments and tactics of the opposition are rather uniform. "We don't need a smarty-pants from out of town to come in and tell us how to manage this town." "There are plenty of good men right here; we don't need to give the top salary to a carpetbagger." "The manager will be a (Mussolini) (Hitler) (Stalin) dictator." "It's un-American."

"All you policemen and firemen will lose your (jobs) (pensions) (civil service rights)." "It's undemocratic not to elect the executive." "The idea is fine but the charter (optional law) is defective."

The Rising Percentage of Victories

In the early years of the movement, adoptions were fewer than defeats at the referendum elections. In 1926 there were twenty-two submissions of council-manager charters, of which eleven carried. In 1950 there were eighty-eight submissions, of which sixty-six carried; in 1951, seventy-four submissions, of which forty-seven (63 per cent) carried. And the defeated proponents sometimes wait awhile and try again with better preparation for the assault.

Deviations from the Model Charter

For a third of a century now the council-manager movement has been kept true to the original concept and few of the hundreds of local charter commissions have diverged into serious errors of principle.

Exceptions from the Manager's Appointive Power

The commonest shortcoming is a timorous failure to bring all existing independent administrative offices, like city clerk, city attorney, treasurer, or money-spending administrative boards, under the manager's control so as to complete the integration of line operations.

When such officers are left elective or otherwise independent in deference to local tradition or personalities, cooperation may nevertheless happen to be genuine and deferential. In some cases, however, the city manager, failing to obtain voluntary cooperation, has felt obliged to set up a complete duplication of services under his own oversight.

Such compromises in charters are failures to carry the council-manager concept to completion rather than deliberate doctrinal divergencies.

Election of Councilmen from Wards

In cities below, say, 500,000 population, where election at large does not encounter Rule Two (unwieldiness of constituency), the

Model City Charter urges election of councils from the whole city at large. Electing all at one time is all right (and so is election in rotation) if the number of councilmen is no more than five. On the other hand, as shown in Reading A, making voters choose nine councilmen at large at one time demonstrates that nine is too many, and making voters each choose seven is *probably* too many for the same reason—the voters will cease to make up their own respective tickets and will take a program from somebody. The common practice with councils of seven is to bring up the renewals of council memberships in rotation such as four in one year for four-year terms and the other three two years later. Or four each biennium for four-year terms except that the candidate elected by the lowest vote serves two years, thus bringing up a majority of the seven each time. Terms overlap in 71.8 per cent of the council-manager cities.

Politicians contend—too often, alas, with success—for election by wards for all or part of the council; 16.9 per cent of the council-manager cities struggle with councils selected entirely from wards and 10.6 per cent more elect in part from wards or by the device of primary elections in wards to reduce the contestants to two per ward followed by an election in which the whole city picks between the two thus advanced in each area. The total, 27.5 per cent, is 3 per cent more than it was in 1939—a slight drift, but in the wrong direction.

The enhanced importance of the councilmanic post fails to overcome the traditions of the title in the popular mind, the politicos know where the boundaries run and how to redraw them from time to time to their own advantage and when to resist their correction, the councilmen get to be regarded by both their constituents and themselves as special pleaders for their districts, and their reelection, like a congressman's, may depend on their successful recklessness in pillaging the general interest for the benefit of their respective constituencies. It is unfair to leave the city manager as the only public officer to be concerned about the combined effect on the city treasury of such importunities and logrolling. Dismal mediocrity of council membership is the usual result of ward elections. In cities where the politicos have succeeded in amending the charter to discard a council elected at large in favor of one "closer

to the people," as they put it, the decline in character of councilmen
has been prompt and dramatic.

In Yonkers, for example, where a council of seven elected at large
by proportional representation gave way in 1950 to election of one
from each of twelve districts (plus a mayor at large), the council
became the scene of such episodes as this:

Twelfth Ward Councilman Ellis D. Allen, Sr. had the "audacity" to
propose a survey of the Waring site on South Broadway with a view to
converting it to a municipal parking area with meters. His knuckles were
cracked by Fourth Ward Councilman Vincent P. Lee who regards his
bailiwick as his own province—not to be made a subject of concern for
any other legislator.

Similarly, Mr. Allen proposed a change in Larkin Plaza to increase
parking facilities, whereupon Second Ward Councilman Alexander J.
Cooke, Jr., promptly scolded him with, "This is pretty far removed from
Mr. Allen's section and perhaps he is not familiar with it." More than
that, he went on, Mr. Allen had better call in the Second Warder when
and if he has "any interest in this part of the city." . . .

Democratic Minority Leader John A. Vaccaro . . . remarked. . . ,
"We had an understanding—certainly among the Democrats and I
thought all of us—about going into another Councilman's ward." [3]

Flint, Michigan, seems to have been the scene of a similar experience where the lower condition after a switch to ward elections
was sharply visible while all other factors remain unchanged.

The reverse movement from ward elections to at-large is familiar
when mayor and ward council plans give way to council-manager
setups, but the improvement attributable to the elimination of wards
and ward-mindedness is inextricably tangled with the benefits from
other features of the plan.

Partisan Elections

"The good old American two-party system" lingers on in 15.4 per
cent of the council-manager cities and automatically delivers a bloc
of docile voters to each set of party managers with corresponding
damage to the cause of those candidates who are advanced on their
simple merits. The practicality of the nonpartisan elections in the

3 Yonkers *Statesman*, April 11 and 12, 1951. Editorials.

other 86 per cent of council-manager cities is exhibited in Reading D.

Protected Tenure for City Managers

Deliberate divergencies range around notions of protecting managers from unreasonable or capricious removal. In a scatteration of unorthodox charters the manager, instead of serving at the pleasure of a majority of the council, is sheltered by a provision requiring more than a majority to remove him. Since the majority usually is left with ample ability to cut his salary, upset his projects, and make him miserable if he should cling to his post, this shelter is obviously a frail one.

In the New Jersey permissive law, as first enacted in 1923, a council majority could remove the manager. This was unhappily amended in 1936 so that removal required one more than a majority after a hearing. Actually no such case ever arose in any of the seven council-manager cities in New Jersey during the twelve years the extra-vote requirement was in effect. Opponents of the council-manager plan in Jersey adoption campaigns often harped on this provision, however, and drew lurid forecasts of entrenched dictators. Undoubtedly existence of the provision deterred consideration of the plan in many New Jersey municipalities. This vexatious detail of the law disappeared for cities adopting the plan in future on the basis of the optional charter law of 1951—the Faulkner Act.

In 1948 in Massachusetts certain revisions of the optional city charters act led to insertion of the requirement of a two-thirds vote for removal—five out of seven or six out of nine—in future adoptions of Plan D (council-manager). The provision may henceforth bedevil campaigns for adoption out of all proportion to the actual probability of the contingency of a resistant manager and an adverse bare majority in council.

Several home rule or special charters also include such protection of tenure. Those brought up by an incomplete dragnet for this discussion are: Saugus, Massachusetts, four votes required for removal of the manager out of five; Berkeley, California, six out of nine; Pasadena, California, five out of seven for both appointment and removal; Petaluma, California, five out of seven; Sacramento, California, six out of nine; Sacramento County, California, four out of

five but only for cause in his first year; San Diego, California, five
out of seven; San Mateo County, California, four out of five by a
1948 amendment; Escanaba, Michigan, four out of five after the
first year in office; Pontiac, Michigan, five out of seven after the
first year in office; Ypsilanti, Michigan, five out of seven; Phoenix,
Arizona, five out of seven or majority "for cause"—1948 amendment;
West Hartford, Connecticut, five out of seven.

Protected tenure appeared in a bill, repeatedly defeated in the
Massachusetts legislature, extending a council-manager option to
towns.

In these cities the total exposure of managers and councils to the
odd contingency of a desire of a majority to remove, thwarted by
lack of an extra vote and coupled with persistence of the manager
in clinging to his office under the circumstances, aggregated 219
city-years up to 1949. To the best of our knowledge, it actually has
occurred just once! That was in Sacramento in 1927.

In that city a new group captured five of the nine council seats
and, according to information obtained at the time from local National Municipal League members, proceeded to try to force the
city manager to make political removals and appointments including the police chief. According to one of these members, they tried
to remove the manager "after a mock trial for alleged incompetence
in which they succeeded only in proving their own incompetence
and emphasizing his accomplishments," but failed to muster the
necessary sixth vote.

The manager stayed through two years of tension.

In the next election, 1929, the manager's four supporters were
reelected but, although all the tickets professed to favor retention
of the manager, he was ousted by eight votes immediately after
election without warning or explanation and a local sponsor of the
principal group was put in as manager. Despite the unpromising
start, he served with widespread approval for fifteen years.

There may, of course, have been other occasions, never brought
to a head, where a quiet count of noses deterred a majority of a
council from attempting to displace a manager in these cities.

Requirement that removal may be only "for cause" lurks in some
charters. Such a phrase in the charter could provide the council
with the alibi that it cannot remove an unsatisfactory manager for

lack of enough definite "cause" to satisfy a court and envisages the possibility of a manager's clinging to his office despite even a unanimous council!

A few other charters impair the council's authority by providing fixed terms for managers. For example, San Mateo County, California, in its 1932–45 charter provided a four-year term for the manager, and a board of supervisors elected in 1936 had to await expiration of his term on June 2, 1937, before it could replace him.

The 1935 state-wide optional manager law under which Monroe County (Rochester), New York, operates provides appointment by the supervisors for a four-year term subject to removal only for cause after statements of reasons and a hearing and subject further to court review by order of certiorari. The first manager, selected in 1936, was still in office in 1952.

Employment contracts are sometimes made by councils to assure a fair trial of a prospective manager's services, especially when he is being induced to come from out of town or to leave another job. Such contracts, not running beyond the term of the council which makes them, seem unobjectionable, but the city managers disclaim interest in even this limited protection.

The International City Managers' Association put a committee on the question in 1935. Two-thirds of the 201 managers who replied to the committee's questionnaire opposed a definite term of office or a contract. Only thirteen had ever served under a tenure contract and nine of these preferred indefinite tenure.

The committee concluded:

Appointment for a definite term, with or without contract, is not desirable from the point of view of either the city manager or the council. The relationship between the council and the manager is largely one of confidence, and when this is broken down because of change in council personnel, or other reasons, an effective working relationship no longer exists. The committee believes that a contract appointment would somewhat discredit the aim and purpose of democratic council-manager government and perhaps bring the manager into politics.

Clarence E. Ridley, director of ICMA, added, in 1949:

I am strongly of the belief that the experience under the council-manager plan in hundreds of cities since 1935 would strengthen and support this statement of the association's committee. One of the most important features of the council-manager plan is that a city manager can be removed at any time or he can be retained in office as long as the council desires. The only protection that a city manager needs or wants would be adequate notice with a statement of reasons for removal along the line of the provisions of the Model City Charter.

Presumably the sentiment of city managers would be even more adverse to the extra-vote-for-removal device that could enable a manager to flout a majority.

Most charters follow the Model Charter of the National Municipal League, which empowers the council to suspend the city manager summarily, with pay, by majority vote. At least thirty days before removal shall become effective, "the council . . . shall adopt a preliminary resolution stating the reasons for his removal. The manager may reply in writing and may request a public hearing," after which a final resolution of removal may be adopted by a majority with payment of his salary for the three calendar months following the adoption of the preliminary resolution.

This provision for deliberateness of procedure does not diminish the responsibility or authority of the council. The thirty days' delay prevents the council from trying to avert a ruction by surprising the public with a *fait accompli*. The public is big and clumsy and requires a little time to get into action and the delay gives it a chance to go to the rescue of the city manager if it wants to do so.

In such an interval public sentiment sometimes is quick to attribute political motives to the council and boils up to the manager's defense. One such hearing in Medford, Massachusetts, in 1950 drew a crowd of 2000 citizens so that the council had to adjourn to a larger meeting room and then to the high-school auditorium amid such signs of indignation that the council reversed itself. Sometimes molesting a well-regarded city manager has resulted in recall petitions and the ousting of the council. Candidates for council frequently find it expedient to make known their esteem for the manager.

Opportunity for the public to take a hand is a desirable detail and appears in most of the newer charters. But any device which so protects the tenure of the city manager as to enable him conceivably to defy or flout a majority of the representative council impairs the unity and discipline of the governmental mechanism and is utterly unsound in principle.

Parenthetically, be it noted that deviations in several charters go the other way and make a manager's tenure more precarious: Dayton, Ohio, and Long Beach, California, make it possible to recall the manager. Recall was tried once in the latter city in 1931 but the petition was thrown out as insufficient. In Bend, Oregon, a vote was required every four years as to whether the manager who happened to be in office at the moment should be retained; on the last such occasion, November 30, 1948, the incumbent's retention was approved three to one. In 1951 this odd invention was amended out of the charter. In San Jose, California, such a vote is required every two years and an attempt in 1948 to remove the provision from the charter was defeated. Such provisions impair the council's proper responsibility and must tend to make the manager a political figure.

Separately Elected Mayors

The Model City Charter and most of the cities using the plan give the chairman of the council the title of mayor. This may have been a tactical mistake; to have had no such title might have been better. For although these mayors are only chairmen, chosen usually by the council from its own membership and having a vote but no veto or separate powers, campaigns for adoption get muddied up by what salesmen call a "talking point," namely, that the people are to lose their former power to elect the mayor. If there just were to be no mayor at all, these protests would have to take some less plausible and mischievous form.

Charter commissions frequently yield the issue by providing separate election of the mayor while faithfully keeping him to the regular *primus inter pares* position. Thus the 1952 *Municipal Year Book* counts 658 council-manager charters, of which 57.2 per cent provide for election of the chairman-mayor by the councilmen from among their own number (it was 56.5 per cent in 1939), 41.7 per cent for his separate selection at the polls, and 0.9 per cent for giving the title to the candidate who gets the highest vote.

In Dallas a local theorist in 1950 campaigned successfully to switch from choice by council to a separate balloting upon a separated group of candidates for mayor although the mayor of Dallas remains simply one of the council in terms of his authority.

The prime virtue of the council-manager plan lies in its ability to produce good councils. Anything which tends to play up one councilman at election time over the others runs wild and, in so far as it overdramatizes one member, diverts public attention from the rest.

Because it equalizes the posts that are up for election and makes every councilmanic seat important, the choice-by-council method is desirable. The Dayton highest-vote method is next best if the "talking point" must be catered to. Other reasons are:

1. It is undesirable to put candidates into two ballot sections, one for mayor and one for councilman. Good candidates who would have made acceptable councilmen may lose because they aspired to the mayoralty.

2. The tendency of voters to be content with an informed vote for mayor and negligent of the equally important councilmen makes for lopsided decisions at the polls and the slipping of undesirable candidates into council.

But how about leadership? Is there a craving of people for someone to follow apart from this craving for drama? Undoubtedly! Sometimes leaders appear and sometimes they don't. Leadership is where and when you find it. It is purely relative; the strong man drops out of the council, the next strongest man takes his place for a while and gets eclipsed by a newcomer a few years later. A man chosen at the polls to be a mayor may not turn out to be the man whom the council or the people feel most like following. Outsiders should not try to single one man from a group and say, "You shall lead!" and "You others shall follow!"

City managers who have worked under both separately elected and council-selected mayors confirm this and prefer the latter. A poll of thirty-five such managers in 1952 by their association inquired, "Under what system did the mayor assume more initiative in determining local policies . . . ?" Nine managers said councilselected, seven said separately elected, and five, no difference. Seven attributed leadership to the method of selection and fifteen to temperament and personality. They had encountered more interference in purely administrative matters from board-selected—one;

from separately elected—fifteen; no difference—ten. The preference was for council selection, twenty-seven to two.

In San Antonio the charter permits the chairman to be chosen by the councilmen from their own number to serve at the pleasure of the council. If the charter had provided separate election of the chairman (mayor), the sponsors of the winning ticket at the 1951 election would undoubtedly have chosen the current mayor. They did elect him to the council and the council did make him chairman. But within four weeks he had changed his attitude, the council repented of its choice, divided against him seven to two, and by threatening his replacement secured his resignation as mayor. Even if he could have held on to his title, the title, in the absence of followers, would not have retained him in leadership.

Surely the sound way is to let the council decide which member to honor. Unless he is one of the majority he cannot be leader, and letting the majority choose is the only way to insure that he will have the predominant following. The need of the moment may be for a highly articulate spokesman who does well in public debate, or for a middle-of-the-road man whom both factions of a divided group consider fair-minded, or for the man with the biggest popular following or greatest intrinsic dignity and eminence. The original thinker who is first to arrive at solutions may be dependent on a slower, less inventive mind to carry the ball for him. Which of them is the real leader?

If it is a good team we want, it had better be allowed, as in football, to choose its own captain. The teammates rather than the constituents have got to work at close quarters with the selectee. The ability to get elected by the people to a separate but empty mayoralty may rest on factors of support that have nothing to do with the candidate's fitness for the chairman's duties; the ability to attract the support of his peers in the council is a good test of leadership in direct intimate relation to his duties.

"Where MacGregor sits, there is the head of the table!"

Four Pertinent Readings

The fullest pictures of local politics under the council-manager plan with nonpartisan ballots are to be found in the historic reports of fifty cities in the 1940 Stone-Price-Stone survey and, as of more recent date, in Readings A, D, H, and I.

The significance of the facts in those Readings is that cities up to 250,000 population under the council-manager plan can and do elect good nonpolitical councils in nonpartisan elections with or without organized leadership by civic committees. They do better with such leadership. Their voters become dependent on such leadership when Rule One is violated by the necessity of each voter to "Vote for Nine." All activity in municipal elections by the local wings of the national parties can be dispensed with for decades, and incidentally, exclusion from participation as a party in municipal elections does not, in Cincinnati, for example, reduce the party vote in state and national elections.

Altogether the progress toward adoption of the Three Rules in the form of the council-manager setup is gratifying.

So is the easy effectiveness of American voters thereunder when old frustrations are thus cleared away!

And as the further fruit of the election of able, public-spirited, nonpolitical councils, it is demonstrated that efficiency is reconcilable with American democracy!

Chapter XIX

PROGRESS IN MUNICIPAL GOVERNMENTS (CONTINUED): IN THE FOURTEEN LARGEST CITIES

IN THE fourteen largest cities (over 500,000 pop., 1950) there has been progress toward simplification and compliance with the Three Rules. Calling the roll in order of size:

New York (pop. 7,385,097), since adoption of the "greater city" charter in 1898, has had a reduction from seventy to twenty-five in the size of the council, extension of its term to four years, and abolition of twenty-four elective county officers.

Chicago (pop. 3,606,436) reduced its council from seventy to fifty in 1923, and Cook County with eighty-five obscure elective offices developed an elective "president" of a few inadequate powers.

Philadelphia's (pop. 2,064,794) progress toward compliance with the Three Rules includes abandonment in 1920 of the two-house council of 145 members in favor of a single house of twenty-one. A council-manager charter drafted by an official commission was derisively buried with funeral ceremonies by the legislature in 1939 although a local public opinion poll indicated it would have passed at referendum. In 1951 a revised charter was adopted; it reduced the ward-elected council to ten from wards and seven at large, voters being instructed to vote for no more than five of the latter, and made the elective receiver of taxes appointive.

Baltimore (pop. 940,205) has also abandoned its two-house council.

Los Angeles (pop. 1,959,692) has made no progress. It has a ponderous administrative setup of departments managed by lay commissions appointed in rotation by the mayors.

Boston, Detroit, Pittsburgh, and San Francisco have in the last fifty years adopted simple strong-mayor and small-council setups which are much alike and all encounter the problem of unwieldy constituencies (Rule Two).

Boston (pop. 790,863) in 1910 adopted a charter with a mayor and a council of nine elected three at a time, afterward, in 1924, enlarged to twenty-two chosen by wards and in 1950 changed back again to nine elected at large at one time. In an effort to make run-off elections unnecessary, its 1910 charter required large petitions which could be obtained by only a few candidates, signature by voters of more than one petition being prohibited. The results for a generation were victories by Democratic blocs swinging about 40 per cent of the votes against divided opposition. In 1950 a charter change provided for runoff elections between the two highest candidates for each office to avert further minority victories.

In 1948–49 Boston seemed likely to be the first big city to adopt the Model Charter complete. "Plan E for Boston," a permissive charter like Cincinnati's with an elective council of nine chosen by proportional representation, a similar school board, and a city manager, was made available by the legislature in 1948. Boston seemed more than ready to adopt it to get rid of the notorious Mayor "Boss" Curley. But Curley's minions by contemptible trickery and connivance in the board of elections headed off the referendum on "Plan E for Boston" contemplated in 1949.

Detroit (pop. 1,838,517) abandoned a council of forty-two in 1918 for a nonpartisan council of nine elected at large, all at one time.

Pittsburgh (pop. 673,763) has a mayor and council of nine elected at large on partisan ballots.

San Francisco (pop. 760,753) has a mayor and a council of eleven at large (reduced in 1931 from eighteen) elected on nonpartisan ballots. The mayor, since 1931, has had a chief administrative officer, appointive by him but removable by the council or by recall, who relieves the mayor of the operation of a number of departments including county clerk, recorder, public administrator, and coroner. The county government was combined with the city government—"the city and county of San Francisco." A string of county officers were left outdoors on the elective list—assessor, treasurer, attorney, district (prosecuting) attorney, sheriff, and public defender, but six others were made appointive and the council doubles as board of county supervisors. These alterations of 1931 have been a highly desirable although incomplete simplification.

Cleveland's (pop. 905,636) story has been told in Chapter XVI. Since discarding the council-manager plan it has had a strong mayor and a ward-elected council of thirty-three with partisan elections.

St. Louis (pop. 852,623) got rid of a two-house council in 1914. It has a mayor and a council of thirty elected in rotation from wards on partisan ballots, plus an elective controller and an elective treasurer.

Buffalo (pop. 577,393) has a mayor and a council of fifteen, six at large and nine from wards, plus an elective controller, on partisan ballots.

Milwaukee (pop. 632,651) has a mayor and a council of twenty-seven from wards, plus an elective controller, treasurer, and attorney.

District of Columbia (pop. 797,670), having not had self-government since 1878, was promised home rule and a vote for its citizens in District government in both the party platforms of 1948. A good charter embodying the council-manager plan with a council of twelve elected at large in rotation and a similar elective school board passed the Senate without an objection in 1949 and died in the District Committee of the House at the end of the 81st Congress in 1950. It was believed that the House would have readily passed it in 1950 but efforts to secure signatures of a majority of the members to a discharge petition fell short of the objective by a narrow margin. The obstruction was not on account of the council-manager features of the proposed setup but related to the prospects of enfranchising the 30 per cent Negro population.

In 1952 the Senate again passed a so-called "home rule" bill, but it provided a mayor selected by the president instead of a manager.

DIFFICULTIES IN THE BIGGEST CITIES UNSOLVED

Application of the council-manager plan to any of these large cities requires sound solution of the problem of unwieldy districts. The ideal solution is proportional representation so that a candidate who has no political machine support need only secure a quota to be elected instead of a city-wide plurality or a plurality in an unreal and artificial small political community called a ward. The Washington, D.C., bill of 1950 called for elections from one or another of four large natural sections by plurality and runoff elections. Hatton's charter in Cleveland used P.R. from each of four large sections but the council of twenty-five turned out to be too large and each membership therefore too small to attract scrutiny. The Boston Plan E or Cincinnati Plan is ideal up to the point where, as still larger cities are considered, a council of nine at large becomes inadequate from the standpoint of sufficient representation. Then invention must begin; such, for instance, as a council of fourteen elected by P.R. seven at a time, at large, to keep public scrutiny focused.

Chapter XX

PROGRESS IN COUNTY GOVERNMENT

> County government is no more fit for its purpose than
> an ox-cart would be fit for the task of supplying modern
> transportation between New York and Chicago.
>
> —GOVERNOR FRANKLIN D. ROOSEVELT
> in the *National Municipal Review,* 1932

OUTSIDE of New England with its township system there are
3049 counties which all violate Rule One and Rule Three and
in some metropolitan and huge area counties—Cook County (Chicago), and San Bernardino County (California), which is bigger
than New Jersey, for example—they are unwieldy districts violating
Rule Two. It is no mere coincidence that counties are also the securest citadels of politicians and their last stand against modernism
or efficiency. The state organizations of the parties are usually
loose federations of the county bosses. The county courthouses are
filled with routineers who learn the business and resist all change
and who constitute a solid team for preserving their party in unbroken dominance for perhaps half a century at a stretch. Their
loyal skill in politics is more potent in protecting their continuance
in their jobs than any economies or efficiencies they might develop.

SAME PEOPLE BUT REFRACTORY MECHANISM

Nor is that ascendancy of the political patronage spirit the fault
of the voters. For the same voters who for decades view with pride
the enthusiasm for fine public service which inspires the men they
elect to city councils under the council-manager plan are steadily
putting into the county courthouse across the street the very political gangs they have successfully excluded from city hall! And the
courthouse crowd provides the base of supplies in patronage and
ward-politics man power at public expense for every sneering attack

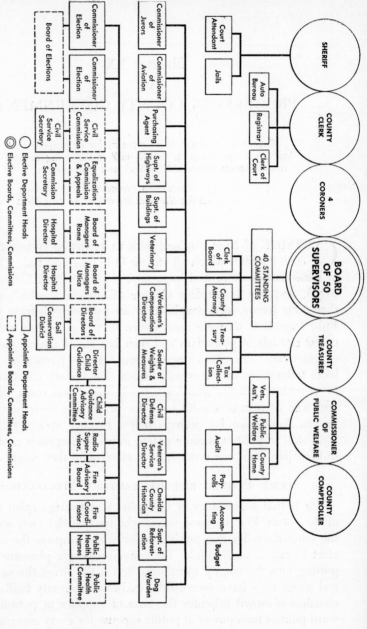

Actual Government of Oneida County, New York.

Typical of counties everywhere except in New England. A board of 50(1) supervisors meeting monthly acts as the executive through 40(1) standing committees to direct 29 operating units and supply funds to 9 separately elected officials. (Municipal Research Bureau, Utica, N. Y., December, 1951.)

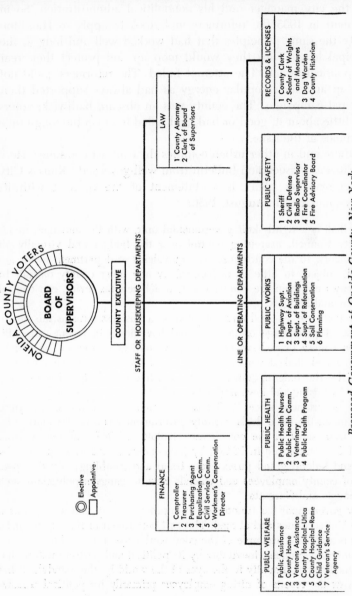

Proposed Government of Oneida County, New York.

A logical integrated short-ballot structure in conformance with the Model County Manager Charter except that the Board of Supervisors remains far too large. (Municipal Research Bureau, Utica, N. Y. December, 1951.)

ONEIDA COUNTY VOTERS

BOARD OF SUPERVISORS

○ Elective
▢ Appointive

COUNTY EXECUTIVE

STAFF OR HOUSEKEEPING DEPARTMENTS

LINE OR OPERATING DEPARTMENTS

FINANCE
1 Comptroller
2 Treasurer
3 Purchasing Agent
4 Equalization Comm.
5 Civil Service Comm.
6 Workmen's Compensation Director

LAW
1 County Attorney
2 Clerk of Board of Supervisors

PUBLIC WELFARE
1 Public Assistance
2 County Home
3 Veterans Assistance
4 County Hospital–Utica
5 County Hospital–Rome
6 Child Guidance
7 Veteran's Service Agency

PUBLIC HEALTH
1 Public Health Nurses
2 Public Health Comm.
3 Veterinary
4 Public Health Program

PUBLIC WORKS
1 Highway Supt.
2 Dept. of Aviation
3 Supt. of Buildings
4 Supt. of Reforestation
5 Soil Conservation
6 Planning

PUBLIC SAFETY
1 Sheriff
2 Civil Defense
3 Radio Supervisor
4 Fire Coordinator
5 Fire Advisory Board

RECORDS & LICENSES
1 County Clerk
2 Sealer of Weights and Measures
3 Dog Warden
4 County Historian

upon the city manager and his nonpolitical administration. So in Cincinnati in 1935 the reformers undertook to apply to Hamilton County the same principles that had worked well and long at the municipal level. Thus they would mop up and protect their rear from political attack. The attempt failed. The reformers could not drum up any such popular energy as had always supported their municipal campaigns. The county was an obscure bailiwick; voters knew little about it, good or bad, and failed to grasp the long-range importance of the issue.

So there and in other urban counties the contrast continues. Here in a Citizens' Association bulletin from well-governed [1] Kansas City (council-manager plan) is a statement of the contrast with its county (Jackson) in August, 1950:

City hall is a tightly-knit governmental unit, with the manager, under the City Council, exercising control over the budget and virtually all departments. In the courthouse the equivalents of department heads are elected, subject to little or no control by any other county official. In some cases not even the county court, which sets tax levies, can control departmental budgets.

City taxes are assessed and collected on a business basis as the steady increase of percentage of tax collected has shown in recent years. By contrast county taxes have been used as political weapons. The county tax-fixing and shakedown racket was called the "most vicious condition found" by the federal grand jury, in which county employees extorted money by raising and lowering taxes.

City government since 1940 has been free from scandals, free from shady under-the-table deals. County government has a record marred by thefts from safes in the courthouse (ballots in 1947 and money from Sheriff Purdome's safe in 1948); by indictments of county employees by state and federal grand juries (vote fraud and gambling); by the spectacle of county employees and officials close to gangster-politicians such as Binaggio and Gargotta.

City government has functioned to improve the city and its reputation in the United States and abroad. The vast betterment of the city financial rating is a clearcut example of the good work done in City Hall.

County government, inevitably by its political and partisan nature, has blackened the community in the eyes of the world by the scandals. It has shown us the results of hiring employees primarily for political reasons.

---

[1] The police of Kansas City are state managed, not part of the city government.

Examples are an assistant prosecutor indicted for failing to pay income tax on his profits as a partner in a gambling game; a chief criminal investigator a pallbearer for Binaggio; a woman friend of Gangster Gargotta working as a deputy county assessor.

CITY GOVERNMENT HAS BEEN CARRIED ON TO PLEASE THE PEOPLE: COUNTY GOVERNMENT TO PLEASE THE POLITICIANS. When the leading politician is a gangster of the Binaggio type the results in county government are disastrous. When citizens band together to support and elect a good City government on a non-partisan basis, we have good government, no matter what the politician of the moment likes or wants. At City Hall since 1940 there has been no Binaggio problem. By maintaining a Citizen Association sponsored non-partisan government in the City Hall we can keep it clean of Binaggio's successors.

Thus, as in the hundreds of cases in which the voters were perennially frustrated before the coming of the better elective process of the council-manager plan and did well for themselves election after election thereafter, we have proof again that the same people will get good results with simple sound mechanism under the Three Rules and sad results with a frustrating, complex mechanism. The people of Kansas City are 80 per cent of the people of Jackson County (439,646 out of 537,550) and there is no reason to suppose that the fringe population is any more interested in supporting low-grade politics than the urban voters or that their participation accounts for the difference. The people were the same before and after improvement of the democratic process, the same in city and the overlapping county. It is the correction of the mechanism that accounts for the improvement in the city.

Typical County Ramshackle

The typical American county sets up an elective board of county commissioners (or board of supervisors or a group otherwise named), three in number in 1500 counties, more in the rest, with about 21,000 members altogether in the 3049 counties. About three-quarters of them are elected from districts or municipal divisions of the county, and rotten boroughs are common, resulting in disproportionate arrays of rural members and minority dominance. Elections are partisan, and sluggish one-party situations persist unchallenged for decades.

The county boards, meeting monthly, are not empowered to govern nor is there any chief executive empowered to administer their expenditures and direct their appointees between meetings. The work of the county is distributed among a series of unconnected traditional officers commonly called sheriff, county clerk, clerk of the court, recorder (or register) of deeds, assessors, county surveyor, and coroner. Also, and for more reason independent, prosecuting attorney and county judge.

The county is thus an illustration of all the favorite American faults of government design, raised to the nth power. It exhibits at its worst every one of the fallacies cherished by our grandfathers and the Jacksonian Democrats. For example, it carries the disconnection of powers to its logical extreme and makes each officer independent of the others and a law unto himself except in so far as he may be restrained from excesses by the fear of prosecution by the district attorney or the governor for transgressing a tangled hedge of legislation. The board of county supervisors, or whatever they may be called, must raise money to pay the bills of numerous officers whose work is laid out by the state and whose conduct they cannot control. The district attorney must work hand in glove with a sheriff who has considerable latitude as to maintaining an *entente cordiale* with him. The state, after making laws, must leave them to the tender mercies of insubordinate agents who are free to exercise a pocket veto by silent nonenforcement if they do not like the laws or think that enforcement will be unpopular in their neighborhood. The clerk who serves the judges may embarrass and annoy his superiors by lax service and yet feel secure in his office. The district attorney may let his cases drag while he goes fishing and the supervisors must helplessly pay the bills for the waiting prisoners in the jail till he finds it convenient to come back.

There is nothing in the county to enforce harmony and cooperation between its various officers except a chaotic mass of printed memoranda, called laws, passed and amended decades ago and quite too numerous to be read.

It is a commentary on the stagnation of county government in general that the preceding two paragraphs were written in 1912 and are still too true. This sketch of the possibilities inherent in the present typical county was purely a work of imagination, but when

I read it to the Los Angeles County charter board that year there was an unexpected roar of laughter, and as I halted in some confusion I was informed that I had exactly described the existing local situation. Mr. Casey of Oakland, who also heard the paper, volunteered, "If I had not known otherwise I would have supposed that you were reporting the results of my own intensive investigation into the workings of Alameda County."

Such a "structure" or archipelago is unfit to carry heavy loads of any kind. But increases of populations have brought to many urban or partly urban counties new tasks and these have involved creation of new county bureaus or offices. Hence the proliferation of special boards or commissions dedicated to the management of airports, highways, hospitals, libraries, recreation, agricultural service, welfare, or what have you. These boards, meticulously described in special or general laws, possess a considerable measure of independent authority, but their appropriations must come, like the sheriff's, from the county board, which may have a tenuous control over their activities. Such semi-independent entities are sometimes separately elected, in other cases appointed with rotating terms by the county board or its chairman, but almost always they are privileged to go their ways in defiant independence.

WOODROW WILSON AND THE COUNTY CLERK

Said Woodrow Wilson to a county clerk who, he correctly surmised, had time enough to talk:

"Suppose you don't do these things that the state law and the resolutions of the county board require of you! What could they do to you?"

"Well," said the county clerk, "I don't know as they could do nawthin'!"

He was at least right enough, for he was fortified on his separate little statutory pedestal further by the fact that "they" would never know whether he complied with the law and, if they did, would never even feel any duty to try to bring him into compliance.

LONG COUNTY BALLOTS

As for the attention the people will pay to the county offices, a glance at the Cleveland 1948 ballot, page 10, will convince. There is the county group far down the long ribbon of paper, as secure from any extensive scrutiny and comparison of the merits as if the candidates' names were printed in Sanskrit. On the 1950 ballot the party circle was omitted, as a result of a change in the Ohio law. The voters, instead of marking a single X in the party circle as most of them always did and thus putting the list into office intact without scrutiny of the stalks in the asparagus ticket, had to mark a separate X for each of the fifty-odd offices. But their votes did not thereby become any more meaningful. Voters could not readily memorize the names of preferred candidates for so many offices and the relative merits of the two submitted for each office; they could not, from their knowledge of local politics, reward virtue any more than they could have each from memory assumed the task of proofreading the list for the printers. And if the printer in honest error had put some Democrats under the Republican label the courts or the election authorities would have been justified in fairness, and possibly in law, in ignoring that long line of X's and reversing the count for each such office, giving each such vote to the opposite unmarked candidate!

Cleveland and Cuyahoga County, with that longest of all ballots, comprise an extreme case, but the unawareness of voters there and elsewhere as to what they are doing on election day in respect to filling elective county offices is all but universal. The politicians in a rural county pursuing the outdoor sport of keeping the other gang out of the courthouse may honestly believe that the mass of the voters are exercising an informed discrimination, but see where everybody would be if party guidance unexpectedly disappeared from the ballots!

In this most refractory of fields progress toward compliance with the Three Rules has been slight and nowhere complete.

Progress in Los Angeles County, 1912

In 1912 Los Angeles County secured a charter with a shortened ballot. The previously elective county clerk, public administrator, coroner, surveyor, recorder, tax collector, treasurer, superintendent of schools, and constables became appointive. The elective list was thus reduced to supervisor, sheriff, district attorney, and assessor.

This change constituted the only recognition anywhere in that decade of the need for shortening county ballots.

RELEASE FROM UNIFORMITY IN TWENTY-ONE STATES

Partial integrations of county administrations in the direction of Rule Three, following no theory except local expediency and good sense, are found in some states. California has encouraged county supervisors to combine statutory offices and functions, and a single elective administrator may thus be, for example, not only treasurer but also assessor, public administrator, recorder, and tax collector. The power has mostly been used to make one full-time office out of several part-time ones. In several California counties there are appointive officers of rather indefinite authority who help the supervisors to supervise and are encouraged to grow in importance and grasp toward managerial functions.[2]

Elsewhere progress for twenty years to 1930 was merely potential although important and basic, namely, the extensive release of counties from old state constitutional restrictions, so that by legislation or home rule procedures counties can progress to more integrated short-ballot forms capable of taking on modern loads of technical duties of the municipal type. In twenty-one states with about half of the counties a fairly complete copy of the National Municipal League's Model County Charter could be adopted now, but unfreezing their structures from constitutions has rarely been followed by action by the counties thus set free. Even in areas like Virginia and New York, where ready-made simplified forms including county manager plans have been dangled before the county constituencies, unawareness, inertia, and inaction have prevailed. New York counties, except Monroe (Rochester), have ignored the options since 1935. In Maryland, Montgomery in 1948 was first to use the 1915 permission.

EFFORTS IN OHIO, 1935

In 1935 in Ohio, promptly following adoption of an amendment which gave to counties power like that of cities to frame and adopt

[2] John C. Bollens, "Administrative Integration in California Counties," *Public Administration Review*, Winter, 1951.

their own charters, there were efforts at simplification of the ancient ramshackle structure in three counties.

The effort in Hamilton County was mentioned in the Cincinnati story, Chapter XVI.

Cuyahoga County, including Cleveland, fifty-four suburbs, and six townships, voted for a charter with an elective county president, an eight-member board chosen by proportional representation, and a county director (manager), who in turn was to appoint six department heads, some of whom replaced offices previously elective. Even the prosecutor was made appointive (by the president) and a controller was provided, appointive by the board. The charter carried by 18,000 votes. But a court declared that it had invaded the field of municipal functions and was therefore invalid. The county commissioners promptly submitted the question of creating a second charter commission to try again but the proposal was defeated at the polls, 146,477 to 149,210, in 1936.

Similarly in 1935 the reformers who had just secured council-manager government for Toledo went after the government of Lucas County, submitting a charter which would have simplified the structure to an elective commission of five and a county manager, the latter appointing all department heads except the prosecutor and the sheriff, grouped under a director of law enforcement, and a director of audits, to be appointed by the commission. It was lost at the polls in November, 1935.

EFFORTS IN MICHIGAN

In Michigan progressive-minded urban reformers have sallied forth in vain to modernize county government. In 1920 and in every legislative session up to 1928 Detroit citizen organizations sought a permissive county home rule amendment and were defeated by rural interests. In 1934 an initiative petition to the same end was defeated by 288,000 votes and in 1936 a less sweeping proposal was defeated by 170,000. In 1942, following some grand jury revelations in Wayne County (Detroit), the legislature submitted an amendment for home rule in that county alone; it was supported by a strong campaign, but rural opposition defeated it by 23,000 and in 1944 the state association of county supervisors beat a similar proposal by 136,000. The trivial net influence of all that battling was installation in 1942 of a civil service system in Wayne, limited by the legislature to that county alone, and a reduction in 1943 of the preposterously large Board of Supervisors of Wayne from 162 members to the scarcely less preposterous number of eighty-four!

So also perished other less valiant attacks on this ivied inner keep of politics in various states or in their constitutional conventions; the alliance of rural county politicians and rural legislators is tough, self-serving, and cynically indifferent to the merits, whereas public concern with conditions in these minor and obscure units of government is always difficult to whip up.

Yet there have been some cases of progress.

ELECTIVE COUNTY EXECUTIVES

In a few metropolitan areas there has been progress toward giving county administrations an elective chief executive on the mayor-and-council plan.

In two populous New Jersey counties, Hudson and Essex, since 1900 there have been single elective county supervisors with scanty powers comparable to those of a weak mayor including veto over the county board.

In Nassau County (pop. 666,252, 1950), adjoining New York City on Long Island, an elective "county executive" was created in 1938 in charge of all departments aside from the old constitutional offices —salary, $20,000.

Westchester County (pop. 622,983, 1950), adjoining New York City on the north, likewise inched forward in 1939 by creating an elective "county executive" in conjunction with its large board of forty-five supervisors. An attempt to reduce the board to twelve failed at the polls in 1941.

St. Louis County, Missouri (which does not include the city of St. Louis), began operations January 1, 1951, under a new home rule charter. A three-member "county court" had served as the executive arm since 1876, when the population was 30,000. In 1950 the population had grown to 404,000. The new charter provides a strong-mayor-and-council setup with an elective county supervisor elected at large for four years and a council of seven, elective one from each of seven districts. But the old county officers were left separately elective—assessor, circuit clerk, collector, four constables, coroner, county clerk, highway engineer, public administrator, recorder of deeds, sheriff, superintendent of schools, and treasurer, controlling 500 of the county's 1300 employees! The *Post-Dispatch* related (December 17, 1950), "Proponents of the charter felt that elimination of elective offices would have doomed the charter at the election because of opposition by office holders and their employees."

Cook County, Illinois, which includes Chicago, is unusual in giving to the president of its board of county commissioners some appointive power like a weak mayor, and a veto.

All these counties have many operating functions of the municipal type, and the improved integration of the administration was impelled by press of business.

NEW YORK CITY'S FIVE COUNTIES CLEANED OUT

New York City includes five counties, and the city's Board of Estimate for half a century or more has been also the board of supervisors for those counties. By the persistent efforts of local reformers, beginning with City Chamberlain Henry Bruère's and Leonard M. Wallstein's report of 1915,[3] with scandals as a jumping-off point, New York has successively disposed of eleven elective coroners (substituting an appointive qualified pathologist from the classified civil service), five elective county clerks (substituting clerks appointed by the appellate divisions of the courts they serve), and four elective registers (substituting an appointive city-wide register from the classified civil service). There are left no elective county officers at all in New York City's five counties except the judges and prosecutors. The specific before-and-after, as shown in the case of the sheriff especially, is in Reading C, a lurid case story of how political machines, helping themselves to a $1,000,000-a-year payroll for their district workers, used it to entrench themselves in power at public expense and carried that to its logical pinnacle by throwing up the figure of Boss Flynn of the Bronx, who makes no bones of the fact that it was originally sheriff's patronage that

[3] "Study of County Government with the City of New York," a report to the mayor, 1915.

established him for a generation as the most powerful boss in the state.

CITY-COUNTY CONSOLIDATIONS

Philadelphia, Boston, San Francisco, Baltimore, and Denver have consolidated various county functions into their city administrations. In Virginia the twenty-seven cities are charged with the county functions, avoiding the double layer of government and taxing power, and all but one of them have city managers.

THE GREAT LOS ANGELES COUNTY MANAGER STRUCTURE

Los Angeles County (pop. 4,125,164) presents an interesting and advanced picture. It has 4083 square miles and engulfs the sprawling metropolis of Los Angeles, forty-four other cities, and fourteen unincorporated areas. Thanks to the shortening of the ballot in 1912, it elects only a board of five supervisors, one from each district, a sheriff, county clerk, and assessor—no more—employs 22,000 people, and had an annual expenditure in 1951–52 of $289,305,525!

Since 1938 the board of supervisors has employed a county manager called chief administrative officer, the "CAO." The twenty-two departmental chiefs are qualified by civil service examinations and are appointed—not, however, by the CAO but by the board. But thus far the board has always accepted the advice of its very able CAO as to which of the eligible list to select, so the deviation from the logic of empowering the CAO to select his own official family has thus far done no harm. The great growth of the county in population—from 936,000 in 1920 to 2,200,000 in 1930, 2,785,000 in 1940, and 4,125,164 in 1950—has produced problems of incredible complexity and difficulty, but the county government contracts with the local governments and special assessment areas to supply and assess for many services and instead of incessant breakdowns and political turbulence there is planning and good order under a single nonpolitical officer of high competence. The original CAO, General Wayne R. Allen, has served for fourteen years at present writing and there is a low turnover in the departments. The supervisors and CAO exercise considerable control over the separately elective sheriff and clerk, so there is admirably complete compliance with

both Rule One and Rule Three and the voters, despite the needlessly numerous other political distractions in California, do rather
well for themselves in this vast unit of government.

San Diego County, California (pop. 535,967), having doubled in
population since 1940, copied the Los Angeles CAO feature in 1947,
and the state exhibits several other CAO's of varied but lesser
powers.

INFORMAL INTEGRATIONS

Here and there, unheralded and unsung, county governments are
carefully and conscientiously operated, despite lack of public scrutiny, by faithful, honest routineers and without serious friction or
waste despite the ramshackle structure. The teamwork may result
from extralegal pressures—the influence of a decent political boss,
the amiable solidarity of a political faction, and a good regional
tradition.

Another type of coordination, developed despite the looseness of
the structure, is seen where one of the county officeholders by
ability, tact, and seniority acquires an unofficial and welcome leadership over the others—the man who knows all the answers, the
man who can quote the law, the man whom the others ask. He may
be the chairman of the board or the veteran member or one of the
separate elective officers. Thus in Wisconsin the elective county
clerk is, curiously, also the accountant and auditor and thereby
may easily become the responsible financial officer and purchasing
agent, preparing budgets for all departments as well as showing the
county board what is to be done by preparing the agendas or con-
vening the committees. A university graduate student visiting
seventy-one of the county seats in search of the working realities
found that seven of the clerks were practically county managers
and twenty-three more were so active and far reaching as to approach that type of authority.[4]

MODEL COUNTY MANAGER PROPOSAL

In 1930 the National Municipal League began pressing for application to county government of the pattern that was proving so

[4] L. H. Adolfson, "The County Clerk as 'Manager,'" *National Municipal
Review*, March, 1945.

triumphant in the cities and drafted a logical short-ballot Model County Manager Optional Law.[5] Several states have since included such plans in ready-made optional charters.

In 1930 Durham County, North Carolina, adopted the principle and the first county manager took office.

In 1933 Nebraska passed an enabling act making the Model County Manager Plan available in that state and Douglas County (Omaha) adopted it in 1934, effective January, 1937, despite a stiff 10 per cent petition requirement and the necessity of mustering a 51 per cent support. The constitution of Nebraska seemed to leave the way clear since it said only, "The legislature shall provide by law for the election of such county and township officers as may be necessary." County officers fought the new plan in the courts, claiming that this meant that all officers must be elective and got the new plan declared unconstitutional; the public energy was insufficient to go after a constitutional amendment.

The further sequence of adoptions is at the end of this chapter.

Not one of the seventeen current county manager counties goes to the full length described in the Model County Charter, falling short of it by leaving traditional constitutional offices such as those of sheriff, county clerk, register, and coroner, etc., outdoors to linger on as little independent units subject to easy direct access by self-seeking political forces through their control of the processes of nomination in an area of low visibility. One county, Lane, in Oregon, submitted in 1948 a completely integrated setup but it was defeated at the polls like the bold pioneer attempts in Cuyahoga, Hamilton, and Lucas Counties, Ohio, in 1935.

The performance records of county managers have been impressive and shine in contrast to the conditions they displaced. An on-the-ground study proved that for three Virginia counties in 1952.[6] The county manager plan has made good in the mighty conurbation of Los Angeles County and in the tiny rural area of Petroleum County, Montana (1025 pop.) but it has yet to attain the advantages of complete integration of all the offices except district attorney under a single board with an appointed chief executive.

[5] Current version, Model County Manager Charter, 1952. See Part IV.

[6] W. O. Spicer, *Fifteen Years of County Management in Virginia,* University of Virginia Extension Division, Charlottesville, 1952.

RURAL MUNICIPALITIES OF TOMORROW

Potentially the county may find a high destiny in suburban areas where the population is large and growing and wants municipal services. Current increases in population in the 1930, 1940, and 1950 censuses were mainly in suburbs, and a fine thing, too! The new homes and the new factories avoid the built-up cities and stream out with automobiles and motor trucks to open countrysides far beyond the reach of annexation. The bright new colonies they form ignore the old village and township boundaries and the village jurisdictions do not conform to the logical areas for drainage and sewerage, or water supply or snow removal or other features of service. Problems develop which relate simultaneously to numerous villages and unincorporated areas. County planning shows the need of moving local services up to larger scale and larger area to support adequate service and sound engineering. So the city hospital, welcoming patients from beyond the city line, stays right on the same street where it always was but is willingly permitted to become the county hospital, with its costs and extensions charged to the county. The county contracts to clear snow on main roads that pass through the villages, to provide health service, or to build a revised highway system. The villages and small cities which, for political and sentimental reasons, resist annexation or consolidation or effacement will more cheerfully surrender to the county one function after another until little is left. If the county in such situations as in Fulton County (Atlanta) is alert and competent, membership in the county board can become a post of high opportunity for service and progress and its managership a thing to aspire to.

Logically the process of passing functions upward from villages and small cities to county governments should await the proper reorganization of county governments to prepare them to assume such multiplied burdens. Actually progress does not, I notice, necessarily work in that logical sequence. The burdens are assumed regardless, the county structure staggers and cracks under the strain, and then, being a sentient living organism, the government strengthens itself under the load and eventually carries it.

As for rural counties of no growth, the prospects for nonpolitical

service may be dim. Certainly there will be cold response to the
logic that urges consolidation of little counties to make up units of
appropriate size for the motor age. But we shall see how readily
the rural town meetings of Maine combine elective local offices into
a single manager serving under the board of selectmen and how
villages under 5000 population steadily move on to the tight efficiencies made possible by council-manager organization.

So the new fashion in political structure has begun to reach the
rural level!

In 1949 the county managers with seven in attendance began annual meetings!

STATE CONSTITUTIONAL PROVISIONS
PERMITTING COUNTY MANAGER PLAN

In the twenty-one following states, county manager government in
close compliance with the National Municipal League's Model County
Charter is possible under the constitution, but no county has used the
opportunity for full compliance:

1. *Arizona.* Constitution provides nine elective county offices "subject to change by law."

2. *California.* Home rule amendment (1911) permits counties to
draft and adopt charters. Three counties had adopted manager forms up
to 1951.

3. *Georgia.* Constitution (1945) requires legislature to provide optional systems of county government. An optional county manager law
was enacted in 1922. A special act for Fulton County was enacted in
1946.

4. *Iowa.* Constitution (1857) is silent on county government except
to require county attorneys to be elective.

5. *Louisiana.* Constitution (1921) requires legislature to offer optional forms. No law up to 1951.

6. *Maryland.* Home rule amendment (1915) permits counties to
draft and adopt new forms. Two counties, Montgomery and Ann Arundel,
have adopted the county manager plan.

7. *Minnesota.* Constitution (1857) leaves county organization to
legislation without restriction.

8. *Mississippi.* Constitution (1890) permits legislature to provide
method of selection of county officers.

9. *Missouri.* Constitution (1945) permits locally prepared charters for three counties over 85,000 population and provision of alternative forms by legislation for the rest. No law up to 1951.

10. *Montana.* Constitutional amendment (1922) authorizes legislature to provide new forms of county government. Optional law (1931) permits county manager form. Adopted by Petroleum County, 1943.

11. *Nevada.* A 1951 act permits counties of over 10,000 population (Washoe, Las Vegas, Clark, and Elko) to adopt a county manager plan described in the act.

12. *New Jersey.* The 1947 constitution permits the legislature to alter forms of county government except that sheriffs and clerks of undefined powers must remain elective.

13. *New York.* Constitutional amendment (1935) required legislature to provide alternative forms of county government and laws of 1935, 1936, and 1937 provide numerous options. Monroe County (1936) adopted county manager plan under the two-option act of 1935.

14. *North Carolina.* Constitution (1876) permits legislature to alter form of county government. Optional law (1927) permits appointment of county managers. Durham adopted 1930 and Guilford County adopted 1942.

15. *North Dakota.* Constitutional amendment (1940) permits, and optional act (1941) provides, county manager form.

16. *Ohio.* Constitutional amendment (1933) permits counties to draft and adopt their own charters by local process and permits legislature to submit optional forms. No optional law up to 1951.

17. *Oklahoma.* Constitution (1907) empowers legislature to change constitutional list of elective county officers.

18. *Oregon.* Constitutional amendment (1944) and enabling act (1945) permit county manager form.

19. *Texas.* Constitutional amendment (1933) authorizes locally drafted charters in counties over 62,000 population and permits other counties to adopt with approval of two-thirds vote in state legislature.

20. *Virginia.* Constitutional amendment (1928) permits and the legislature has provided (1932 and 1938) optional forms of county government. Five counties—Albemarle, Arlington (by special act of 1930), Fairfax, Henrico, and Warwick—have county manager or executive forms. Twenty-seven cities of Virginia are independent of counties; city managers exist in twenty-six of them and exercise county manager functions.

21. *Washington.* Self-executing amendment (1948) permits locally drawn charters.

In the six New England states, with their important town system, county government is only vestigial; Connecticut has one elective county officer (sheriff); no Rhode Island county officers are locally elective.

In the twenty-one remaining states, county government provisions embedded in state constitutions prevent full compliance with the Model County Manager Charter. County manager plans of varying degrees of incompleteness are permissible in some states of this group, including *Tennessee,* where a special act (1947) provided such a plan for McMinn County.

CHRONOLOGY OF THE SEVENTEEN COUNTY MANAGER PLAN ADOPTIONS

(From *Digest of County Manager Charters and Laws,* National Municipal League, 1951)

In effect

1930   Durham, North Carolina

1931   Santa Clara, California

1932   San Mateo, California; Arlington, Virginia

1933   Sacramento, California; Albemarle, Virginia

1934   Henrico, Virginia

1936   Monroe, New York

1942   Guilford, North Carolina

1943   Petroleum, Montana

1945   Fairfax (revised, 1950), Virginia; Warwick, Virginia [7]

1947   Fulton, Georgia; McMinn, Tennessee

1949   Anne Arundel, Maryland; Montgomery, Maryland

1952   Elizabeth City County, Virginia [7]

Under incomplete charter authority to manage, county managers are also found in Robeson, North Carolina, 1929; Los Angeles, California, 1938; Hamilton, Tennessee, 1942; San Diego, California, 1947; Charleston, South Carolina, 1950.

[7] In June 1952 Elizabeth City County and Warwick County voted to become cities.

Chapter XXI

PROGRESS IN TOWNSHIPS AND VILLAGES

IN THE middle Atlantic and north central states from New York and Pennsylvania west to Kansas, Iowa, and Wisconsin, there exist in eleven states most of the 17,338 townships and their estimated 138,704 elective officers. In New England, towns are important and counties are trivial but elsewhere counties are standard equipment and in the presence of municipalities make townships unnecessary.

The midwest townships are often products of the same T-squares which marked off on level prairies the 160-acre quarter-sections offered to immigrants from the east under the Homestead Act; four quarter-sections made a square mile and an area six miles square became a "congressional township," sometimes before there was any population in the region. The population, when it came in, clustered around railway stations and river landings and many of the townships were left as almost meaningless lines on the map and gave way to civil townships. Then the clusters of population became incorporated villages or cities and proceeded in a far more natural and urgent progression to take care of their own needs. Many of the townships which were thus created never acquired much population but they apparently had to have governments, no matter how feeble and impecunious. Others, of course, secured population, and perform diverse services.

But even the latter began losing their importance with the coming of good roads and automobiles. These made it feasible for counties to take over or duplicate township services and to do the work better because of the pooling of the work and ability to pay full-time employees. In the modern world the township is too small to do anything well and has become in great part perfunctory and trivial in its functioning. Hence officers elected to nonsalaried township jobs fail to qualify and offices stay vacant sometimes for years. The taxes they collect are sometimes all used for overhead with next to nothing thereunder. Most of the states get along nicely without this needless layer of government and never miss it—the counties take care of the unincorporated areas outside the cities and organized villages. In Illinois seventeen counties have no townships and in 1931 the Illinois Tax Commission demonstrated that eleven sample counties without townships had a per capita cost for general governmental services of $1.84 whereas in seven counties with townships the cost was $3.83.

A committee of the National Municipal League in 1934 checking the services performed by townships found that every one of those services—justice, health, welfare, highways, fiscal, records, elections —was inappropriate and impractical when thus decentralized to such small areas and populations, the remedy being complete abolition of most of the townships and transfer of their duties to the county governments.[1] The constitutions of Illinois, Missouri, Ohio, and Nebraska make specific provisions facilitating abolition.

In 1938 Oklahoma abolished all its townships.

In 1948 Iowa abolished 1600 township assessors, nearly all elective, in favor of appointive civil service men under elective county auditors. In 1952 the township functions had been so completely absorbed by the counties that the census dropped them from its count of governments.

Nebraska in 1951 abolished 962 elected precinct assessors.

MANAGERS IN MAINE HAMLETS

The remaining item in this calendar of progress toward simplification and the Three Rules is the somewhat unexpected extension of the council-manager plan into villages, particularly in Maine, where over 100 communities have adopted the plan, bringing professional management to over 50 per cent of the state's population. A state law in 1939 made it feasible for towns by action of their town meetings to authorize the usual board of selectmen to hire a manager and combine in him the functions previously distributed among several independent elected officers. Such town meeting

[1] "Recommendations on Township Government," *National Municipal Review*, February, 1934.

action proved easy to get and even in hamlets of as little as 500 population managers were created who were forthwith titled also commissioner of roads, overseer of the poor, town clerk, treasurer, and tax collector. In some cases managers serve two towns or even three. One manager oscillates between two villages fifty-eight miles apart. In Vermont one manager frequently serves a village and a surrounding township of the same name. The jobs pay only small salaries but provide an entrance into the profession of city manager-ship. The University of Maine, training postgraduate students in special courses, with field work, has been placing all the graduates promptly in jobs. The selectmen thus provided with a full-time agent are relieved from importunities and drudgery and the young managers learn to handle the diverse detail to local satisfaction. Sometimes the village manager is the whole pay roll; sometimes he has a girl to keep the office and answer the phone. The concentra-tion of the numerous duties in one office insures teamwork and fa-cilitates switching of help to the seasonal peak points. Says one manager, "When as overseer of the poor I receive a plea for relief from an able-bodied man, I proceed as commissioner of roads to give him a job!"

Chapter XXII

SCHOOL SYSTEMS VS. THE THREE RULES

NOW we come with our Three Rules to the field of public education and encounter a body of professional doctrine sincere, resolute, of long standing, and not primarily self-serving, a doctrine whose program resists integration and proposes, as the lawyers in so many constitutional conventions and charter commissions have vainly done, to assign to voters an array of duties without ascertaining whether the voters will actually accept and perform the assignments. The people, in the view of most educators, should elect an independent state board of education and independent local boards, and both should be free of restraint by other branches of government; the local boards should levy their own taxes and have their own borrowing power. This of course at some points would increase the number of elective officers, increase the number of governmental units, lengthen the ballots, and block our whole program of sweeping simplification of the voters' business in the very field where there might seem to be the most room for progress toward compliance with the Three Rules!

The Educators' Position

The great National Education Association, to be sure, does not officially go quite the whole way. The NEA platform, adopted in 1932 and reaffirmed each year, does not explicitly advocate turning school systems into separate governments everywhere by making their boards elective; it uses the word "chosen" and "selected": "Local, district and state boards of education should be chosen on a nonpartisan basis, selected at large. . . ." But other educator groups press further, as we shall see.

215

STATE BOARDS OF EDUCATION

In thirty states all or a major portion of the members of the state boards of education are appointed by the governor. Two, Utah and Washington, let a convention of local elective school boards make the selections. New York has a board of thirteen regents selected in rotation for thirteen-year terms by the legislature with a requirement that there be one from each of ten judicial districts.

Nine states have no state boards of education.

As to elective state boards, the preference of educators is quoted thus by the U.S. Office of Education in a pamphlet describing "a composite of good practices which now prevail in some states":

The State Board is composed solely of able laymen who serve long overlapping terms and are not subject to reappointment or election. Members are selected at large in the state in a manner which frees them from partisan political control and makes them truly representative of the will of the people. ["Selected" again!] Election by the people of board members furnishes a sound method of freeing members from any allegiance except that which they owe the whole public. . . . This method of election is in accord with the American democratic tradition and has much merit.[1]

In a later bulletin (No. 12, 1950, pp. 107–108) the published conclusions of the Office admit a doubt:

Appointment by the governor is in harmony with the theory that full responsibility for each branch of state government should be centralized in the executive of the state. This theory, however, is opposed by legislative trends and views of school authorities. Election by the people on a nonpartisan ballot represents more nearly than does appointment by the governor a direct expression of the people's interest in the control of the state school system. This method, however, if it requires its candidates to campaign, is likely to cost the state board some highly qualified persons who would accept an appointment by the governor but not a candidacy that involves campaigning.

The National Council of Chief State School Officers also goes further than the NEA platform, stating in 1950:

In each state there should be a nonpartisan lay state board of educa-

---

[1] *The Structure of State Departments of Education*, U.S. Office of Education, Washington, 1949.

tion, composed of 7 to 12 able citizens elected by the people in a manner prescribed by law, broadly representative of the general public and unselfishly interested in public education. The members of this board should serve for long overlapping terms without pay.

The Office of Public Education pamphlet admits:

Practical difficulties are frequently present in the election of members of the state board of education which are not likely to be present in local school board elections. These include (1) the difficulty of persuading the most able persons to run for election and (2) disseminating information about the candidates.

Completely ignoring the further dubious question of whether the sovereign people will accept the assignment or be any more aware of the contests than they are of those for the post of state treasurer!

DIFFICULTIES OF DIRECT ELECTION

Added difficulties are these: The interest of the voters in the contest would be slight, the press unless there were a religious tussle or some dramatic scandal would give scant attention, and few voters would go to the polls at a separate election for state board members; if there were other more truly political contests to draw them there, the board contests would be overshadowed and neglected. The difficulty of dissemination of information about the candidates is part of the unwieldy-district problem (Rule Two). How to make a dent in the consciousness of a busy state-wide constituency without raising and spending large sums and organizing energy! And all to win an unpaid office! Under those circumstances, if there be any patronage, plunder, or religious advancement at stake, a trivial political or special-interest group may easily win most of the time unobserved by the people. Thus violation of all Three Rules makes the concept anything but democratic, although it is, alas, "in accord with . . . tradition," and a bad tradition too!

The evidence needed to support the unwary political science of the educators is to be sought in the experience of four states— Louisiana, Michigan, Nevada, and Texas. They (plus Colorado, which began in 1951) elect some or all of the members of their state boards of education. How much scrutiny do candidates for these offices usually get from the voters of those states? Are they

not so lost in the shuffle on the tail of the state ticket that voters pay
scant attention and are unable to name the man they vote for or tell
anything about him? Is the problem of getting nominated and
elected to the office made so difficult and professional a task by
reason of its state-wide basis that no one can hope for election unless
supported by the managers of one or the other of the standing
armies of the parties? And what about dividing the state government in such fashion that the board can safely defy the governor,
quarrel endlessly with his financial officer, and lobby for its own
appropriations? Perhaps in one or another of these states candidates
for board membership are adequately scrutinized by the voters as
well as by the relatively small group of interested educators. If so,
good. I doubt it, but it would take a Gallup poll to find out. The
influence of the educators is likely to be good as far as it can
reach but if educators think that other voters are as aware of the
issues involved as they are, I suspect they would be in for a surprise if they began to ask men in the street at random, "Whom do
you expect to vote for for member of the state board of education?"
shortly before election. The answers in effect might be "How should
I know?" If so, that fact should be completely decisive! To say "The
voters *ought* to take an interest" is begging the question: if it
doesn't "democ," it isn't democracy! The selection of members must
not be left in the hands of party managers or even coteries of professional educators in the obscurity which commonly characterizes
minor overshadowed elective posts; that's undemocratic!

It cannot be contended that power of appointment of educational
or other boards and department heads by governors is not frequently abused and misused for political advantage. But, with or
without confirmation by the state senate, appointment by the governor, the conspicuous, best-scrutinized officer of the state, lodges
the choice of state boards in a safer place than in the obscurities
that will surround it under any elective system. As all new state
officers are nowadays made appointive by the governor while minor
elective officers no longer grow in importance, the experience, as
well as the influence of political scientists, runs counter to the hopeful proposals of the educators which follow the old follies at which
this book is aimed.

STATE SCHOOL EXECUTIVES SHOULD BE UNDER THE BOARDS

Twenty-nine states elect their executive commissioners of education. On a preference for appointment rather than election of the state commissioner of education, both educators and political scientists agree. Direct election of the commissioner along with a board obviously erects a two-headed setup even if the commissioner sits as an ex officio member of the board. Twelve states empower the board to appoint the commissioner, but only Texas and Colorado actually have the combination of an elective lay board and power in that board to appoint the chief school officer as favored by the educators. It is due to work better than the elective boards of Louisiana, Michigan, and Nevada, which deal with separately elective state school commissioners, since the greater power should make the Texas and Colorado boards more attractive to good men, and able professional candidates for commissioner will not be deterred from aspiring to the post by a necessity of seeking state-wide election and reelection. The new Colorado setup is at best more promising than what it replaced, namely, an ex officio board from the tail of the elective list—secretary of state, attorney general, and superintendent of public instruction; this was next to the last of all such ex officio boards, of which there were twenty-one in that state in 1900.

LOCAL SCHOOL BOARDS IN GOOD REPUTE

The 63,407 school districts with taxing power are more numerous than all the other American units of government put together. Their usual structures are like those of the council-manager plan of municipal government; in 85 per cent of the districts the school board is elective. It usually has three to six members. Eighty-six per cent of the boards are chosen in nonpartisan elections, 86 per cent are elected at large, and 74 per cent [2] are unpaid. The school districts in more than half the cases [3] are not coterminous with any

[2] "Status and Practices of Boards of Education," *National Education Association Research Bulletin*, April, 1946.

[3] "Fiscal Authority of City School Boards," *National Education Association Research Bulletin*, April, 1950.

other local government area, and 72 per cent of them have complete control of the school budget.

The typical board hires—from out of town, if it likes—a professional school superintendent. Writing in 1914, A. Lawrence Lowell, president of Harvard, testified:

Twenty years ago the power of the superintendents of schools was as a rule extremely small. I remember it was commonly said at that time that the only function of the superintendent of schools in Boston was to write an annual report. Within the last 20 years the position of superintendent of schools has changed very much. It has become a profession in which a man is sometimes employed who is not an inhabitant of the city, who has been superintendent of schools in some other town. The feeling against that is rapidly diminishing. The influence of the superintendent as an expert has become very much greater. Instead of the members of the school board trying to select teachers and manage the schools directly they employ a superintendent who has had years of experience, has expert knowledge, and then back him up; keeping him, however, in touch with public opinion, with the result that the relation between the schools and the people is much better, much closer than it was 20 years ago.[4]

The promotion of school superintendents from small cities to larger ones was essential to creating a real profession and, in the years since, transferability has become commonplace and the profession is well established. Such superintendents, selected by the school board, proceed in turn to give full time to the work, to appoint teachers and preferably all other staff and direct the whole performance of the department.

Voters are a bit more touchy about the appearance of self-serving politics in school boards than in city councils. Fine citizens with no personal or partisan axes to grind are usually more willing to serve on a school board than in the typical and much weaker city council under the mayor-and-council plan. School systems are less commonly utilized to strengthen the dominant political party than the adjacent municipal administrations are. All in all, school boards are, I have seen, in such superior repute that it is usually pretty safe to cite the school system as the local precedent where adoption of the parallel council-manager plan is up for consideration.

The personnel of any independent unit of government is likely

[4] *National Municipal Review,* January, 1915.

to defend its independence with fierce jealousy. The tendency appears in the stubborn resistance of little incompetent one-room school districts to efforts to bring about consolidation into larger · districts with the advantages of graded classes—a resistance which the rural school bus and good roads are steadily helping to reduce with useful results in diminishing the number of independent taxing units; the 1952 census count shows fewer school districts than the 108,579 figure of 1942.[5] It appears likewise in resistance to making the school system merely a municipal department with an appointive board and in resistance to any yielding of partial control to "the politicians in city hall." There is a common assumption among teachers and school board members that they are outside of politics and maintain a purer atmosphere in their affairs. Certainly in many communities the school boards do attract selfless and able men and women who, in devotion to the public welfare, contrast sharply with the city councilmen. Often they are protected by the influence of live parent-teacher associations, which are more numerous by far than the "good government" associations which argue with the other municipal officers.

The idea that the schools should thus be somehow set apart from city halls has sometimes been reflected in parallel demands for independent status by park and recreation personnel and by librarians and library boards.

As to elective local school boards, the American Association of School Administrators, a department of the National Education Association, in an Official Report, 1939 (p. 246), is more explicit than the NEA, saying:

The Association recognizes with pride that the American system of electing boards directly by the people to control public education without interference from city councils and commissions has been responsible for a large share of the independence of the schools and the educational achievements of the country. The Association condemns vigorously recent attempts to break down this system by subordinating the control and support of education to boards charged with many other responsibilities in government.

[5] U.S. Bureau of the Census, "Governments in the U.S. in 1951," March 1952.

The Connecticut report of 1951,[6] least inhibited of recent state reorganization studies, followed the doctrine of the educators to logical completion. It proposed to establish small elective boards in all school districts, boards of five, seven, or nine members with overlapping terms elected on nonpartisan ballots with power to appoint and remove professional school superintendents as chief executives. The report further proposed to snip the various existing controls over budget totals and bond issues now exercised by some municipal governments so that the school boards need no longer come in at budget-making time to petition for appropriations and permission to issue bonds for new construction, as other municipal departments must do, and face the chance of their requests' being cut down to keep the total tax levy from running beyond reason. The report advocates letting the school boards tax, spend, and borrow with the same freedom as the municipal governments, leaving the constituency to say which of the two is being extravagant and subject to correction at the next election or the next bond issue referendum.

My challenge to this deference to the comfort of the educators is that there is no consideration of the diversity of the constituencies to which this uniform rule would apply. In a compact homogeneous suburb or in a simple rural district, its results may be quite ideal. In a large city the contests for the board can be hopelessly obscured by more dramatic contests and long ballots. A strong tradition, working well, may induce self-seekers to keep hands off, despite the apparent vulnerability of the school board to political capture. The question of whether to retain the school board as a separate elective government where it has usually worked well and attracted adequate voter scrutiny can be answered affirmatively. But where there is perennial trouble and criticism, the remedy of making the board appointive has certain extraneous advantages—it would provide one less separate government for voters to keep track of, one less separate taxing and bonding power with its vested interest in getting as much money as it can regardless of the grand total levied on the area and regardless of the needs of other equally important activities such as health or sanitation. But the use of such a remedy is sharply curtailed by the fact that a minority of the

[6] "Education in Connecticut," by the Governor's Fact-Finding Commission on Education, January 3, 1951.

school districts are coterminous with cities. That circumstance may leave only the county to tie them to and geographical factors may sometimes make such a solution absurd.

The elective school board with its professional appointive super-intendent is ideal as to form—it has a short ballot of equally im-portant board members, it is tightly and correctly integrated, and the district is usually wieldy. It provides conditions of service that are attractive to high-grade candidates. For us here, its problem is in its context: Are its board memberships important enough rela-tive to other offices put up for election at the same times to attract adequate scrutiny by voters? (Rule One) Or if chosen at a separate election, nonpartisan or otherwise, do the voters turn out? Can the community afford to have two governments and two tax levies with-out the minor economies and the concern about the total tax burden that might be achieved if the school board were made appointive by the mayor? (Rule Three)

THE CASE AGAINST SEPARATENESS

Marshaling now the viewpoint of political scientists, we turn first to the eminent William Anderson:

> It is generally agreed every clearly defined urban community should be organized as one local government, and not split into a number of layers such as county, city and school. . . . In the United States the idea has not been fully accepted because school administrators . . . have insisted upon separate school corporations. . . .

In canvassing the problem of reducing the number of taxing units to a national one-ninth of the current total, Anderson says:

> . . . There should be no separate school districts in the country what-soever. Under state control and supervision the several counties, cities, larger towns, and larger villages should administer the local schools within their limits. Advisory and even administrative school boards might exist in many places, but not separate corporate school districts.
>
> It is recognized that this is an advanced proposal, but it follows from the principle of having only one local government in each area. The exist-ing separation between school government and other local government, however much it may have been justified in the past, now stands in the way of adequate local governmental organization. To separate the func-tion of education from other functions of government, to give school

authorities and teachers a feeling of irresponsibility for the rest of the
government, to permit school budgets to be made, school taxes to be
levied, and school bonds to be issued without reference to other governmental needs is in the long run unwholesome for the educational system
itself and for the political institutions of the country. Education will
always be one of the important functions of government, but it will not
fare the worse and probably will greatly benefit from being more closely
articulated with all the other activities of state and local government.[7]

The Model City Charter is silent on the question of the relation
of the schools to city hall, leaving local custom, whatever it may be,
unchallenged. Cities commonly adopt the council-manager plan
with charters that merely restate and leave undisturbed the separate position of elective or appointive school boards.

In a circular issued by the NEA in 1939 entitled "Relationship
of Local School Systems to Council-Manager Plan of Municipal
Government," it was concluded from a survey of forty-four such
cities that "school administration in council-manager cities does not
differ markedly from that among cities in general." The Tennessee
optional law of 1921, which offered council-manager plan with the
school superintendent as a simple department head under the
manager, resulted in few adoptions.

But the council-manager governments are now attracting superior
public-spirited characters to the councils, just as school boards do,
and in those cities the superiority complex of the school boards as
to freedom from politics of the baser sort is ceasing to be justified
by any facts. If the school systems of council-manager cities became
as they are in many cities municipal departments with or without
an appointive lay departmental board intervening, they could press
for their share of the revenues and bond issues on equal terms with
other departments rather than as importunate outsiders and would
be appealing to the same type of board member. Joint purchasing,
joint use of buildings, joint pay roll and financing service would be
facilitated. And the enhanced importance of councilmen in a municipality that thus controls the $\pm$ 40 per cent of the total tax levy
devoted to schools would attract an intenser scrutiny to the office
at election time. With continued good traditions under the council-
manager plan, the advocates of separateness for school systems lose
their favorite argument.

[7] William Anderson, *The Units of Government in the United States,* Public
Administration Service, Chicago, 1949, p. 41.

A report in 1938 by members of the Department of Education of the University of Chicago covering cities of over 50,000 population found advantages in closer cooperation of school and city administrations and hopefully predicted:

As the city governments improve in efficiency and responsibility, the question of coordinating school and municipal functions will arouse less opposition. The firm belief that this will be the case is founded upon the respect which school authorities and citizens have for the city government in the manager cities. In such cities, respect for the city government is as great as if not greater than, that for the school administration.[8]

An important Minnesota study [9] relates how in the course of representations to the legislature re new revenues in 1947

There was a considerable amount of resentment aroused among city officials by the independence with which the school officials formulated their requests to the legislature and by their staunch refusal to cooperate with the city in a joint request unless one-third of all new revenues were dedicated to school use.

The same report cites the efforts of school officials, during a campaign to reform an antiquated city charter in Minneapolis in 1947–48, "for what they called greater independence . . ." and "for the highest possible limit on the taxing power of the school board." Further regarding "the familiar long standing controversy between political scientists and educators over the relative merits of the dependent and independent school systems," the report remarks:

Most professions have certain standards of orthodoxy, deviation from which is looked on with extreme disfavor. The absolute desirability of independent school districts is such a standard among educators, even though not quite universally agreed upon within the profession. It is an article of faith, a creed to which one subscribes if he is to be considered a member in good standing in the fraternity. Its precepts are passed on from one generation to another, being inculcated in every neophyte as a part of the regular ritual in the colleges of education throughout the country.

[8] Henry and Kerwin, *Schools and City Government,* University of Chicago Press, Chicago, 1938.

[9] Robert L. Morlan, *Intergovernmental Relations in Education,* University of Minnesota Press, Minneapolis, 1950.

Dependent Boards in Half of the Major Cities

Of the 191 cities of 50,000 population or over about half have dependent school boards. "The experiences of superintendents in charge of school systems operating under the plan known as fiscal dependence do not support the contention . . . that the welfare of the schools demands a complete separation of school fiscal affairs from those of the local government," said a 1933 field study.[10]

Morlan concludes:

. . . The trend is gradually and painlessly toward greater integration. It is true, however, that a case can certainly be made against complete integration when the municipal government concerned is a weak and decentralized type in which it is virtually impossible to fix responsibility. Not only would relatively little be gained by integrating the schools into a city government that does not even provide centralized budgeting, purchasing, reporting and so on for existing departments but there would also be grounds for contending that in such a situation the schools might easily be lost in the shuffle. In a type of municipal government in which a single administrator can be held clearly and definitely responsible for efficient and economical operation of all departments, the schools can be certain to receive fair treatment and to be subject to popular control. . . . Opposition to dependent school districts in council-manager cities tends to be relatively less. Furthermore, some school administrators of dependent systems in cities without the council-manager form have indicated that their objections to the system, however slight, might be largely met if council-manager government were to be installed.[11]

It has always been a vulnerable argument to plead that while all other municipal departments are under tight central administrative and fiscal control the school system ought to run free. In Massachusetts, where elective school committees prevail, the Federation of Taxpayers Associations in 1950 "came out in favor of wresting control of public school spending from the hands of school committees. . . . Representatives of teachers' groups and school committees vigorously objected to the proposal."[12] The spokesman for the Federation

[10] Henry and Kerwin, *op. cit.*
[11] Morlan, *op. cit.*
[12] Boston *Globe,* March 10, 1950.

. . . took issue with the propriety of state law permitting school committees to set their own budgets without interference. "The question to be decided," he said, "is whether we are to permit a group of self-styled professionals working through school committees to continue control of our public schools. We remain unimpressed by the contention of educators that municipal control of school budgets spells politics in the schools. Too often we have seen the school committee, according to local custom, accepted as a necessary rung up the political ladder. Neither do we think school committees are always wise and pure while mayors, city councils and town meetings are stupid and nefarious."

England abolished all separately elected school boards in 1902.

LOCAL SCHOOL EXECUTIVES SHOULD BE APPOINTIVE

Some local (county, town, or city) school systems do not vest appointment of the school superintendent in the elective school board but elect him separately. Educators and political scientists agree that this deviation from the favorite practice is unsound. The Governors' Conference survey of 1949 said:

. . . It is important that the superintendents be appointed by school boards on the basis of personal and professional competence and given salaries in line with the professional qualifications expected. Most serious deterrents to the exercise of continuing and effective educational leadership are the election of superintendents by popular vote for short terms and salary schedules too low to be attractive to persons of professional competence.[13]

VISIBILITY ESSENTIAL

So, while we seek no alteration in the *internal* organization of local school systems with boards and appointive executives, the facts remain that there are too many of them, that thousands of them should be consolidated for their own sake, that thousands more of the school boards can be acceptably and advantageously made appointive in municipal or county governments, and that getting school boards and other school officers off ballots is one of the ways of getting ballots short enough—five contests or less—to come within the actual effective scrutiny of voters.

[13] *The 48 School Systems,* The Council of State Governments, Chicago, 1949.

Chapter XXIII

PROGRESS IN THE CORONER'S OFFICE

O N THE long ballots of county elections the coroner, by some psychological instinct or sense of appropriateness, seems always to be placed at the bottom of the list. He is treated separately here for it happens that making him appointive by some other county authority is not the correct way to get this obscure figure off the ballot.

INCOMPETENCE IS CHARACTERISTIC

For at least two generations the typical elective county coroner has been the despair of all qualified observers. The position calls for an unheard-of combination of medical and legal knowledge, neither of which could be competently appraised by a county full of voters even if the voters ever looked in that direction. Election to this office violating Rule One reflects no popular opinion whatever; the office constitutes a little undesired bit of patronage which the party managers distribute, practically unobserved, to one of their supporters. Technical competence by any modern standard is not to be expected under the conditions, and few prosecuting attorneys take seriously the coroner's jury proceedings in the areas where such juries survive.

Complaints within the last decade consist mainly of an eighteen-page report published by a committee of the American Medical Association in 1945 exhibiting the common incompetence of the medical evidence produced by the county coroner system, where "medicine participates less effectively in the administration of justice . . . than it does in any comparable country in the world," which undoubtedly predisposes to (1) the nonrecognition of murder, (2) the unjust accusation of innocent persons, etc.

From time to time lurid magazine articles jeer at coroners with dramatic stories of ineptitude, as the recent titles indicate: "How Murderers Beat the Law," *Saturday Evening Post,* December 10,

1949; "Murder by Courtesy of the Coroner," *Cosmopolitan,* November, 1949; "They're Getting Away with Murder," a 1949 United Feature Syndicate series for newspapers; and "The Coroner Racket; a National Scandal," *Coronet,* June, 1950.

CONDITION OF THE CORONERS IN NEW YORK CITY, 1917

Reform of the office in New York City was instigated in 1917 by the New York Short Ballot Organization and was pushed further by the City Club, which induced Mayor Mitchel to put Leonard Wallstein, his pungent chief investigator, on the task of examining conditions in the offices of the eleven elective coroners. There had never been any attention given to the candidates by voters; the office had been used as direct patronage for decades by the five county machines and the service was no less than filthy.

Wallstein reported:

1. Candidates for coroner are nominated to balance the ticket or to represent a given race, religion, class, political faction or geographical portion of the city. Thus almost every consideration except qualification for the position determines his choice.

2. Of the 65 men who have held the office of coroner since consolidation, not one was thoroughly qualified by training or experience for the adequate performance of his duties.

3. Most of the coroners' physicians in New York City have been drawn from the ranks of medical mediocrity.

4. Such disciplinary power as the Manhattan Board of Coroners possesses over its physicians has been used, not to improve the character of their medical work, but rather to harass and embarrass the most competent of all their physicians.

5. An analysis of 800 inquisition papers made by Deputy Health Commissioner Emerson finds that in 320 cases, or 40% of those examined, there is a complete lack of evidence to justify the certified cause of death.

The incompetent medical work of the coroners' physicians persists in the investigation of criminal deaths and deprives the community of an absolutely necessary deterrent to crime.

6. So far as the activity of the coroner's office in New York City is concerned, infanticide and skillful poisoning can be carried on almost with impunity.

7. At least one coroner's physician has no conception of the functions

of his office, denying that it is part of his function in first instance to detect crime by medical examination.

Wallstein's disclosures made it impossible to defend the system, and a single medical examiner appointed by the mayor from classified civil service lists for an indefinite term replaced eleven transient politicos. Thereby as many as four coronerships in some boroughs disappeared from the ballots. The voters never missed them. The office of medical examiner has enjoyed high repute ever since. The skill of the medical examiner and his staff, likewise chosen from civil service lists, has uncovered an annual average of fifty otherwise unsuspected deaths by violence since the political hacks were ousted.

Competence in technique is to be found in a few metropolitan counties even when, as in Cook (Chicago) or Cuyahoga (Cleveland), the coroner is elective—the volume of cases develops expertness among the subordinates. Los Angeles County has had a coroner appointive from civil service eligible lists since 1913.

COUNTIES ARE TOO SMALL TO SUSTAIN MODERN TECHNICAL SERVICE

But provision of adequate medicolegal investigative service for about 3000 non-metropolitan counties requires taking the task out of such counties entirely. Most of them indeed may have no physician within their boundaries who could pass a logical examination in modern legal medicine for the post. And if an adequately trained person were brought in from outside, he would have too few cases to justify the salary and laboratory costs. Pooling of the "business" over a larger population is essential to justify provision of adequate laboratory equipment and to develop the expertness which can accumulate only from daily practice of this grisly art.

CONSTITUTIONAL OBSTACLES

Unhappily the coronership is frozen into the constitutions as an elective county officer in over half the states and is actually elective in twenty-five. In several more the coroners (or equivalent officers) are appointive but are used as political patronage without tests for competence. Where constitutional difficulties prevent abolition of the office, deliberate duplication by modern services may be the only feasible correction.

FOUR STATES SHOW THE WAY

Four states have shown the way—Massachusetts (1877), Maryland (since 1939), Virginia (since 1946), and Rhode Island (since 1949). Massachusetts finds the distances from the laboratory no barrier these days to a prompt service which commands the respect of physicians, prosecutors, and courts, and the briefer experience of the other states is gratifying. Dr. Alan R. Moritz of Harvard Medical School contributed to setting up the sound systems of Maryland and Virginia as well as helping in abortive attempts at correction in various other states.

ADVANCES IN MEDICO-LEGAL SCIENCE

In recent years the gap between coroner standards and medical science has been widening by reason of the development of advanced methods of plucking dependable evidence from corpses. The advance has been led by the little pioneering Department of Legal Medicine at Harvard Medical School headed by Moritz and his successor as acting head, Dr. Richard Ford, and aided by Mrs. Frances G. Lee of New Hampshire, a great lady whose curious hobby has made her an authority in the field and has included construction in a shop of her own of a fine array of dioramas of murder scenes in miniature for the Department's museum to illustrate to students and police seminars the importance of sound autopsy evidence.

A recital of the modern technical medico-legal fact-finding methods accumulated and taught at Harvard would dazzle any ordinary practitioner and obviously go far beyond the resources and imagination of almost any county coroner or his best available local medical advisers.

MODEL MEDICO-LEGAL INVESTIGATIVE SYSTEM REPORT, 1951

In 1949 the National Municipal League assembled the best authorities to agree on what ought to be done with the coroners, and Dr. Richard Ford acted as chairman of the League's committee, with cooperation from the National Civil Service League on the civil service provisions, the American Judicature Society, the Criminal Law Committee of the American Bar Association, the American

Medical Association, and the newly founded American Academy of
Forensic Sciences. These became additional sponsors of the re-
sultant report, published in 1951 and called *A Model Medico-Legal
Investigative System.*[1]

The report quotes discriminately significant parts of the successful Virginia and Maryland laws but differs in some respects from
both. It (1) establishes adequately the classes of death to be inves-
tigated (to the extent of autopsy when necessary), including deaths
incidental to employment and deaths in public and private custodial
institutions; (2) creates an unpaid supervisory medico-legal commission, including ex officio members such as the attorney general,
chief of state police, and medical society officers, to establish qualifications for appointment within the system, help to rate applicants,
make regulations, and review the condition of the service; (3)
creates a chief state medico-legal investigator (salary $10,000 or
more) who must be an M.D. and pathologist, appointive from civil
service eligible list, and regional investigators similarly chosen; (4)
establishes a central state laboratory; (5) authorizes the investigator
to determine the necessity of autopsy; (6) requires the investigator
to furnish the prosecutor with records of cases requiring further
investigation (thus obviating coroner's inquest and coroner's jury
proceedings); (7) makes such records acceptable in the lower
courts without personal attendance.

The gist of it is to transfer the function to the state and thus pool
the medical business of the coroners' offices sufficiently to justify
employment of experts and keep them busy, the trivial vestigial
judicial and legal aspects of the office being abolished or transferred to the prosecutor and the courts. The current small scale of
operation in a typical county and the obscured application of the
elective process to what nowadays can and should be a highly
technical office are both incompatible with competence in this
function.

The much derided elective county coroners themselves should
welcome relief from impossible positions wherein they are vested
with highly technical duties in counties which cannot afford to provide them with the resources requisite for modern service.

[1] National Municipal League, 50¢.

Chapter XXIV

SHORTENING BALLOTS BY LENGTHENING TERMS

THE federal government, electing president and vice-president for four years, senators for six, and representatives for two, was not generally followed as to length of terms in states and cities. Until recent years there were many cases of one-year terms for mayors and councils and legislators and an array of two-year terms for governors. The short terms helped to make ballots needlessly long, brought into one ballot the task of manning two to five layers of government in a single day, led to elections in both spring and fall to secure separation of the contests, made the elective officers' burden of campaigning twice what it had to be, and kept the average tenure of office low. All this was to the detriment of work requiring an ever increasing amount of experience as governments took on heavier and increasingly technical loads.

One-year terms for some reason persist in Canadian cities—Toronto citizens have twice defeated referenda for extending them— and in other cities up there longer terms are suggested with great caution. In the United States the once common one-year term for mayor has almost completely disappeared. The 1951 *Municipal Year Book* shows only 2.4 per cent of one-year elective mayors under the mayor-and-council plan, and a good thing, too!

The two-year terms have been changing to four for governors— there are twenty-eight now. Four-year mayors, 37.6 per cent, are increasingly familiar. Montana in 1938 moved up all county officers from two years to four. One-year legislators are giving way to two-year.

Two- or four-year terms can be scheduled to bring local or state elections in off years from national elections, separating the contests to facilitate settling of each on the unconfused merits. When the Greater New York charter was written in 1898, the separation

233

of the municipal elections from state and national by putting the former into odd-numbered years was hailed as a great advance, as subsequent experience showed, although as late as 1945 Eleanor Roosevelt, in unawareness of local history, could anachronistically be persuaded to urge the election of a Democratic mayor so as to strengthen the party for the congressional election due twelve months later!

EASIER ELECTION SCHEDULES IN NEW YORK CITY

How much lengthening of terms can help toward shorter and more comprehensible ballots is exhibited in New York City since 1917. Progress there toward the adoption of the short-ballot principle has seemed glacially slow, but a backward look over thirty years shows that the continued pressure of local civic organizations has achieved important reductions in the ballot load by lengthening of terms, transfers from elective to appointive basis, and a drastic reduction in the size of the city council.

Governor, lieutenant governor, comptroller, and attorney general are now elective for four years instead of two.

Secretary of state, state treasurer, state engineer and surveyor, formerly chosen every two years, are no longer elective.

Sixty-seven assemblymen from the city are elected for two-year-instead of one-year terms.

The city council has twenty-five members elected for four years instead of seventy elected every two years.

Appointive expert sheriff, register, and medical examiner are under civil service competitive system instead of the five sheriffs, four registers, and eleven coroners, formerly elective.

Five county clerks are now appointed by the appellate divisions of the Supreme Court instead of being elective.

Thus the total elective in New York City in a four-year cycle has been brought down from 578 to 293—just about half!

The individual task which confronts each New York voter on his voting machine each year calls for selecting ten to fourteen as compared with twenty or more a generation ago. Federal, gubernatorial, and municipal elections are almost completely separated.

But ten to fourteen is still too many! Several of these on every ballot are judges, obscured by the fact that as many as thirty out of 136 such elective judges come up for election in one part of the city or another each year to divide the public's languid scrutiny. A switch to appointive judges—one-third of the city's judges are appointive already—would bring the ballots down to five in 1952, six in 1953, eight in 1954, and none in 1955.

DRIFT TOWARD FEWER ISOLATED OFFICES IN CITIES

Partly as a result of the adoptions of the council-manager plan, there is a definite and gratifying drift in the whole municipal field toward shorter ballots (Rule One) and integration (Rule Three) by transfers of isolated municipal elective officers to appointive status. In 1933 Merriam reported that "the number of elective officers in 202 cities decreased from 3118 to 2343 in the period from 1915 to 1929." [1] The 1941 *Municipal Year Book* showed that 60 per cent of all cities over 5000 population under all the forms of government were then electing one or more of such officials as auditor, treasurer, clerk, assessor, attorney. In 1951 the figure dropped to 53 per cent. [2]

---

[1] *Recent Social Trends in the United States*, President's Research Committee on Social Trends, McGraw-Hill Book Co., New York, 1933.

[2] *Public Management*, June, 1951.

Chapter XXV

PROGRESS IN INTRAPARTY ORGANIZATION

STATE and urban nominating conventions in political parties came into widespread disrepute and disfavor at the beginning of the century. They were easily and shamelessly manipulated by invisible governments, and insurgency was confronted with the mechanical obstructions of having to organize and elect delegates through numerous local unregulated caucuses which all party voters were nominally free to attend. But the party voters commonly never heard about the caucuses and did not attend. Delegates, when elected, furthermore, did not always stay faithful to the purposes of their sponsors in the course of the convention proceedings. Delegates served too briefly to be held to account—they served a single day or two and adjourned sine die. And who was to say that the rightful delegates were seated? Control of the credentials committee was often a key point and, in the great turbulent quadrennial national conventions, still is. Witness Edward J. Flynn of the Bronx, leading Democratic party figure, who candidly relates in his autobiography [1] how in the 1932 credentials committee "we decided to support (Huey) Long's slate (of delegates) because he had pledged himself to the candidacy of Roosevelt."

CONVENTION CONTROL IN WESTCHESTER, 1950

As recently as 1950 in New York, where state and judiciary conventions still survive, we have a fresh case. In Republican Westchester County (just north of the New York City line), the party leaders rather incautiously let out on February 22 the information that a certain three men would receive the party's nomination for judges in the November election. When it was remarked that the nominations would be made by conventions to be held in September following election of the delegates in the August primaries, a party

[1] Edward J. Flynn, *You're the Boss*, The Viking Press, New York, 1947.

236

leader corrected the announcement by describing the names as only "conjectures." But in August lists of proposed delegates appeared uncontested on the primary ballots, and whether they were pledged to those three candidates or not the few voters who voted in the primary had no reliable way of knowing. The delegates met and, sure enough, did vote unanimously for the men mentioned in February. The convention, ostensibly representative, democratic, and consulting, protected control by the party managers. For if the names of the three nominees had been on the primary ballot, they could have been attacked by candidates otherwise brought forward and the contest for the party's endorsement would have become a clear and relatively visible conflict with all cards on the table face up. But contra-nominations of a set of delegates pledged to rival candidates would have presented the voters with a doubled array of would-be delegates on the primary ballot, unidentified as to their allegiance, in alphabetical order. Guiding voters through that blind barrier—a barrier of faceless names different in each voting precinct —was an impossible task for any latent insurgency. And the barrier was undoubtedly set up for that very purpose.

Combined with the difficulties of unwieldiness of Westchester as a constituency (pop. 623,000) and the undebatable and secondary character of the offices, the system lost all trace of democracy.

Direct Primaries, 1910 and Since

So, going back to about 1910, a widespread spirit of insurgency turned to governmental regulation of intraparty operations and nominating procedures to simplify that battleground.

Forty-seven states (Connecticut is the exception) regulate and conduct the internal "direct primary" elections of political parties for party offices and nominees. Several varieties of direct primary exist and some states have restlessly and discontentedly tried them all. The history and the present condition of intraparty structure and methods have not been examined for decades; the latest books on the subject are black with dust.

The widespread disappointment of reformers with the direct primary as successor to the old convention system is basically due to the long ballots, which, in both final and primary elections, violate

Rule One and ask the voter more questions than he can possibly be expected to answer. The net result is not popular apathy really but unawareness and lack of information about most of the nominees and a trivial attendance at most primary elections.

For the conspicuous offices like governor or senator, however, party voters can and do express their opinions in primaries since, for these offices, they have opinions to express.

REGULATED PARTY PRIMARIES ESSENTIAL IN UNWIELDY CONSTITUENCIES

National Municipal League programs propose *nonpartisan* elections or proportional representation at the municipal and county levels and 59.4 per cent of American cities have the former, regardless of whether they operate under the mayor-and-council, the commission, or the council-manager plan. So our area for discussion of direct *party* primaries can be narrowed to the unwieldy constituencies—congressional districts, large judicial districts, metropolitan and state-wide elections. The feature of election on these levels is the great size of the constituencies in area and population. Mere size gives overwhelming advantage to permanent electioneering machines and effectively debars insurgency and improvised one-time-only organizations.

Rarely has insurgency within a party been successful in a state-wide contest; the exceptions are so scarce that they merely prove the rule. There was, as an exception, the candidacy of Gifford Pinchot for the Republican nomination for governor of Pennsylvania in 1922. Efforts to buck the machine under the 1913 primary law had failed dismally in 1914 and 1918 and Pinchot would have had scant hopes in 1922 had there not been a deep split in the regulars fighting for the crown of the late state boss, Boies Penrose. In the three-cornered contest, the weaker faction abandoned its candidates and swung in back of Pinchot. He won, 511,377 to 502,118, with 20,000 votes scattered. The Republican State Committee, elected in the same primary, three weeks later, gave Pinchot's candidate for chairman only thirty-two votes out of 114, which situation reflects how a convention would have voted and also how, despite his national eminence, he would have fared in the primary if there had been no split.[2]

So, in such unwieldy constituencies, the binopoly of the party managers in selecting party nominees is complete even for top offices of maximum natural visibility.

MODEL PRIMARY ELECTION SYSTEM

No abandonment of election at large in unwieldy constituencies like states is in prospect. We can hope for abandonment of election of *minor* state administrative offices for such constituencies. And we are attempting to mitigate the evils of binopoly by regulation of the party internal mechanisms and elections. The objective is to give insurgents a decent break. They should be released from undue difficulties in getting on the party primary ballots and from fraudulent counts. The League's Model Primary Election System [3] goes further and stipulates a short ballot for party offices in a simple structure. It follows Rhode Island's adventure dating from 1948 in letting those designated by the party officials be identified as such on the primary ballot and goes another step, as Governor Charles Evans Hughes ardently advocated a generation ago in New York, by providing a time interval after publication of the official designations by party managers during which the offerings may be scrutinized and counter-nominations may be gotten up by petition.

Finally, the model abandons the idea that American parties are parties in the English sense. In Great Britain a central nucleus writes platforms and recommends party nominees in all the parliamentary districts, thus facilitating consistency of party character and doctrine. Whether we like it or not, however, American parties are unofficial mechanical extensions of official machinery for producing election duels and majority decisions.

INTRAPARTY MECHANISMS AND BALLOTS MUST BE SIMPLE

The necessity of imposing ultra-simple structures of party government on the parties is exhibited by the condition of the Demo-

[2] "Gifford Pinchot and the Direct Primary," *National Municipal Review*, October, 1922.

[3] *Model Direct Primary Election System*, National Municipal League, New York, 1951.

cratic party in Manhattan—Tammany Hall. A group of insurgents there has recently demonstrated how party leaders empowered to draft party rules entrench themselves behind intentional complexity. The enrolled Democrats of each little voting precinct elect at the primary not one but ten or twenty county committeemen, making a total of 38,086 (in 1950) for the city (9000 attended on the exceptional occasion in 1949 when the committee did meet). There are over 1000 on the "committees" in many of the assembly districts. That duly elected thousand are notified (in so far as they *are* notified) and gather (to a fractional extent) around a motor truck on the street in front of district headquarters or elsewhere and are treated to some mumbo jumbo; a quorum is declared present, some stalwarts yell "Aye" and the district leader is declared reelected. The district leaders constitute the executive committee (in Manhattan "the Hall"), which can split districts to the disadvantage of rebels, change the rules, reject unwelcome newly elected members, control the funds, and pick nominees. And pick the slates of their successors which go unlabeled on the various precinct ballots next time! As long as the mechanism stays so complex, the committees are impregnable! In the other boroughs and in the Republican party, with a city committee of 13,397 (2000 attended in 1950), the rules are, at least, simpler than that. The Citizens Union program would substitute election of one captain and a woman co-captain from each precinct and one leader and a woman co-leader from each assembly district, letting these latter constitute the party management for operation and for submission of designees for nomination; in that simplified battleground Tammany and many a similar gang would melt away!

The story of how Tammany Hall uses its power of making party rules to entrench itself behind complexity is given in Reading F. A similar story could be told of Philadelphia, where party rules shelter the fifty-two Republican ward leaders behind 2800 committeemen.

Tammany, of course, is only one example of how the practice of letting parties make their own rules for their internal governance results in rules that protect the party managements behind deep jungles of obscuration and needless complexities of procedure wherein only the habitués and professionals know the rules. There are no field studies to provide comparisons of the realities among the states, but I dare say there are long ballots, unwieldy districts, and scatterations of power in state party structures from coast to coast, all of them ostensibly democratic and open to all comers. Individual self-seekers and gangs can filter in and gain access to great power, but a frank frontal attack based on public opinion and seeking to install new management requires more skill than can usually be found among insurgent amateurs. Primary fights are usually mere splits within experienced managements. The terrain favors the defense.

The state which undertakes to provides an honest count in the intraparty contests should go further and mow the whole jungle from the battlefield by drastic simplification of the duties laid upon the party voters so that the latter "can obtain a right understanding."

In *wieldy* districts, parties, however organized internally, are vulnerable to latent competition by insurgents if they affront their constituencies. In the *unwieldy* districts, parties and party managements are binopolies, if not monopolies, and must not be private clubs governed by their own rules; they are, in those larger constituencies, unofficial but essential mechanical extensions of the governmental structures as deeply affected with public interest as the official structures. That condition necessitates their effective regulation by law to keep their procedures not only honest and fair but simple.

Chapter XXVI

PROGRESS TOWARD PRECISION IN REPRESENTATION

IN 1857 Thomas Hare, an Englishman, devised and published the Hare plan of proportional representation. Of several such mechanisms this is the only one which has been tried in this country and is probably the best. It was at a little International Congress on Proportional Representation at the Chicago World's Fair in 1893 that a small group including John R. Commons, William Dudley Foulke, Stoughton Cooley, and others started a quarterly publication in its behalf. A few years later Robert Tyson of Toronto became the active spirit, yielding in 1913 to C. G. Hoag, University of Pennsylvania professor, who published a *P.R. Review.* It was pretty academic then. There was no promising place in the United States to fit in P.R. until the council-manager plan came along in 1912. Then P.R. had to wait again until the little council-manager movement had become strong enough not to be sunk by so novel and unfamiliar a supplement.

But in 1915 there were twenty-five council-manager charters and dozens more in sight and the idea of coupling the plan with P.R. for the council elections could be advanced as an added feature without confusing the issues.

Mr. Hoag Stops in Ashtabula

Mr. Hoag relates that in 1912, in the course of a journey to Cleveland, he found himself with a day to spare and, quite at random, made a stopover at Ashtabula, Ohio. Knowing nobody there, he walked up the street, saw the sign of the Chamber of Commerce, walked in, got the staff to listen to some talk on proportional representation, and ultimately ignited a friendly labor leader, one William E. Boynton. The latter went on to lead a successful local campaign for addition of P.R. to the council-manager plan after the latter was adopted there in 1914 but before it was due to go into effect. Professor A. R. Hatton went down from Cleveland to help and announced that Ashtabula would have the best and most advanced charter in the country if it adopted the combination, and in August, 1915, P.R. was carried at referendum.

So began a series of trials of this voting system in American cities, all of them successful but with a high mortality, as time has shown.

THE FIRST AMERICAN PROPORTIONAL REPRESENTATION ELECTION

There were seven to elect to the Ashtabula council—no wards, all members chosen at large but requiring for election only a quota instead of a plurality. There were 2972 valid votes cast in the first election and the quota was arrived at by dividing 2972 by eight (one more than the number to be elected) and raising the quotient, 371½, to the next number, 372. This unfamiliar but simple enough arithmetical formula supplied the quota, the smallest number of votes which could be won by each of seven without leaving room for an eighth, with each voter helping to elect one.

There were fourteen candidates including persons well known to be Republicans, Democrats, and a Socialist, but nomination had been by a 2 per cent petition and no party labels appeared on the ballots; the local wings of the national parties did not attempt to identify any of their fellow party members as orthodox, and party allegiances and habits were only one of the influences to which voters responded. The voters marked the names of candidates on the ballot with numbers 1-2-3 in the order of their favor, and (as in ward elections) each ballot counted for one candidate.

When the ballots were sorted according to the first choices marked thereon, one candidate, McClure, was found to have 392 whereas he needed only 372 for election, so his twenty surplus ballots were not wasted but were, as the next step, distributed to other candidates according to the second choices found marked thereon. Then the lowest tail-ender, having the least chance of election, was declared "out of the count" and all his ballots were redistributed to other candidates still in the running as the voters had, by their numbering of the candidates, instructed. As successive tail-enders were thus declared out of the count, the tallies of other candidates rose to quota until elimination of the eighth man left seven in the race and made it unnecessary to carry the sorting further—the race being over.

The resulting council was an accurate and interesting reflection of the diversities of the population: a young business manager of a department in a large store, never in politics before, a leading physician, a greenhouse man, an assistant bank cashier, a clerk-paymaster in a large ore company, a newspaperman, and a saloon-keeper. The Irish, Swedes, and Italians each were represented by one member. The Socialists elected one. Four were "wets" and three were "drys." Three were businessmen. All parts of town, all religions were duly represented. And there was a marked enhancement in the quality of the council over previous standards. It worked without any organized political intervention by politicians or citizens' association, but the result could have been improved if a group of respected citizens had gotten together to enlist as candidates and publicly sponsor the kind of persons who would never come forward unless responsibly asked.

My chronological chart at the end of this chapter condenses the subsequent history of P.R. in our country down to 1952. Other reforms have a way of staying put—cities hardly ever go back on nonpartisan elections or council-manager charters or the merit system in the civil service or shortened ballots. But P.R. greatly irritates the politicians and they come back at it unceasingly, as the chart shows.

OPPOSITION OUTCRIES

Typical opposition assertions in campaigns for repeal are:

1. "It encourages new little splinter parties to the detriment of the familiar (or as the orators say, the American) two-party system." Answer: P.R. does end the artificial repression of new party groupings and gives them for the first time equal chances. It loosens the old binopoly, letting in independents and non-subservient party members moving under their own steam to the chagrin and disconcertment of party managers. The experience, however, in Cincinnati, for instance, does not show that reduced access to power and patronage in city hall impairs the showing of the dominant party vote in state and national elections. Nowhere in the American experience has the splinter party factor hurt anybody but the poli-

ticians. If your mind flies to the circumstance that Communists with help from many non-Communists won places in the New York council in 1943 and 1945, be assured that the population (as I saw) took no trace of alarm at the time and came to no harm by what those two Communists did or said in the council. They would not have been reelected in the changed temper of the public in 1949 or thereafter if P.R. had been retained. Tammany's successful whipping up of the Communist scare to secure the repeal of P.R. in 1947 was bluster for the simple purpose of regaining (as it did) the permanent prospect of winning twenty-four out of the twenty-five seats at $5000 salary, one for each district.

2. "P.R. ruined European politics." Answer: In some countries politics were ruined indeed in the presence of—but probably not because of—another system of P.R., while some other countries (the Scandinavian, Swiss, Dutch, and Belgian, for example) fared very well. History has to be strangely distorted to support opposition to the Hare plan here, and the American municipal experience with P.R. affords no examples of calamity thereunder.

3. "P.R. foments division on religious or ethnic lines." Answer: Where's the evidence? Nonpartisan ballots, which in local elections discontinued the rather meaningless groupings of citizens around national party names, do turn the voters loose toward more meaningful allegiances. But the record in nonpartisan P.R. elections exhibits no deepening of such divisions; such divisions are always sedulously catered to by ticket makers, and leaving those pressures to resolve themselves automatically under P.R. results in greater accuracy. The mild and natural tolerance of Americans frequently has revealed itself most interestingly and unpredictably in the course of the P.R. counts; the ballots given to a Negro on first choice may go more numerously to a white than to another Negro still in the running as second choice. The Catholics or the East Siders or the Italians roam easily over the whole list with their ballot numberings. No city can be pointed to as having suffered an aggravation of such political factors under P.R.

But the Experience Has Been Good

On the other hand, P.R. in practice in about 120 American municipal elections so far has given minorities their share of seats, has prevented minorities from ever capturing a majority of the seats, has released voters from having to estimate a favorite candidate's chances to avert wasting a vote which might be helpful to a second-choice candidate, has enabled prominent figures, too independent-minded to be subservient to party managers, to run and win against party hacks, has ended gerrymandered districting scandals and saved the expense of runoff elections.

P.R. since 1915 has been included as first alternative in the National Municipal League's Model City Charter and since 1921 in the Model State Constitution for its single-house legislature. The League supports it as the ideal way to make policy-forming bodies truly representative.

The common alternative is the prevailing practice under the council-manager plan of election at large of the five (or more) members of the council. On the nonpartisan ballot, the voter is instructed to "Vote for Five"; if five do not win majorities, as in three-cornered contests, the two highest for each office go to a runoff election two weeks later. The defect of this is that a 51 per cent bloc of voters may elect all five and leave the other 49 per cent without any spokesmen at all at the council table to plead their viewpoint or watch the operations of the majority at close range. And ward elections are worse, for to a board of five, one from each ward, 51 per cent of the voters may elect all five again, or three, or only a minority of two. Such irrelevance of the outcome to the division of the people is due to the fact that wards are easily mapped to give unfair advantage to one party or another, the ideal of the plotters being to gerrymander the wards so that their adversaries will be wastefully massed in one ward while the plotters' party is producing modest but safe majorities in four wards. Such unfairness, once established, becomes a vested interest of the beneficiaries and may, and indeed often does, reverse the popular verdicts of the elections.

In New York City's Board of Aldermen chosen from single-member wards, the dominant party up to 1936 commonly elected sixty to sixty-four of the sixty-five members. Under P.R. in 1937 it polled 49.6 per cent of the votes and elected 50 per cent of the council, whereas on the same day it won 80.6 per cent of the district-elected delegation to the state assembly and 87 per cent of the district-elected delegates to the constitutional convention. In 1939, again under P.R., the dominant party won fourteen out of twenty-one seats; [1] in 1941, seventeen out of twenty-six; in 1943, ten out of seventeen; in 1945, fourteen out of twenty-three. The term having been extended to four years, there was no election in 1947. Then in 1947, taking advantage of the fact that Communists, duly labeled as such on the ballots, had won 9 per cent of the votes and elected two (9 per cent) of the members in 1945 when Russia was an ally, the dominant party assailed P.R. and got it ousted in favor of a council elected from twenty-five single-member districts. Whereupon in 1949 that party won twenty-four of the twenty-five seats, and the salaries. Thereupon New York City lost the only series of competent legislative bodies it has had in a hundred years.

USEFUL THOUGH LESS ESSENTIAL IN SMALL CITIES

In the cities below 250,000 population, with nonpartisan elections, the business of a council-manager council may not produce the sharp cleavages of public opinion, the competing schools of thought, the mustering of rival clans requiring the precision of representation which P.R. can provide. A nominating committee in putting forward a ticket or slate will need no coaching to be aware that its list must not be all Catholic or all Democratic or all employer class or all from east of the railroad tracks. Or if there be no sponsoring committee to present a balanced ticket, candidates of all self-conscious groups will come forward independently. Furthermore, the custom of councils is to let citizens beyond the rail come forward at meetings and be heard, usually in protest and sometimes with cheering groups of supporters. Such demonstrations do not represent any single minority party—there is commonly no such—but only the diverse specific opposition groups aroused by specific pending measures. Even where the town is one divided by a river, a railroad track, a racial or religious difference, an unrepresented segment is usually not being denied consideration by reason of its lack of representation nor does such a segment usually have any different or characteristic philosophy as to what ought to be done. When a

---

[1] The number of seats varied with the turnout of voters inasmuch as New York used a permanent quota of 75,000.

frankly Socialist effort in Kalamazoo in 1919 proposed municipaliz-
ing the electric light plant, the voters defeated the proposal and reelected its sponsors. In other words, true parties and doctrinal
divisions on the municipal level are not a feature of the American
scene in most cities and P.R. is left to solve the minor problems of
balancing more authoritatively the conflicts of ethnic and geographic groups whose members seek office as councilmen. But there
are many cities below the 250,000 size where P.R. can be highly
useful because they are the scenes of perennial divisions and mutual
fears or jealousies among the people, and it is always well to have
all such groups represented in due proportion to their members.

P.R. Would Solve the Unwieldy Constituency Problems of Metropolitan Cities

In large cities above 250,000 P.R. provides the only dependable
way of avoiding the sordid evils of ward systems without encountering the great partisan monopolies or binopolies characteristic of
unwieldy constituencies (Rule Two). A council of nine can be
elected in a city of a million voters by P.R.; the quota will be
$\frac{1,000,000}{9+1} + 1$ or 100,001. Any candidate getting that many ballots
will be elected; he need not set forth to get a plurality which might,
in a two-sided contest, be as much as 500,001. In New York, despite
the minor powers of its council, and the correspondingly slight
scrutiny which the contests for membership attracted, various outstanding individuals were able to get the quotas of 75,000 votes
without organization help, and others won with the support of relatively small groups, breaking into the old Democratic-Republican
binopoly even while those potent labels were being shown attached
to the candidacies of their opponents.

Even in our fifteen biggest cities there may not always be true
local parties with diverse philosophies seeking realization and de-
serving of proportional shares of the council seats. But there is always the inevitable struggle for power between the ins and the outs,
the self-servers and the good-government forces and the further
conscious or unconscious groupings of great religious, racial, and
economic clans characteristic of a cosmopolis. P.R. takes the chess

play out of politics in such situations, for the solidarity and purposeful discipline of a group do not give it any added power in such elections against an opposing group that is less united. A voter does not have to worry about wasting his vote, for if his first choice has no chance, the fact will be verified in the counting and his ballot will be passed to the rising pile of ballots supporting his second choice. Accordingly the voter can vote for a Socialist and that party will exhibit its full strength, whatever that may be, undiminished by defections of those who, in plurality elections, prefer not to waste their vote on a hopeless cause.

P.R. vs. Binopoly

To the veteran of binopoly politics—the two-party system—the fact that the situation is no longer rigged against small or new parties is disturbing. Where may not voters wander away when alternatives to the two standard parties become available? Such potential fluidity scares politicos accustomed to seeing one solid phalanx of party voters matched against another under banners that are meaningless on the local level. So in Massachusetts when a run of seven cities had adopted the Model Charter, P.R. and all, and in 1950 several more adoptions were in prospect, legislators tried to reverse those adoptions by prohibiting P.R. Finding that such intervention encountered stormy opposition in the seven cities, the legislature settled for prohibition of any more adoptions of P.R. in Massachusetts. Which may be esteemed as a compliment to P.R.!

Eire Uses P.R. in All Elections

In Eire every city, every county, and the nation itself has elected its representative body by the Hare plan of P.R. since 1922 and there are indeed no other elective officers there and no other kind of elections. They told me in Eire P.R. is secure and upheld by all parties. But the few tapers of faith in it which waver here in the vast windy spaces of our plurality politics are having a hard time because they are isolated, novel, and easily misrepresented. It takes a good deal of telling to explain the principles of P.R., especially to such as prefer not to learn. And there is no catching up with all the sneering half-truths about it which can be plausibly uttered by

A—ADOPTED BY REFERENDUM   IN EFFECT   ?—REPEAL REFERENDUM FAILED
R—REPEALED BY REFERENDUM   C—DECLARED UNCONSTITUTIONAL BY COURTS   L—BANNED BY LEGISLATURE

Cities (1915–52):

ASHTABULA, OHIO
BOULDER, COLO.
KALAMAZOO, MICH.
SACRAMENTO, CALIF.
WEST HARTFORD, CONN.
CLEVELAND, OHIO
CINCINNATI, OHIO
HAMILTON, OHIO
TOLEDO, OHIO
WHEELING, W. VA.
NEW YORK, N.Y.*
YONKERS, N.Y.
CAMBRIDGE, MASS.
LOWELL, MASS.
LONG BEACH, N.Y.
COOS BAY, ORE.
WORCESTER, MASS.
MEDFORD, MASS.
QUINCY, MASS.
REVERE, MASS.
SAUGUS, MASS.
HOPKINS, MINN.

The stormy experience of proportional representation in American cities, 1915-1951, exhibiting thirty-four attempts to repeal, of which ten succeeded. One hundred and twenty P. R. elections, including nineteen for school boards in the Massachusetts cities, had been held up to December 31, 1951.

* The 1938 repeal referendum was statewide, on a proposed constitutional amendment which would have banned the use of proportional representation in any city in New York state. It was defeated.

a politico who fears and hates it. While it remains a novelty, expounding it is as hazardous a task as expounding baseball to a hostile and derisive-minded Englishman; the latter can easily interrupt to prove in a few tart words that so complex a game could never be understood by a crowd. So P.R. spreads slowly with three steps forward and two back! Since the Irish are bright enough to use it, we are too! It has no fault but its unfamiliarity. Its virtues are mathematically provable.[2]

[2] The specialist on P.R., since Mr. Hoag's retirement, is George H. Hallett, Jr., secretary of the Proportional Representation League, which is located in the offices of the National Municipal League. *P.R.—The Key to Democracy* (pamphlet; 177 pp., 1940, with 1948 addenda) is the handiest current statement of the subject. (National Municipal League, New York.)

Chapter XXVII

DEMOCRATICS IN UNWIELDY PRIVATE CONSTITUENCIES

IN THE HUGE LABOR UNIONS

IN THE CIO and AFL groups in 1951 were fifty unions with about 12,000,000 members, the largest being the CIO United Auto Workers with about 1,200,000 and the AFL Teamsters with about 1,000,000. The total net worth of these unions, according to *Business Week* (November 19, 1949) was $339,000,000. Outside of their insurance funds, which would raise the total to about $1,000,000,000! Another 4,000,000 union members with assets in the same order of magnitude are to be found in fifty-five unions outside the CIO and AFL groups. One out of every six American adults is a union member.

Here then are vast membership organizations comparable in size of constituencies to cities like Baltimore (940,205) or Pittsburgh (673,763); larger indeed than any American city except New York, Chicago, and Philadelphia in numbers of voters (since not all the city population may vote) and larger too than the voting electorate of most of the states, violating Rule Two. Furthermore, the importance of unions to the members may well seem nearer to home and to the standard of daily living than the services of government in normal times.

The internal government of these great aggregations is set up in their constitutions defining various and not always adequate rights of the members over their local and national officers and governing boards. The members function largely through meetings rather than ballot elections, including periodic national conventions with an attendance of delegates comparable to those of national party conventions. The finances of the unions have commonly been secret from the members on the plea that employers must not be able to watch the state of the union's resources for sustaining a strike. There is no equivalent of a free and informed press for discussion of union affairs and the behavior of union officers. Finally, the members of a national union are not compactly grouped in a town but are scattered through the states and not easily reachable by insurgents seeking to oust the union management. The mechanics of democracy in a nation-wide union are thus even more difficult than those of a city or state government and may operate in greater obscurity and with less chance for investigation or independent audit.

The contests for union office invite individual self-seekers just as those for public office do. There is the same problem of securing a high percentage turnout of the members at critical meetings. There is the same possibility that a compact purposeful minority acting in self-interest to secure the salaries or the power to blackmail employers may grasp control and misuse their authority and the treasury to entrench themselves against dislodgment for decades. And alas, all such things have happened and have persisted, checked rarely by resort to the courts to repress frauds.

The challenge to public sovereignty implicit in the mere size and mobility of great unions and their grip on essential services like coal production or transportation has impelled the government to recognize the fact that what the unions do affects the public interest and justifies legal intervention; they cannot be left as mere private clubs as once they were.

Frustration of the Democratic Process

But behind the problems of how unions throw their weight in their bargains and contests with employers is the question of whether their leaders always are the true choice of the rank-and-file union members. The Taft-Hartley Act aroused great umbrage among union leaders, but Senator Taft reported receipt of private cheers from some of the rank and file who welcomed government regulation to strengthen and protect the rights of members against excesses and manipulation by their union officers. There is, for instance, the practice of the hod carriers union officials of rarely holding any elections at all (two conventions in forty-five years)! Or locally elective officials are made removable by the president (Mu-

sicians)! Or district officers in twenty of the thirty districts of the
United Mine Workers are appointed by John L. Lewis!

Among the less obvious ways in which union politicians can entrench themselves and frustrate the ostensible democratic process
of union elections are long ballots, indirectness of authority, complex divisions of authority, secretiveness as to facts and finances,
secretiveness as to membership lists and lists of locals; also the
holding of local membership meetings so frequently that members
get tired out in the effort to watch against surprise action and, by
absence from meetings, inadvertently relinquish control to con-
spiratorial and purposeful minorities such as the Communists or
other self-serving groups.

We will not linger here to try to draw up a model constitution
for a national union with, as first concern, the providing of reality
to the powers of the members and a democracy that can "democ."
But the problem of facilitating control of unions by the mass membership and preventing union managements from eluding or defy-
ing insurgency by unsportsmanlike maneuvers is of proper public
concern, and efforts to protect the rights of members by law should
recognize our Three Rules of democracy and acknowledge that
government by elected officers is not inevitably democratic unless
it is designed with full deference to the actualities of probable
voter-member behavior and information.

As a problem in political science—which gives me my license to
venture in—it is more difficult than setting up a workable government for a constituency clustered in a geographic area. In a nation-
wide union the members and locals may be widely scattered, and
who but the officers, with their interest in resisting ouster, can
know where they are? In a city the voters' list is a public document
and can be addressed by mail, or circularized by house-to-house
canvass, or shouted to in press and local radio, but these methods
will not find a union rank and file scattered through perhaps thirty
states. So a right of access needs to be established whereby any
local may demand in good season, before the annual conventions
or before elections of national officers, a list of those qualified to
vote so that they can be addressed directly on behalf of candidates
for union office or on behalf of policies or new bylaws. Independent
tellers of election are likewise logical parts of the machinery to

assure honest count. Similar provisions would give every member of a local the right to get the list of names and addresses of his fellow members and protection against being intimidated or counted out by the "ins" at the election—as in corporations, where any stockholder has the right to obtain the whole list of fellow stockholders on demand and to look to independent tellers for responsible tally of the votes and proxies!

To mitigate the clumsiness of a union's far-flung constituency, the nominating committee should be required to make known its recommendations in time for scrutiny and for the presentation of a rival ticket, as in the National Municipal League's Model Direct Primary System. There will remain the obstacle of cost in trying to reach and influence a great union constituency. The normal habit of having no contest might still handicap insurgency and make it seem like revolution unless provision were made for minorities to form and to grow peaceably if they cater successfully to some constituent sentiment from year to year. To such ends a crude system of proportional representation could be applied. For instance, let each local send two delegates to the national convention or board, each union member voting by secret ballot only for one, each of the two highest delegates to be accredited with multiple votes in the convention, e.g., one for each 100 of his home supporters.

The wholesome conditions which prevail in most trade unions are vastly important in the modern scene. The occasional ascendancy of spectacularly reckless racketeers and self-servers endangers the public as well as blackens the cause of unionism. No way can be contrived of keeping union leadership in the hands of true friends of unionism just as there is no way of automatically producing good government. All that can be done is to aim at democracy in a truly workable form with confidence that a union management vulnerable to easy correction by union rank and file will average better than that of the self-serving and arrogant leaders who sometimes clamber into power and entrench themselves by methods like those of political bosses elsewhere.

Corporation Democratics

Ostensibly the stockholders of a corporation elect the board of directors, and the directors, from their own number or otherwise, select the officers. The design of the corporation structure is old as Rome and even where it fails to work as intended there is no better structure conceivable. Protection of the stockholders against misrepresentation by their servants, the directors, is built into the structure, the redress being the annual chance to oust and replace the directors. The law fortifies the rights of stockholders by identifying the tellers of the elections, requiring certain reports, making the charter and bylaws accessible in public records, providing independent audit and penalizing favoritism between stockholders, and restraining officers, directors, and major stockholders of unregistered corporations from secret playing of the market for the stock, etc.

In a small corporation with a few stockholders the powers of the latter are adequate and are freely and effectively used. The stockholders usually include some who hold important percentages of the stock and they come to annual stockholders' meetings and vote competently and informedly even if they do not have the further frequent advantage of participation in active management. They lead minor stockholders whose interests are identical. The setup works and the management moves in consciousness that the owners of the business are actually looking over its shoulders and are capable of ousting it.

Unreality of the Democratic Process in Large Corporations

But how about the American Telephone and Telegraph Company, which in 1951 made a fuss over its millionth stockholder, and more than half of them women! Or the next largest, General Motors, with 460,000! Here is a case where Rule Two comes in—the constituency is unwieldy; mere bigness has altered the principle. To be sure, stockholders' meetings are called. Sometimes a collation is served; officers make speeches and submit to random sarcasm from odd cranks. Everybody knows that such an affair is a mere gesture devised by the public relations officer. The reality is in the bale of proxies, gathered by mail and sometimes by telephone calls to large holders, which the management has obtained and presently casts for reelection of the incumbent board. Insurgency is made barely possible by the right of any stockholder to obtain the list of stockholders and their respective holdings but the ousting thus of an administration is practically unheard of. Ordinarily in the large national corporations an assistant secretary journeys to Wilmington, Delaware, or Flemington, New Jersey, or wherever the corporation has established its legal nominal head office and, after looking around for a possible stray stockholder, gathers a few dummies, goes through a few moments of mumbo jumbo, following pre-written minutes he has brought with him, and returns. Since the stockholders almost never have any useful opinions to express, the failure of the democratic machinery to function is not too significant.

More significant is the disappearance from large American corporations of any large shareholders who can lead the smaller ones and bring to the directors' table competent creative concern of the principal owners of the business. The management may hold no more than 1 per cent of the stock, and the largest single holding anywhere, including holdings owned by trustees of financial institutions, may also be no larger than 1 per cent. Corporation officers accordingly are immune from stockholder assault and can view with polite concealed amusement the occasional sputter of letters from disappointed investors whose dividends fall below their expectations. The corporation officers and directors renew themselves in office and fill their own vacancies for decades on end. They can feather their own nests and confer handsome salaries and bonuses on themselves, and sometimes they do, but the stockholders of successful companies cheerfully turn in favorable ballots if schedules of such rewards are submitted to them for prior approval. The rareness of justified complaint from the defenseless stockholders is an outstanding fact and a remarkable one in American business history. Our great corporations serve their stockholders in complete honesty and legality. Truly independent auditors measure and report the profits. They pay their taxes correctly and in fabulous amounts. The principal deviation of managements from the desires of stockholders is in a disposition to seek to enlarge their empires toward long-range objectives, ever improving the security of salaried management behind vast reserves, immune from the yearning of typical stockholders, with a few current years to live, for immediate dividends. Intervention by government through the Securities and Exchange Commission has checked some of the maneuvers by which controlling stockholders and officers can use inside knowledge of the corporation's affairs to the relative disadvantage of casual investors in the stock market whose respective voting powers are obviously insufficient to enable them to protect themselves. Other factors than owner control via stockholders' elections keep American corporations the most effective organisms in the world: the fact that managements come into control mostly by promotion for merit, an intense and proper self-interest in the progress of the enterprise which pays their salaries and supports their future, a fierce jealous rivalry with competitors whose relative success might imperil the ship, and finally the spacious personal rewards to successful managements.

No Remedy!

I see no reason to suppose that the democratic process can be revived or made effective in big corporations with no major stockholders; only the form exists and can exist. The stockholders do have interests but they do not and cannot know each other, work with each other, or learn enough about the company's affairs to know what ought to be done. Most of them, seeking diversification of risk, are owners of stock in several corporations; they cannot be imagined as pursuing their interests into each of the annual stockholders' meetings where they are entitled to enter and doing themselves any good there. I have seen the larger turnouts of stockholders in British corporations; they only proved that the Britons hold on to fictions longer than we do, for those meetings were no more meaningful than our perfunctory ceremonies.

Breaking the big corporations into little ones would not restore the democratic process to reality nor would it benefit the stockholders if the holdings of the stock continued to be scattered in 1 per cent bits without any big stockholder with sufficient at stake to provide knowledgeable leadership. Further devices of regulation to protect stockholders may be justified from time to time but restoration of primitive conditions to provide a better field for the democratic process in corporations is not in the cards. Decadence of managements by misuse of their independence is not in sight and the democratic process would not cure it since the democratic process is crippled when the constituency is unwieldy (Rule Two) and, in this case, scattered geographically and made up of persons most of whom are unprepared by training or information to use their rights to their own benefit.

OTHER PRIVATE DEMOCRACIES

There are other big groupings—great fraternal orders, church systems—where the democratic process is depended upon under conditions that present unsolved difficulties of realistic operation. I think of the American Medical Association, serving 150,000 physicians, which has been the scene of stormy divisions of policy, the National Education Association with nearly 1,000,000 members, the American Legion, and the American Bar Association with its dues-paying membership of 44,000. Such groupings may be unaware of any inherent difficulty because the prizes of office are too small to make capture attractive to self-serving interests. They go along easily, the "ins" each year selecting their own successors, deferring to opposite opinion among the rank and file, if there be any, only because of not caring much; they could easily parry and evade and resist if they chose and insurgency could not do much about it. The constituency is unwieldy!

We need not linger here to speculate on conceivable mechanistic solutions. Our excursion from the governmental field in this chapter has been made merely to exhibit the parallel violation of Rule Two.

Chapter XXVIII

OTHER FRUSTRATIONS OF THE DEMOCRATIC PROCESS

VIOLATIONS of the Three Rules frustrate the process of making governments by elective officers responsible, but there are additional ways of bedeviling the democratic process and they must at least be listed here to complete the picture. They too are mechanistic, not moral, and help to demonstrate that our difficulties, being mechanistic, are responsive to mechanistic corrections.

Efforts to correct an unhappy political condition may be baffled, intentionally or otherwise, by needless obstacles and the long-windedness of corrective procedures. Obstructionists can be provided with a terrain in which they can almost defy popular assault since the public energy available is unlimited neither in amount nor in pertinacity. The situation appears most often when reformers bring forward projects which might be upsetting to the incumbents of public office and to their backers in the party machines. Reformers with overwhelming latent support may spend a lifetime disposing of an entrenched self-serving opposition comprising no more than 2 per cent of the electorate because the political terrain so favors the defense.

RIGID AND RESTRICTIVE STATE CONSTITUTIONS

In some states the constitutional conventions of past generations, with unjustified confidence in their foresight or in fear of progress, froze their judgments into documents which are unduly difficult to amend. Just as they overestimated the readiness of voters to concern themselves with all the contests on long ballots, they overestimated the readiness of voters to bestir themselves about future constitutional amendments. Or perhaps they were taking pains to lock up existing practices against correction.

Thus in November, 1948, 302,250 Michigan voters said yes to a proposal to call a constitutional convention whereas only 164,241 said no. But the yes vote fell short of the majority of those voting for public officers at that election required by the constitution. In Illinois and eighteen other states constitutional amendments required a two-thirds vote of all the members of each house of the legislature to submit an amendment. Furthermore, the Illinois legislature could not propose amendment of more than one article at the same session or of the same article oftener than once in four years. Thereafter ratification by the people required a majority of all those voting at the election (as distinguished by those voting on the question). Behind that barricade the Illinois constitution of 1870 remained substantially impregnable down to 1950 despite ample and visible preponderances of public opinion for amendment from time to time. One bottleneck was in the difficulty of inducing a high percentage of voters to cast any vote on amendments. This bottleneck was broken finally in 1950 in favor of a gateway amendment relaxing the restrictions. A prodigious citizen effort urged voters not to neglect to vote "the blue ballot." Voters were bombarded with letters on blue paper, Leagues of Women Voters gave "blue ballot" parties and served blueberry muffins, and in some voting precincts voters were given the separate blue ballot and sent into the voting booths to mark it and got their regular ballot only after depositing the blue one in the box. Difficulty of amendment obviously entrenches beneficiaries of existing procedures and practices whereby a self-serving minority can and does stand off majorities for decades!

States thus snagged to ancient *status quo ante* can find an ample array of good precedents in sister states where more reasonable provisions have permitted sensible readjustments from time to time; included are those states whose constitutions provide for routine submission every twenty years or so of the question of having another constitutional convention, thus getting around the reluctance of legislatures to call conventions.

Constitutions of thirteen states can be amended by initiative petition when legislatures prove resolute in slyly pocketing measures that threaten political privilege. This alternative to self-serving legislators is an urgent need and perhaps the only hope in many states. Although in one state, California, with its long detailed constitution, the device has sometimes been abused, its usefulness is abundantly established. How else can misrepresentative legislatures be dislodged from their undue grip on the control of cities and counties? How else can judges be gotten out of partisan politics? How else can we force fair apportionment or abolish one house of the legislature or cut off the sacred political tail of a state ticket?

Mal-Apportionment of Legislative Seats

State constitutions commonly require legislatures to reapportion legislative and congressional districts immediately after every federal decennial census, but the legislatures neglect to do so for thirty or forty years at a stretch and go unpenalized. An obsolete districting, failing to recognize shifts of population, becomes a vested interest for the districts which thus retain more than their share of the legislative or congressional seats. In Chicago within a few years the largest congressional district had about eight times the population of the smallest; in New York City the largest had thirteen times that of the smallest; in Philadelphia one legislative district in 1945 had 9618 population and another had 177,522! Commonly partisanship is the unabashed motivation of resistance to correction in district lines and utilizes the opportunity to entrench itself by gerrymander.

A major issue is the ancient array of rural versus urban districts. The great growth of city populations has not been accompanied by parallel growth of representation in the state legislatures and the distortion has been allowed to grow to fantastic extremes. Over-represented rural districts cling to their outdated voting power regardless of fair play. In New Jersey in 1946, where 20 per cent of the population chooses 62 per cent of the state senators, eleven senators from as little as 15 per cent of the population scattered thinly through the state's southern pine barrens successfully blocked the creation of the 1947 constitutional convention until a stipulation was attached to the legislation pledging, in effect, that this over-representation should not be corrected!

Connecticut, where reapportionment has been neglected since 1901, gives two representatives in the lower house to Colebrook with 547 population and the same to Hartford with 166,000. If the little rural towns be ranged in the upward order of their populations, their representation will provide a majority of the house before 10 per cent of the population is covered! The six smallest towns, with 2312 people, outweigh the people in the five largest cities! In New Hampshire the dwindling little community of Livermore had a right to have a state representative at least once in ten years and kept that right until in 1950 when its turn came around there were no residents left.

Such statistical inequities were devastatingly portrayed in colored graphs by the U.S. Conference of Mayors in 1948. Added up they showed that the rural 41 per cent of the United States population elects 75 per cent of the members of the state legislatures.[1]

Nor is this any mere theoretic or academic grievance! Correction of such inequality is resisted to preserve the entrenchment of the benefited political party for generations. Rural dominance in legislatures explains legislative readiness to levy on city dwellers an unfair share of the taxes and sometimes to leave the municipalities with revenues inadequate to their needs and turn a deaf ear to the pleas of their numerous and infuriated but helpless urban citizens. The cities provide disproportionately large parts of state revenues and commonly receive disproportionately small shares of state services or state aid. In Connecticut, for example, Canaan and its 555 residents pay the state about $6000 toward the state aid fund for road maintenance. The state turns around and pays Canaan $26,000 for the upkeep of its twenty-eight miles of highway. Waterbury, on the other hand, is a community about 180 times as big as Canaan with more than 200 miles of roads. Waterbury pays in upward of a million dollars toward the state aid fund. But this city, too, is entitled to get back only $26,000.

The remedy of this inequality is mechanistic, not moral; it involves getting the power to reapportion legislative and congressional districts into neutral and impartial hands instead of those of the legislative beneficiaries themselves. The Model State Constitution with its proposed single-house legislature elected by proportional representation requires only a simple mathematical distribution of more seats to districts which have grown in population and less to those which have shrunk, a task assigned to a unique officer, the

[1] *Government of the People*, U.S. Conference of Mayors, Washington, April, 1948.

secretary of legislature; district boundaries can be altered by law but gerrymander thereby is not possible under P.R. A legislature elected from single-member districts which failed to reapportion as required by the state constitution could be corrected by the governor, who is given power in the model to act when the legislature neglects a constitutional duty. In Maryland the governor reapportions one house; in Ohio, the governor, auditor, and secretary of state may apportion; in Arkansas since 1936 the function has been vested in the governor, attorney general, and secretary of state subject to compulsion and review by the state's supreme court; in California since 1942, if the legislature fails at its first session after the census, the six minor elective state officers take over the task; likewise in South Dakota since 1936 and in Texas since 1948.

All these setups are as vulnerable to self-serving political influences as the legislature is, although not necessarily to just the same influences. In the New York 1938 constitutional convention a remoter control was devised; if the legislature twice failed to reapportion, a commission, appointed two by judges in New York City where more than half the state's population lives and eight (!) by upstate judges, might submit a reapportionment at the polls. It was not passed.

Recourse to the courts on unfair or delayed legislative apportionments is ineffective; courts can mandamus executives to obey the state constitution on pain of invalidation of their acts but have always felt impotent to dictate legislation affirmatively. Hence when the courts throw out a legislative apportionment as not complying with the state constitution, the prior apportionment is left still in effect.

Congressional districts have been sometimes boldly gerrymandered by the state legislatures or left for decades in obvious inequities. The Ohio fifth district of 1951 had 167,000 population and the twenty-second had over 600,000.

Congress as judge of the election of its own members has power to stipulate that such conditions be repaired, and legislation requiring that districts vary not more than 15 per cent from an equal share of the population is under consideration; if enacted it may influence the apportionment of state legislative districts also. It can result in creation of a few districts that are awkward—very large in area with poor communications like the state-wide constituency of Nevada's single representative—but such difficulties are minor compared with apportionments which may have the effect of distorting or even reversing the verdicts of the people.

The problem of mal-apportionment is not being argued out here; it is listed to get it enumerated and remembered as being not only a scandal in itself but one of the far too common additional mechanistic frustrations of the democratic process.

When legislative imbalance thus becomes a vested interest, the only remedy may be use of the initiative; Washington in 1930 won in that way the first reapportionment since 1901.

Frustration by Remote Control

For a long time cities not only were the legal creatures of the states but were treated like conquered provinces by rural-dominated legislatures. In many states, especially the southern states, the legislative delegation from a given county will be permitted to have its way on its local bills in return for similar "courtesy" to the delegations from other counties with similar projects. Then if the legislative delegation happens to belong to a different faction or party from that controlling the local government, the former can and often does rake the latter, even to the extent of ripper bills cutting short the terms of its opponents in the local offices and naming in the law new personnel to replace them! It was done in Bradley County, Tennessee, in 1943 and again in Polk County, Tennessee, in 1951. In the latter county citizens formed a Good Government League which crusaded successfully against the long-dominant local political boss-sheriff and elected in 1948 a ticket of county officials dedicated to improving schools and roads. A ripper bill was passed by the legislature in 1951 abruptly ousting some of the new county board, board of education, and other elected officers and naming in the law their successors, including some of the candidates who had been defeated at the polls. The bill was put through by the delegation from the district which under a rotating system included at the moment no member from Polk County; the members of the delegation, being from adjoining counties, were indeed beyond reach of even ultimate political reprisal from the Polk citizens. When the officials thus imposed went to the courthouse to assume their powers, they encountered an armed and angry mob which for a time blocked their access to the offices and produced talk of calling out the militia.[2] A few weeks later the four-four tie in the board was broken by a murder which left control with the Good Government forces.

Knoxville shook off its local politicians and installed a council-manager charter in 1924. In 1937 the district's legislative delegation procured repeal of the charter without giving the local voters anything to say about it. The voters at the next opportunity sent up representatives who secured restoration of the council-manager plan in 1939 but in 1946 another delegation, despite local outcry, again procured its abolition!

Atlanta is in two counties with eight legislators; the opposition of any one of the eight could have blocked the 1951 annexations which tripled the area of the city!

Another spectacle of the same sort developed in Massachusetts in 1949–51. Cambridge, Worcester, and five other important cities adopted Plan E, a ready-made optional plan made available by state law which provided nonpartisan proportional representation elections for councils and a council-manager plan. From those cities the control of local officers by one or the other of the local wings of the national party organizations promptly dwindled out rather completely and civic organizations manifested an unprecedented ability to win successive elections. The successes threatened to cause a swift spread of the plan to other cities, including Boston. The nourishment of the old two-party setups by municipal patronage was threatened, a bill to prevent further spread of Plan E was passed, other bills to reverse its arduously won victories in the seven cities which were happily living under it appeared in the legislature, and proponents in the latter cities had to gird for battle again to elect sympathetic legislators and defend their gains.

In such states the bound volume of petty special acts of remote control will often outweigh the volume of the general laws of a session. In Alabama 68 per cent of the 1947 laws were merely local in application; in South Carolina in 1949 the percentage was 84; in Tennessee in 1946 it was 75. Accordingly an affirmative effort of public opinion must not only achieve a local victory but persist to

[2] New York *Times,* March 25, 1951.

insure a like-minded delegation to the legislature, which thus becomes a second battleground on the same issue. On the legislature itself the effect is calamitous, for each legislator, with his pocket full of private bills essential to his political standing at home, becomes the docile prisoner of the legislative leaders on major measures.

How precious to legislative politics the grip on local governments must be is illustrated by the spectacle of Pennsylvania's slippery legislatures. In 1922 the cities in a paroxysm of effort secured passage by a majority of 132,490 of an amendment granting them freedom from legislative interference and the right to write their own charters and manage their own affairs. But the amendment was not self-executing; it required implementing legislation before it could take effect. The effort which won passage of the amendment was insufficient to force suitable enabling legislation through the committees and procedural snags of two legislative houses. And despite the popular mandate, no such legislation except one measure for Philadelphia was passed in the thirty years thereafter!

There is a drift toward broader grants of power to cities by legislatures, making resort to the capitol for special enabling acts less frequent.

In twenty-three states cities have won their freedom from legislative interference by securing constitutional home rule. In seven other states where constitutions were not in the way legislatures have enacted general laws providing for local drafting and adoption of charters and/or making available ready-made optional forms. (The similar progress in releasing counties is exhibited in Chapter XX.) In such free cities—Mott counted 646 of them in 1949 [3]—and in free counties, a local constructive effort can be advanced in the local arena and will not have to be fought out all over again in the remote lobbies of the state capitol. Thus progress is less impeded, especially progress against the political beneficiaries of the *status quo,* and public opinion can get its way without mustering so much persistence against mechanistic procedural obstacles. Needless hurdles not only encumber public business; they frustrate the democratic process!

[3] Rodney L. Mott, *Home Rule for America's Cities,* American Municipal Association, Chicago, 1949.

Obsolete Local Boundaries

When factories were located in cities to be close to the labor market and workers went to live in cities so as to be close to the factory jobs, the adjustment of political boundaries to growth of population could be solved from time to time by annexation of closely contiguous areas. But since the full development of good roads, motor trucks, and automobiles enough to provide one for about every four persons, a new factory will almost invariably locate in open country, remote even from the railroad, and the workers come easily to the parking lots from a ten-mile radius, thus having a choice of home sites over 300 square miles. Hence the modern phenomenon of "urban sprawl" far beyond the reach of ordinary annexation procedures by the nucleus city.

The new settlements streak out into field and hill and woodland according to the developer's opportunity to get acreage at a bargain, without any regard to old village and township lines and without regard to the logic of water supply and sewerage engineering. The problems of serving the new congeries of population tangle with the old governments whose joint consent is needed in the economic solutions, and situations may arise where so many consents are required that even with universal good intentions progress is infinitely difficult. When a natural constituency with common problems is thus divided into units that no longer fit over common interests, the mustering of public opinion toward a purpose may become such a technical tangled task that the clumsy public is like a lion in a net. A requirement of many concurrent consents here as elsewhere is enough to defeat any contentious measure and becomes another mechanistic obstacle to the democratic process.

Another type of obsolete boundary trouble is the financial plights of areas which are unable to take good care of themselves. A case in point is Hoboken, New Jersey, a square mile of rundown, smoky working-class neighborhood amid a much larger population strung along the heights opposite Manhattan. The population of the larger area includes wealth, leadership, and education but little of those is enclosed by the obsolete lines in the middle of streets which form the outlines of Hoboken. Its per capita wealth and taxable base being low, its neighbors have no wish to annex it and spread the costs of redeeming it physically or improving its shabby political condition.

Then there are the lean-to communities that lie profitably against the boundaries of large cities separated only by an invisible legal line. Eastern Massachusetts provides an extreme case; numerous suburbs encircling congested Boston house the employers and constitute most of the high-value residential areas—spacious patches of costly homes with a high per capita taxable base, no industry, no poverty and little need for service.

MISFIT PRESS COVERAGE

A newspaper, and preferably more than one, is all but essential to the democratic process of filling the elective offices, but thousands of communities have none or none that is read by a high percentage of their inhabitants. In suburban communities, for example, most residents read only the metropolitan papers. In Greenwich, Connecticut, a community of commuters, the local five-days-a-week paper reports a circulation of 5870 in a population of 35,600, whereas in New London (pop. 30,456), beyond the orbit of metropolitan papers, the local daily reports a circulation of 19,844. A community of 5000 to 20,000 with no press of its own and mere occasional mention in the metropolitan press may be too big to substitute neighborhood acquaintance and gossip effectively for the steady stream of objective, professionally gathered information which informed voting requires. Consider the area of the Chicago metropolitan press which by a 1933 count covered 1600 governmental units with 7700 elective officials! Again the result is obscuration and a degree of frustration of the democratic process. The existent newspaper coverage thus becomes a factor to be remembered as pertinent when satisfactory territorial consolidations with effective and natural constituencies are being sought.

NOMINATION TECHNICALITIES

Obviously elective officers must not be entrenched against dislodgment by devices which encumber latent insurgency at elections. The instinct of lawmakers desirous of protecting a dominant group sometimes takes the form of establishing stiff requirements in nominating petitions. The number of signatures required to get a candidate's name on a primary or election ballot may be made unduly burdensome or almost prohibitive. To such odds add the pettifogging technicalities which law and officialdom can invent to bedevil political amateurs and invalidate signatures for wrong color of paper, abbreviation of a street name, use of an initial for a first name that was written out on the poll book, and scores of other ways wherein the election authorities can vent malice and finesse against any who threaten established power.[4] At the same times petitions for friends of the authorities may be swiftly accepted despite obvious and outstanding insufficiencies. The procedures can be made into a game for experts only and free competition for office can be mechanistically frustrated.

Petitions are a wasteful nuisance anyway. They do not represent sponsorships but only the diligence of canvassers doing dull meaningless buttonholing of the neighbors until enough names are accumulated. Boss Crump of Memphis in 1939 got up his petition for mayor in blank and filled in a candidate's name later. The cost and effort are purest waste. Election authorities in the rest of the English-speaking world—Great Britain, Canada, Australia—accept cash deposits which are returnable if the candidate proves his right to his place on the ballot by obtaining a sizable vote at the election. For the British Parliament a deposit of £150 puts the name of the nominee (without party label) on the little 5″ × 5″ official ballot (see p. 15) and the money is returned if he gets one-eighth of the total vote. In Canadian Dominion Parliament elections a nominee deposits $200, returnable if he gets half the number of votes polled for the winner.

In this country the principle has been used for some years in Detroit as an alternative to petitions, the returnable deposit being $100 for candidates for offices with $3000 or more salary. The experience has been bewildering in some respects; Detroit's local political scene is complex and bewildering anyway, with long ballots. But in 1947 the system was extended to include legislators and county officers throughout the state, the $100 deposit being returnable if the candidates run first or second.

[4] See Reading F, "How Tammany Holds Power."

BALLOT FORMS THAT INFLUENCE THE VOTING

When voters have no opinion to express, they proceed to vote nevertheless, and in the absence of other guidance a position at the head of the list is commonly alleged to be advantageous. Thus Nebraska's party primary election law of 1907 was hastily altered in 1909 "because the originally provided alphabetical arrangement of aspirants' names under each office almost caused the nomination of a few Messrs. A. . . . It was estimated that first place on the ballot for a state office was worth from 20,000 to 30,000 votes." [5] The altered law provided rotation of the candidates' names so each might have top position on an equal number of the ballots.

So, lest the Aarons get an undue advantage over the Zyggs, provision is sometimes made to rotate the names on the ballots or voting machines and give every candidate an equal chance with the voters who vote for the top name because they really have no choice. (See also Chapter IV.) But such procedure does not reach the real difficulty.

Official paper ballots or voting machine façades follow one or another of four styles of layout:

1. In the ideally fair Massachusetts office-group form (used in eighteen states in 1950) each office is named along with the candidates, each having his respective party label or labels, in a box or grouping. The voter proceeds from group to group, picking his candidate for each office. It is as easy thus to vote a split ticket as an all-Republican ticket and each candidate's name appears only once even if he exhibits more than one party endorsement. Little party emblems—"the bird with pants" or a star—are frequently authorized.

2. The Massachusetts form may be used plus a "party circle" or "party square" (Pennsylvania only) wherein one X or finger pressure votes for all the nominees of one of the parties. The voter may thus vote the straight ticket and make exceptions by also voting specifically in the office groups for nonparty candidates, with the risk that, on paper ballots, the exceptions may be overlooked by the counters. Or the voter, ignoring the party circle altogether, may vote sepa-

[5] Ralph S. Boots, "The Career of the Direct Primary in Nebraska," *National Municipal Review,* November, 1922.

rately in each office group all the way through the list. Three ways of voting, one being easier than the others!

3. The party column or party line type lists the party candidates in a straight vertical or horizontal party line. If a candidate has the support of both the principal parties the name appears on both lines and if there is a third party, or if he has the support of an independent group, it may appear again therewith. There being no separate party circle where a single mark votes the whole party column, the strict party voter puts an X opposite every name down the column but has no reason for trepidation if he wants to make an excursion into another column to benefit some candidates of the opposite party.

4. The party column or party line type plus the party circle is used in twenty-seven states. As in 2, this provides three correct ways of voting, the straight ticket circle providing the easiest way, and a candidate's name may be in more than one place if he is sponsored by more than one party.

Party managers deplore any tendency of party voters to make exceptions from the straight ticket; the party circle (2 or 4) suits them to perfection and they bitterly resist its abolition. Undoubtedly its use facilitates the count of paper ballots and the early reporting of results, for the counters can sort out the "straight" ballots and then turn to the scatteration of "split" ballots as a minor task. Next in favor with party managers comes type 3, where the ease of moving in a straight line must have some tendency to repress divergence. In New York City's voting machines (type 3) a ripple sweep of a finger across on the party line turns all the little levers of one party in a single gesture. On the other hand, getting a candidate's name on more than one party line is advantageous enough to induce minor parties to linger on far beyond their natural life and to induce managers and candidates of major parties to seek to capture them or secure their endorsement. That creates opportunity for finesse.

Regardless of the ballot form, a candidate for mayor or governor or president will often run ahead of or behind his ticket by impressive percentages. Not so the candidates for obscure minor offices like those on the tail of the state ticket; they run in lock step and, even with allowance for the fact that there must be some immeasurable neutralization of divergences from one party ticket by contra-divergences from the other, the symmetry of the returns is one of the available demonstrations that most voters have no opinions to express on those contests and have, in effect, declined to accept the assignment of scrutinizing and differentiating between the candidates.

When the Massachusetts form is adopted and split ticket voting becomes exactly as easy as straight voting, variation from the straight tickets increases and becomes more likely to affect the outcome of a close party contest.

In 1949 Ohio, with a long ballot of state and county offices, and with legislative delegations of as many as twenty-three chosen at large by counties, shifted from type 4 to the Massachusetts type (1) by constitutional amendment. The reform, long contended for, was bitterly resisted as likely to help the reelection of Senator Taft (R.) in the face of the great popularity of Governor Lausche (D.), running for reelection on the same ballot. The new ballot made it exactly as easy for Lausche supporters to vote for Taft as for his Democratic opponent. Taft's opponents disparaged the adventitiousness of the timing of this reform but could not prove that the change gave him any unfair advantage. Support of the measure came from Republicans in sections where a rising level of straight Democratic voting in state and national elections was gradually engulfing the Republican candidates for county and legislative offices. So in November, 1950, Ohio voters for the first time grunted their laborious way down through the too-long ribbon of paper to make forty or more separate X marks.

How much the vote was altered by the new form from what it would otherwise have been in that bitter election no one can be certain. In 1944 when Lausche was also running for governor, Taft ran 180,000 votes ahead of the Republican candidate for governor, whereas on the new ballot with different issues in 1950 he ran 580,000 ahead. Senator Taft himself before election thought the new ballot form might help him but was never certain of it. After his election he observed, "If I were to guess, I would think that the new ballot was responsible for something between 100,000 and 200,000 of my total majority of 430,000." [6] The totals were Taft,

---

[6] *National Municipal Review*, July, 1951.

1,642,000; Ferguson, 1,212,000. The difference attributable to the mere form of the ballot is obviously enough, on some other occasion, to frustrate a latent majority.

In that same 1950 Ohio election there was, as compared with 1946 and 1948 results, an immense increase in the falling off of the vote for minor positions, since many voters failed to mark any choices as they came to the lower lines on the long ballots. Thus in the most populous county, Cuyahoga, the lowest Democratic candidate (one of the twenty-three legislators) got 136,000 votes to the gubernatorial candidate's 237,000 in 1946, 223,000 to the latter's 304,000 in 1948, whereas in 1950 with the new ballot the low candidate with 155,000 lagged much further behind the gubernatorial candidate's 338,000. In the Republican party the corresponding lag of the bottom legislator behind the top man was 165,000 versus 212,000 in 1946, 163,000 versus 203,000 in 1948, but, with the easily split and easily partially voted new ballot of 1950, 127,000 versus 262,000 (for Taft who ran far ahead of his ticket) or versus 212,000 for the next best. Thus, by a mere ballot form in this sensitive area of voter behavior the voting for the lowest legislator compared with that for the party's best performer had been artificially held up by influence of the party circle to 58 per cent, 73 per cent, and 80 per cent but dropped to 46 per cent and 47 per cent when the party circle was removed.[7] Mere mechanism again distorting the democratic process!

GRAFT AND PATRONAGE

The secret under Cheops hid
Is that the contractor did
Pharaoh out of millions.

It is an ancient problem, but graft and simple thievery from the public purse is in most American communities the exception and a cause for shock. Tightened controls and procedures to identify wrongdoers are the effective administrative deterrent; even a bank cannot prevent a clerk from strolling out with a roll of its currency but it knows how to be certain who did it.

[7] From data kindly assembled by Ray W. Bronez, Western Reserve University.

Graft used to reward political workers and contributors at public expense and win elections is a frustration of the democratic process in addition to its other more obvious demerits.

But far commoner is the unabashed use of patronage to buttress the "ins" against the assaults of the "outs." When the party in power distributes a million dollars in municipal salaries to ward heelers as a reward for their labors in winning elections, it perverts the democratic process itself, and the opposition, grubbing for $5.00 volunteer subscriptions, is relatively crippled. The process is cumulative. Buttressed in power, the "ins" attract followers as sugar attracts flies —their party waxes rich and generous, their rivals dwindle and despair. The patronage-buttressed party may spend no more in electioneering than the "outs"; it doesn't need to, for an army of mercenaries troops out of city hall especially at election time, to ring doorbells, warm up the interest of the neighbors, and get them down to the party clubrooms for a party. Their contribution to victory is ostensibly volunteered; it does not show in campaign expenditure reports.

After seventy-five years civil service reform still has an uncompleted program. The federal government has its merit system, which covered 73 per cent of its employees in the continental United States in 1941 and 92.7 per cent of its nonmilitary employees in 1950, but there is still enough left exempt to influence elections.[8] In the forty-eight state governments employing over 1,000,000 people and paying them over $2,000,000,000 [9] only nineteen have general inclusive civil service laws. These cover 87 per cent of their employees.[10] Partial merit systems covering certain functions to satisfy stipulations of federal aid are to be seen in other states. There are still states, Oklahoma, for instance, where changes of administration bring a sweeping out of whole staffs and substitution of green new personnel of another political complexion, and the same is true of counties and cities by the hundreds. But a 1938 Gallup poll showed 88 per cent of the voters hostile to "patronage."

On the other hand, civil service reform not only has made patronage old-fashioned but has won notable specific victories. The first

---

[8] National Civil Service League bulletin, New York, January, 1951.

[9] *Book of the States, 1950–51,* Council of State Governments, Chicago.

[10] National Civil Service League, New York, 1951.

civil service constitutional amendment in New York State in 1883 still stands and 87 per cent of the state's 57,265 employees win and hold their jobs on their merits. The turnover is negligible. In New York City and its five counties with over 131,000 employees (outside the 44,000 in the schools) less than 600 are exempt; the others can do political work if they want to but they are under no serious compulsion to do so, and elections bring no earthquakes in the personnel below the bureau chiefs.

The civil service status of employees in all the states varies from 97 per cent protected to 7 per cent protected, with the country-wide average 58 per cent. Recent federal aid stipulations are responsible for a sharp increase in protection in some states. When New York City in 1942 replaced its five highly political sheriffs with the first civil service sheriff in the United States, there was one classified employee on the pay roll—a telephone operator. Soon thereafter there was only one unclassified employee, the sheriff's counsel. The patronage had been so securely in the hands of the party district leaders that they sometimes put deputies on the pay roll for sinecure service without telling the sheriff. The change took away from the dominant party nearly $1,000,000 a year in pay rolls previously utilized in compensating party committeemen. (Cf. the full story, Reading C.)

Almost daily the press in some areas gives realistic accounts like this from New Jersey:

Hudson County Sheriff Thomas F. Fleming . . . who was denied support for reelection by Mr. Kenny, began a campaign of retaliation by removing three Kenny supporters from his payroll and replacing them with men friendly to the forces that would unseat the mayor from leadership.[11]

Thus in spots public pay rolls are still used as pawns in the game of politics and, at public expense, unbalance the free play of public opinion and entrench the "ins"! The damage to the taxpayers is secondary to the fact that the practice frustrates the operation of the democratic process.

Eight ways in which the democratic elective process can be frus-

[11] New York *World Telegram,* December 13, 1950.

trated are listed in this chapter. The list is not complete, and the description given of each is merely intended to be sufficient to make the neglected point that their mechanistic faultiness impairs and betrays the proper operation of government by elective officers. Most of them have been explored fully elsewhere and are less fundamental than the frustrations which develop from violation of the Three Rules and which justify, as I hope I have demonstrated, the major emphasis they have received in this volume.

L'ENVOI

THERE stands the panorama of the program of the modern political reformer! There is no competing school of thought, no contrary program. You will find it scattered through every university textbook on government and even in high-school texts, stated with approval but with less completeness and urgency. Opposition appears only when the program encounters in specific battles the self-serving sputter of local beneficiaries of needlessly complex "democratics." But this book is the first documented statement of the whole uncontested creed.

When my *Short-Ballot Principles* was published in 1911, it related at this point that the National Short Ballot Organization had been formed with Woodrow Wilson as its president and myself as volunteer secretary to advance the "short-ballot" principle. To most people the principle had the impact of a new and convincing idea and the organization's propaganda efforts were warmly received. The efforts went on until the First World War and were then suspended. In 1920 after the older National Municipal League had committed itself to the doctrine, altered its Model Charter to the council-manager plan, enlarged its scope to include state and county government, and developed a more vigorous policy of pamphleteering and field service, the League's office was brought to New York, and the Short Ballot Organization turned over to the League its files, its stocks of pamphlets, and its dreams.

In the many years since and in the time available away from my successive business connections, I served the League irregularly and fitfully as an officer until my retirement from business in 1947. Now as "guest artist" in the League's busy office, I find opportunities to reassert with fresh evidence the theories which the League's objective model laws and lay pamphlets have faithfully pursued to abundant trials and proofs in the forty years since 1910.

Anyone interested to get into step with the efforts to advance the acceptance of the Three Rules in cities and states can join the Na-

tional Municipal League by filing his autograph (on a check for
$10.00) at 299 Broadway, New York 7, N.Y. That will bring him the
National Municipal Review each month with its reports from all
parts of the nation of local efforts and methods of combating foul
politics (1) by *frontal* attacks to turn the rascals out at election
time and (2) by *technical* attacks to improve the openness of the
battleground in the interest of ordinary citizenry by the principles
of reform subjectively explained in this book.

Objectively stated, the program of the League is to carry toward
complete coverage the council-manager plan of municipal and
county government, secure strong single-house state legislatures, reduce the needlessly numerous array of elective taxing units of government, simplify the internal organizations, as well as the tasks
(and opportunities for mischief) of political party managements,
get selection of judges now elective into official instead of private
political control, get rid of obscure elective offices everywhere and
bring the few elective offices that remain into the comparative
safety of focused public scrutiny.

These proposals are all supported by varying degrees of actual
successful trial and are further definitized in the League's pamphlet
series of models—Model State Constitution, Model County Manager
Charter, Model City Charter, Model Direct Primary Election System, Model State Civil Service Law, Proportional Representation,
Model Election Administration System, Model Registration System,
and Model State Medico-Legal Investigative System. For local campaigns for adoption of the Model City Charter the League carries
a stock of popular material ready-made for local voters and the
press, backed up by technical materials to facilitate the work of
charter revision committees and lawmakers.

In all this the objective is simplification, in confidence that when
the most intelligent, best-educated electorate in the world is thus
provided with a sound mechanism for its democratic processes, instead of with the stupidest and most unworkable system on earth,
it will, in visible self-interest, find its own way out from subjection
to self-serving, self-anointed political cliques.

By that route our children may be free!

Part III

Readings

Stories from the Civic Battle Front

A.

WE MUST KEEP BALLOT SHORT

*Survey shows that ticket makers step in
to "help" in cities where voter must vote for nine for
city council.*

By Richard S. Childs
(From *National Municipal Review,* July, 1949)

The short ballot doctrine calls for making minor offices appointive and getting the ballot down to not over five offices at any one time and place, five, according to classic opinion, being about as many candidates as a voter will select for himself without becoming blindly dependent on ready-made tickets prepared for him by interested leaders.

From the beginning the short ballot principle was advanced as an essential factor in the council-manager plan; in fact, the latter was first advanced as an application of the former. So the early council-manager charters provided for councils of five members elected at large. In most of the cities where the councils have been made larger than five proportional representation was adopted or terms were rotated or some members were chosen from wards, so that now, in fifty such cities of over 10,000 with councils of from nine to twenty, the ballot is in practically every case not over five.

The purpose of this article is to examine the experience in Fort Worth, Dallas, Long Beach (California) and Sacramento, the four council-manager cities which have been for some years off the rails of the original concept by providing for councils of nine elected at large at one time on nonpartisan ballots.

When the typical voter in these cities has faced the alphabetical list of candidates on the ballot with no party labels to guide him and the injunction to "Vote for Nine," did he have nine opinions of his own to express? Or did he, in fact, characteristically, accept proffers of complete tickets or slates, vote a straight ticket and let his power gravitate into the hands of interested ticket makers? Did candidates who were unable to get on such a ticket have much chance for election?

Now tickets are not objectionable and will exist and ought to exist as

283

features of natural leadership. As in a social club, there may properly be a nominating committee to interview logical candidates, ask them to serve, obtain their consent and sponsor their candidacy. The best citizens are properly reluctant to seek the post unasked or to advance their own claims to consideration.

The shortest ballot still requires such a nominating function for best results and in Dayton, with only three or two to elect each biennium, at least one citizens' committee has sponsored candidates every time. But when the citizens of Dayton follow, as they almost always do, the recommendations of their principal civic group, it is with a concentrated and ample scrutiny of the tiny list and the citizens' committee must cater carefully.

Such scrutiny is diluted when the voter must vote for nine and some of the nine must be mere names to many voters, requiring a pocket list, homemade or ready-made, to avert errors of recollection during the hurried moments in the voting booth.

So goes the theory!

The narratives which follow are based primarily on the news story reporting each election on the following day in the leading local daily. Quotations not otherwise attributed are from those news stories. In watching for the influence of tickets and ticket makers, observe that sometimes the nine incumbents ran as a group for reelection and constituted in effect a mutually sustaining ticket in addition to those groupings of candidates identified with sponsoring organizations. Incumbents were frequently persons who had entered the council by cooption to fill vacancies created by resignation or death.

To easterners, to whom nonpartisan ballots are less familiar, the failure of the local Democratic or Republican city committees to throw their weight, covertly or otherwise, will seem astonishing; the full news accounts of the elections in only two cases mention activity by the local wings of the national parties!

WHAT IS EXPERIENCE?

And now see the part which tickets played in these elections and how often they went intact to victory or defeat by similar votes for each candidate thereon!

FORT WORTH, TEXAS. Population in 1926, 106,000; now 268,000. In 1924 the treasury was empty and payrolls were in arrears, resulting in adoption of the council-manager plan in December of that year.

1925. Council of nine elected, consisting entirely of successful businessmen, all but one selected by the *Citizens Association* that had procured adoption of the charter. Candidates ran for Place Number 1, Place Number 2, etc.; six had one opponent each, three had none. The first manager collected $729,000 in delinquent taxes, cut expenditure for supplies by 10 to 20 per cent by centralized purchasing, and secured better paving at 20 per cent less cost.

1927. *Incumbents* all reelected. Five were unopposed; one, the mayor, barely won, 6,513 to 6,340.

1929. *Incumbents* reelected without opposition with only 700 perfunctory votes cast. Some of the nine members had entered the council by appointment by the remaining members to fill vacancies.

1931. *Incumbents* reelected without opposition, a few more than 700 votes (out of 34,400 eligible) being cast.

1933. Three or two candidates for each of the nine places. Eight *incumbents* were reelected against opposition of *Citizens Ticket* and *People's Ticket* and two *independents*. One man endorsed by both tickets beat out an incumbent. The *Telegram* in the neighboring city of Temple said editorially: "The men who were elected again are successful businessmen, all of high standing."

1935. Six candidates drafted by the *Good Government League* (friends of the charter) were elected and three of a new group called *People's Progressive League*. One incumbent was unopposed; the others had two or one opponents. The new council included seven *incumbents*. Two were elected on reckless promises of cheap gas, cheap electric lights and lower carfare.

1937. *"People's Progressive League* wrested control of the city council from the *Good Government League,* taking six of the eight contested places and unseating five incumbents. One man was endorsed by both groups and had no opposition. . . . Progressives waged their campaign on an eight-plank platform including a demand for a five cent bus fare and substantial reductions in utility rates."

George D. Fairtrace, city manager for six years, was promptly ousted. In August another city manager was ousted by five votes including those of the Good Government League members, "after he refused to recommend the reappointment of R. E. Rover as city attorney."

RECALL ELECTIONS

In December 1937 a recall election altered the balance of the council, which thereafter numbered four *Progressive Leaguers,* four *Good Government Leaguers* and the mayor who was entreated by a councilman "to join with Progressive League councilmen in voting to put future recall balloting on a *party* basis. . . . He argued that there were 'parties' in city politics and that last Friday's election was a travesty and a hoax." Council wrangles became incessant and resignations brought the council for a time down to five members.

In February 1938 deadlocks in the council and "continued turmoil since last April" were advanced as reasons for a short lived effort by a *Women's Patriotic Association* to get up a mass meeting and petition for reversion to the commission plan.

1938. In July a *Citizens Recall Committee,* making a more determined effort than the one the previous December, filed petitions for the recall of five councilmen and succeeded by a heavy vote, replacing them with a majority "pledged to non-interference with the manager . . . a good sound council." The new council members in a caucus voted "to function as originally intended under the new city manager form."

1939. About 11,000 voters turned out and reelected all nine members of the council supported by *Council Reelection Committee* "to keep the politicians out of city hall," overwhelming one to three opponents for each place described as representing the Davis *ticket,* the Crowley *ticket;* also A. J. Lee, "the only *independent* in the field."

The "chairman of the Council Reelection organization said . . . our citizens were appreciative of the splendid record made by our council in the eight months they have been in office."

1941. "City council gained a new member in a mild election that offered a sharp contrast to turbulent recalls and strong opposition tickets of recent years. H. Malvern Marks, Jr., an *'independent,'* nudged out incumbent A. B. Smith by 151 votes for the only contested post. . . . Only 2,413 votes were cast in contrast to the 1939 election that offered two complete *tickets* and drew 11,229 people to the polls."

1943. All *incumbents* reelected unopposed; 724 votes cast.

1945. A *Citizens Ticket* opposed the *incumbents* for eight of the nine places. No independents ran. All *incumbents* were reelected with votes of 6,300 to 7,210 over *Citizens Ticket* candidates whose votes ran from 3,805 to 4,655. It was noted that only in a certain twelve of the 79 ballot boxes "the voters showed a disposition to split the tickets widely giving majorities to some candidates from each group."

1947. Nine *incumbents* reelected including Marks, the independent of 1941, only four being opposed; 4,000 votes cast.

1949. The *Greater Fort Worth ticket* brought five new faces into the council; 18,039 votes cast. For one of the nine places this ticket made no endorsement but won the other eight over four other *tickets* (not all complete) by 15 to 25 per cent margins over the next best *Independent Voters Committee* candidates.

The story of Dallas is closely parallel except that the raiders lasted two terms.

DALLAS, TEXAS, population 294,000, elects to nine places. Places 1 to 6 are in six wards but candidates are selected by the voters at large. The two highest candidates in each ward in the primary go to the final election. Places 7, 8 and 9 are nominated and voted upon at large in the primary and if a candidate for any of these gets a majority, he need not run again in the finals.

1931. *"Charter Slate* Wins Election with Big Vote." "The *Citizens Charter Association ticket* for members of the first city council under the city manager plan of government were swept into office by majorities that almost approached unanimity." Light vote. Result conceded in advance. Winners 10,050 to 8,560; next highest 1,203; fifteen candidates.

The Charter Association had had long battle to secure the charter, using the initiative to pass 39 amendments, two to one. "Each of the nine men elected was drafted after the hardest effort on the part of the association leaders and their friends, agreeing to serve only through a sense of civic duty." "Efforts of the old line politicians to nominate a *ticket* against the charter group failed after numerous caucuses had been held, with most of the men sought to be nominated in opposition declaring their allegiance to the *charter's slate*. A unique feature of the campaign was the fact that none of the charter candidates made a speech nor any promise. . . . The Charter Association did not issue a platform."

1933. "Council Reelected on Majority Vote without Runoff." Eight *incumbents* and one new *Charter Association* replacement of an incumbent who refused renomination; 35 candidates. Opposition by *Home Government Association, Progressive Voters League,* and *Socialist party.* Opposition stressed failure to lower utility rates and employment of City Manager John N. Edy. "Mr. Edy was charged with hardness of heart, discourtesy, the fact that he is not a native of Dallas and that he received $16,500 salary. The 26 opposition candidates were agreed on one thing—that they would 'get rid of Edy' as their first official act." Former Mayor Tate and three others ran independently and got light vote.

1935. *"Civic Ticket* Runs Away with Election; Edy Quits Today. Complete Change in City Council is Dictum of Voters." Nine candidates of a *new group* called *Citizens Civic Association* won each of the nine places in the primary election over *Citizens Charter Association* candidates. Forty-five per cent voted three to two. Charter group and Edy, city manager for four years, showed balanced budget and depression economies in contrast to prior deficits. "Opposition kept its movements clothed in secrecy for the most part; promised repeal of new sewer tax." Civic candidates 11,952 to 10,550; Charter 9,734 to 7,723. Charter forces did not take alarm until near end of campaign.

1937. Primary election: *"Charter* and *Forward Dallas* Candidates Go into Runoff." Forty-four candidates, five for each of eight places and four for the ninth. *Citizens Charter Association* candidates led five of the groups; *Forward Dallas Association—Legion of Honor,* four. *Utility Rate Reduction League* got no places in the runoff. Light vote. The *All Dallas Association* and the *Dallas Democratic Association* also endorsed candidates. Only one candidate had endorsement of two groups.

VOTERS SEEK HELP

"Election judges caught many voters trying to enter the voting machine enclosures with cards bearing the names of candidates used in guiding them. . . . Whenever these cards were seen they were confiscated." [!] "A few voters came to polls and asked officials to tell them the names of candidates on a certain ticket so they could vote for them. . . . This wish was not complied with."

Editorial: "The implication is clear that Dallas is best satisfied with the efforts of the mayor and P. M. Brinker as a minority to close the city against the invasion of the gambler, the bookie, the slot machine and street solicitation. The responsibility of a majority of the present council for existing unsatisfactory conditions cannot be evaded."

Runoff Election. "Five *Forward Dallas* and Four *Charter* Candidates Elected." Seven incumbents including the mayor. Thirty per cent voted. "A determined fight likely will be made to unseat City Manager Moseley by leaders in the *Forward Dallas—Legion of Honor* organization." "A large number of cards bearing names of candidates were taken up by judges. Proponents of the *Forward—Legion* organization had distributed thousands of these cards and other devices to help people *vote that ticket straight.*" Both the *Charter* and the *Forward—Legion* received support from the *Utility Rate Reduction League* and the *All Dallas Association,* but "the *Dallas Democratic Association* members will begin a campaign for a referendum to revert to the commission or aldermanic form of government soon."

Editorial: "While the belligerent opponents of organized vice hold only four of the nine places on the council, they should have a more effective voice than during the last two years, when they could count regularly on only two votes."

1939. "Smashing Win Puts All *Charter* Candidates on Council." Thirty-three candidates, three or four for each place, all but five described as *"Charter," "Non-Partisan"* or *"Progressive."* Only one incumbent ran. No runoff needed. Candidates of the *Citizens Non-Partisan Association* took second place in all the council races but one. Lethargic campaign until *Non-Partisans* "began charging that the *Citizens Charter* ticket was banker-inspired and banker-controlled." The *Progressive Civic Association* "wanted a full-time mayor and councilmen elected by districts instead of from the entire city." City Manager Moseley "openly was marked for dismissal by the *Progressives*" and the *Non-Partisans* promised to oust him also. Second high man, W. B. Johnson, "was one of the charter candidates attacked by the *Non-Partisan* campaign speakers for alleged banker connections."

Editorial praised "the exceptional strength of the group of representative citizens named to the council places, the united support of the daily newspapers of Dallas, the constructive program."

1941. "Mayor and Council Reelected by Overwhelming Vote."

1943. "Dallas's Quietest Election Returns Council to Office." No opposition except a few odd write-in-votes!

1945. All *incumbents* reelected without opposition.

1947. In the primary two *Citizens Charter Association* candidates got a majority. Other seven went to runoff against *All Dallas, G. I.* and *Veterans party.* Forty-six candidates of five parties and one independent. The *All Dallas* seven faced the *Charter* seven for the runoff.

Runoff Election. Six out of the seven remaining *Charter* candidates were elected. "Dallas voters Tuesday *returned the Citizens Charter Association to power.*"

1949. "Charter Slate Wins All Nine Council Jobs." Votes ranged from 13,285 to 15,527 for *Charter* candidates, the three other candidates for each place getting from 7,344 down, and representing three other parties, namely *Dallas County Democratic Association* (frankly partisan), *Dallas Voters Association* and the *Change the Charter Association*. Two *independents* polled 1,916 and 1,254 votes. A *Times Herald* editorial referring to the appearance of the *Democratic Association* said, "For the first time in nearly 30 years, an effort to inject national politics into the city government is being made."

Two California Cities

LONG BEACH, CALIFORNIA, population 241,000. A similar chronology (which we condense) begins in 1921, with the election of the whole *ticket* of the group which had promoted the council-manager charter. In 1924 all *incumbents* who desired it were reelected by long leads. In 1927 a new group, the *Straight-Eight Ticket*, captured the city hall and their conduct led to their ousting by recall two years later. In 1930 a man who "was on none of the political *tickets*" won "as an *independent*" and with the others made a "good council" which withstood a recall attempt in 1932. In 1933, four incumbents, four opponents on a *United Citizens* ticket and an independent were elected and all were recalled next year and replaced with civic leaders who withstood a recall, three to one, the following year.

At that election, recalls and efforts to switch to other types of charter having been too frequent, the process of stirring up such attacks by small petitions was made less easy by charter amendment. In 1936 *incumbents* were easily reelected but in 1939 they were ousted, the manager was fired, and a *Solid Five* councilmen, who had campaigned together, won and won again in 1942 and 1945. Change of districts brought a special election in 1947 when the *Solid Five* were defeated by the revived *Citizens Charter Committee* whose *ticket* was reelected in 1948.

Long Beach has resort town problems which are reflected in the political turmoil yet the charter survived several attacks and its friends won eight of the fifteen elections.

SACRAMENTO, CALIFORNIA, population 120,000, puts *incumbents*, labelled as such, at the top of its nonpartisan ballot, so that they have frequently constituted in effect a *ticket*. Here is a condensed story. 1921: the freeholders who had drawn the charter elected four of the nine under proportional representation, which was declared unconstitutional before the next election. 1923 saw in the field two full *tickets* sponsored by the *Civic League* and *Good Government League* respectively and two partial tickets. The *Civic League*, friends of the charter, won eight of the nine places and in 1925 won seven.

Then in 1927 came a successful raid, the *People's Ticket* winning five places and trying vainly for two years to oust a well regarded manager who, under an unorthodox provision in the charter, could only be removed by six votes. He stuck unhappily to his post amid disorder for the next two years.

In 1929 a *Unity League* ticket, heir of the *Civic League* and friends of the charter, elected seven. In 1931, 1933, 1935 and 1937, nine *incumbents*, including some mid-term replacements, were reelected, always with *Unity League* backing. In 1939 eight *incumbents* and one *independent* were elected. In 1941 seven *incumbents* were elected and the same thing happened in 1943, although the *Unity League* had folded up. In 1945 eight *incumbents* won and five won in 1947.

A story of good government interrupted only once in 26 years!

Summary

Obviously candidates who campaign as a group with organized backing may thereby improve their chances over individuals running alone; this is true even under the very short ballot of Dayton.

Is it too invariably true when the voter must "vote for nine"?

The evidence demonstrates that tickets were a feature of the scene; when the voters did get along without them it was usually because the group of incumbents running for reelection constituted a ticket automatically. Of 477 posts—53 elections for nine offices—persons significantly called *independents* did get some but their percentage was no more than 2 per cent if *incumbents* be counted as being on *tickets*.

. . . .

Following leaders is all right if you have looked at what they offer but blind and uncritical following of even good high-minded leadership is hazardous and is not quite democracy. One-ninth of the public's scrutiny, I submit, makes too pale a spotlight on a candidate! Better not monkey with the short ballot principle!

B.
PUBLIC AWARENESS OF STATE OFFICES

In a poll, 96 per cent of Michigan voters could not name the state treasurer whom they had elected four times!

Report of the Michigan Legislative Committee on Reorganization, 1951.
Appendix XI *

Many Michigan voters, when confronted with a ballot full of little-known candidates, refuse to vote for them. Many others, it is believed, vote in these contests whether or not they are familiar with the offices to be filled or the candidates. The study on which this material is based was conducted to obtain some estimate of public acquaintance with state offices and office holders by going directly to the people concerned.

Citizen interest in and acquaintance with the lesser state executive offices have a direct bearing on state reorganization. In fact, the matter of citizen concern about these offices might well have more weight in determining how an office should be filled than the usual arguments—that an office should be *appointive* for greater administrative efficiency or *elective* because it would preserve a proper balance of power. With adequate citizen attention, the election of any official becomes feasible and significant; without that attention it becomes an empty form and a travesty on the democratic process.

Although much is written about voter fatigue and the impossible task that voters are expected to perform with our long ballots, studies with a direct approach to the subject are lacking. This investigation was intended to make a beginning by interviewing the people who render decisions at the polls. The interviewing began just seventeen days before the 1950 election, an election which, as it turned out, was to attract more voters to the polls than ever before in a non-presidential year.

METHOD

To survey the state as a whole was beyond the resources of the investigation. Therefore, a study was made of the voting records of all the

* The survey upon which this material is based was conducted by Donald S. Hecock of the Wayne University Department of Public Administration and financed by the Citizens Research Council of Michigan.

counties in recent elections in an attempt to find a barometer county, one which could be used as fairly typical of the state. A county was sought in which the percentage which the winning candidate for each statewide office received of the total vote cast for that office came within 3% of the percentage in the state as a whole. Only Bay County fulfilled the requirements, so it was chosen as the territory to survey.

For example, these election results, expressed as a percentage of the total vote, are typical:

1948	State	Bay County	1946	State	Bay County
Governor	53.4	53.9	Governor	60.2	58.3
Treasurer	49.6	49.0	Treasurer	62.6	61.0
Secy. of State	50.8	49.1	Secy. of State	62.8	60.7

While a sample of Bay County was not regarded as a sample of the state, the results here were considered to be more significant for a pilot study than they would have been in any other area.

The sample was made up of 371 interviews of which 31% were made in rural areas and 69% in the urban parts of the county—chiefly Bay City. Based upon 1948 vote, this distribution over-represented the rural interviews slightly. In that election rural voters cast 25% of the vote. There were 32 calls involving persons not at home and 16 persons who were at home refused to be interviewed. This left a total of 323 interviews which resulted in answers to part or all of the questions.

For the rural areas, a random sample of the 1,058 one mile stretches of road, as shown on the county road commission map, was chosen and one adult was interviewed in each house on the roads selected. For the City, election districts were selected by a system of random numbers. Each district was then divided into quarters and again the quadrant to be polled was selected in random fashion. Within the quadrant approximately every third house was used, leaving little discretion to the interviewer.

All of the interviews were conducted on Saturday, October 21, 1950. The key questions were questions of fact rather than opinion. These were presented together with requests for opinion in order to elicit a maximum of response and to avoid the appearance both of an election poll and a bare test of information.

RESULTS OF THE SURVEY

In order to minimize a possible feeling of frustration on the part of persons being interviewed a few questions were asked which did not have a vital relationship to the main point of the investigation and are not reported here.

The first key question was: Which one of the state offices do you know most about? Each person interviewed was given an alphabetical list: attorney general, auditor general, controller, health commissioner, highway commissioner, police commissioner, secretary of state, superintendent of public instruction, and treasurer. At a later point, to serve partially as a check on other data obtained, the question was asked "Which one of the offices do you know least about?"

In other words, each person interviewed was asked to pick the officer who was best known and least known. The table below shows the distribution of the responses among those who had opinions:

	Percentage of Responses	
	Best Known	Least Known
Highway Commissioner	26.	0.
Health Commissioner	16.3	1.6
Secretary of State	14.	4.
Police Commissioner	10.	3.
Treasurer	7.4	2.6
Attorney General	7.	9.4
Superintendent of Public Instruction	4.	13.
Auditor General	0.3	7.
Controller	0.	37.
"I don't know" or "I don't know about any of them"	15.	22.4
	100%	100%

The inverse correlation between the two sets of figures is readily noted. The fact that the highway commissioner was most generally familiar and the controller least familiar is understandable in terms of the direct services furnished to the public and publicity attached to the offices. The position of the controller had existed for only about three years.

It is to be noted that 15 to 22% apparently felt their knowledge of the offices to be so limited as to prevent them from making a choice.

Perhaps most significant, in terms of the argument advanced in favor of elected offices, is the fact that two appointed offices ranked well above four elected officers in being best known to the citizen and that one of those offices—health commissioner—was picked more often than the elected secretary of state, in spite of the publicity attaching to the latter office through administration of the motor vehicle laws. From this, the question may well be asked: "Should the health and police commissioners then be elected or should the other elected offices be filled by appointment?"

As soon as the "best known" official was indicated, each respondent was asked to tell about that office. If no answers were forthcoming, specific questions were asked as to the functions, present office holder, whether elected or appointed, how long in office, term of office and time of next election or appointment for that office. In effect this was an appraisal through the use of six standard questions of how well the respondent knew that office which he had said he knew best.

There were 228 individuals who had answers to these questions of fact. If all six items had been answered there would be a total of 1,368 answers. Actually there were 780 answers of which 553 were correct.

The percentage of those responding having one to six correct answers on the six questions about the office they said they knew best, is shown below:

Number of correct answers	1	2	3	4	5	6
Percent Responding	29.5	29.5	21	8	8.5	3.5

Again recalling that each individual was talking about only the office he said he knew best, 59% could answer only one or two of the questions and only 20% could answer more than three.

Responses to two of these substantiating questions were examined in detail—who holds the office now? And, is he elected or appointed? The results were:

	Number Choosing Each Office As Best Known	Number and Percentage Correctly Identifying Method of Selection		Number and Percentage Correctly Identifying Incumbent	
	No.	No.	%	No.	%
Highway Commissioner	79	52	66	20	25
Health Commissioner	50	23	46	0	0
Secretary of State	44	27	61	12	27
Police Commissioner	30	15	50	4	13
Treasurer	23	19	83	1	4
Attorney General	21	11	52	4	19
Supt. of Public Inst.	13	8	61	3	23
Auditor General	1	1	100	1	100
Controller	0	0	0	0	0
Totals	261	156	60	45	17

In respect to identification of present office holders, it will be recalled that the secretary of state had campaigned for the nomination for governor just a few weeks earlier. The election for highway commissioner and superintendent of public instruction was last held in April 1949 and they might be considered as being at a disadvantage in the survey because of this.

The above data also show that in identifying the incumbent in the office chosen as the one they knew most about, 73% of those who chose the secretary of state could not name the incumbent, 75% could not name the highway commissioner, 77% could not name the superintendent of public instruction, 81% could not name the attorney general and 96% could not name the treasurer, who had been in office the longest of those on the list.* From this it is interesting to conjecture what the results would have been if each person interviewed had been asked to identify the incumbents in the offices other than the one he said he knew most about!

. . . .

While this may be disheartening to those who hold elective office, it would seem to raise a serious challenge against the validity of electing officers to fill such positions on the theory that election keeps government close to and responsible to the public. It would seem to be obvious that if the general public were so uninformed about an office that not more than 10 or 15% could even name the incumbent, and two weeks before an election, an incumbent has to have only a small but solid core of followers (perhaps based on private interest?) to create a large factor in determining the outcome of an election. It also means that success to such offices is likely to be determined merely by trends in "party" popularity, influenced by national trends.

It is needless to point out that neither of these place any accent upon good performance of the specific function in question.

* Elected four times, 1943–51! R.S.C.

C.

FIRST CIVIL SERVICE SHERIFF

*New York politicians controlled the overshadowed office
of sheriff so completely that they sometimes installed
deputies without telling the sheriff!*

By Richard S. Childs

(From *National Municipal Review*, June, 1948)

McCloskey is a good traditional name for a sheriff, but the keen-eyed,
sandy-haired young sheriff of New York City is not the traditional type.
He serves in place of five former sheriffs, since he manages the errands
and mandates of the local courts in all five of the counties embraced
within New York City. In a quiet and noticeably clean carpeted office at
the top of the massive Hall of Records, he does this with obvious competence and orderly efficiency—*and* without benefit of politics. Most remarkable of all, he was selected by careful written and oral civil service
examinations from among 335 applicants—the only sheriff ever to be so
selected in the United States.

Municipal offices in New York City had moved toward efficiency and
businesslike atmosphere by steady process decades 'ago, and 99⅔ per
cent of their employees are under civil service now—out of 160,000 only
446 are exempt. But none of this progress had reached into the political
citadels and spittoon traditions of the five county sheriffs' offices before
January 1942.

Sheriffs were elective in their respective counties. The voters paid no
attention to the contests for their offices and neither did the newspapers.
So party leaders filled the obscure posts subject to perfunctory ratification at the polls as part of a long ticket.

In the days when "Al" Smith took the post in New York County, it
was paid by fees and was reported to net something like $50,000 a year
to the occupant. It was at any rate a plum if the beneficiary could avoid
dividing the proceeds too heavily with the political backers who put him
there. When fees were made payable into the city treasury, however, the
profits became deep annual deficits and political interest centered in
patronage.

In 1936 Mayor La Guardia turned his investigators into this pasture and they came back with mud galore. In cool objective detail they related that there were 100 deputy sheriffs in the five counties who handled each month an average of three papers that required any work beyond simple filing; that came to, at most, fifteen hours of work monthly to earn $2,000 to $3,000 a year. And, lest he faint from toil, each deputy in most cases had an assistant! "The assistant deputies, if they work at all," said the report, "do not need to spend more than five or ten minutes at their tasks."

Clerical payrolls were similarly loaded: a bond clerk "handles approximately ten papers per month, requiring little effort." Bookkeeping entries over 30 months were at the rate of seven per day per bookkeeper. In one division "at least 60 per cent of the employees have been unnecessary." The Bronx clerical division in 1934 and 1935 received on the average eight papers per day, a number which must have facilitated their equable division to the eight employees!

POLITICAL APPOINTMENTS RIFE

Appointments to such sinecures were commonly made by district leaders who, when their turns came, sometimes put their protégés on the payroll without even telling the sheriff; the latter did not even swear them in! Of the New York County office employees 75 per cent were party committeemen; 90 per cent in the Bronx, 68 per cent in Kings, 57 per cent in Richmond, and 39 per cent in Queens. In other words, the dominant party manned its organization thus at the taxpayers' expense and buttressed its tenure of power with 360 salaried workers.

Looking back 25 years to his younger days as an incumbent of the office, ex-Governor Smith testified: "I was sheriff myself and I was busy looking for something to do and, if it had not been for the war and the time I put in selling liberty bonds and war savings stamps and seeing the boys off, I would have had nothing to do."

Edward J. Flynn, who became Bronx sheriff in 1922, tells in his recent autobiography how the 62 exempt jobs thus placed at his disposal provided him with such a grip on the party machinery of the county that he was able to announce his intentions to elect himself county leader in defiance of all other aspirants. And this he did and, by later admittedly utilizing similar exempt places in the district attorney's office and elsewhere, made his position as boss of the Bronx impregnable for 25 years.

A constitutional amendment in 1935 . . . established a single city sheriff to be appointed from a list chosen by competitive civil service examinations. Of the 335 persons who took the written examinations about 40 qualified for the second stage oral examinations.

Under the law, the mayor had the power to choose one of the first three. He took John J. McCloskey, Jr., a lawyer then serving as deputy commissioner in the city department of investigation, and McCloskey took office on January 1, 1942.

The new sheriff's first duty was to restaff the service from new civil service eligible lists. This involved a clean sweep since, in the five sheriffs' offices, only one employee, a telephone operator, was a member of the competitive civil service and available for retention. Some of the old staff lingered to help him, but only one of the 100 deputies, despite their presumable experience, passed the civil service examinations. The requirement that they pass the same physical examination as rookie policemen was enough to discourage most of the old deputies; their ability to chin themselves on a horizontal bar was not worth exhibiting!

It took six hectic months to complete the transition to a new high grade staff. Only one member, the sheriff's counsel, is exempt, a precise reversal of the old situation. The total payroll thus abruptly lost to the political machines was nearly $1,000,000 a year.

Clerical staffs were sharply reduced. At the central office a chief accountant and a few clerks now operate the fiscal routines on a uniform basis. Under-sheriffs operate each of the five local county offices; the one in charge of the New York County office, which handles half the total business, is located next door to the sheriff and has power to act in the latter's absence.

The examinations for under-sheriff and chief deputies, limited to members of the bar, brought in experienced young lawyers of top caliber and the educational pedigrees of the five incumbents include Phi Beta Kappas, *summa cum laudes*, an M.A. degree, a doctorate of juridical science and editor of the *Columbia Law Review*. Two are graduates of Columbia Law School, two of Brooklyn Law School and one of Harvard Law School. One man who had served for twenty years as assistant counsel in the office of one of the old sheriffs, an acknowledged authority on sheriff's law, qualified for retention.

In place of the 100 deputy sheriffs who served processes, etc., a force of 49 now does the work. They include 33 with college training. Seventeen are lawyers. Comparable costs were immediately reduced $300,000 a year; a $650 cost-of-living salary raise all around has since reduced that gain. . . .

D.

500 "NON-POLITICAL" ELECTIONS

*Model Charter cities find choosing a good council needs no
selfish guidance; but high-minded leadership helps.*

By Richard S. Childs

(From *National Municipal Review*, June, 1949)

In its attempt to make life so easy for the voters that the whole mass
of them can do what they please and know what they are doing on
election day, the *Model Charter* [1] provides a "short ballot" for the election
of a small number of councilmen, whose importance is calculated to be
sufficient to attract intensive public scrutiny.

This condition facilitates the use of *nonpartisan* elections since the
voter can accumulate and carry in his head his brief list of personal
preferences and do without guidance of party names and symbols on the
ballot or voting machine. Nonpartisan elections are in use in 61 per cent
of American cities and, in the southern one-party states, the Democratic
primaries provide a similar condition in many more.

A questionnaire from the [National Municipal] League's office to newspapers, chambers of commerce and managers in January 1949 brought
replies from 48 cities of over 5,000 population which have had ten years
or more experience with the nonpartisan council-manager plan.

I

The answer to the query, "Do Republican or Democratic city committees throw their weight, officially or unofficially, openly or covertly,
despite the nonpartisan theory of the elections?", was universally "no"
with these three partial exceptions:

AUBURN, Maine, (population 19,817; plan adopted 1918): "Sometimes the
Republican or Democratic committees will take a hand in the election and endeavor to get a particular candidate to run but we believe that this is the exception rather than the rule."

DUBUQUE, Iowa, (43,892; 1920): "There was an unexpected shake-up in
the March 1948 elections. A young attorney and a filling station operator were
elected to the council with the backing of the Democratic central committee in
Dubuque County . . . the first time there was any contest."

[1] National Municipal League, 1948. 172 pp.

CLIFTON, New Jersey, (48,827; 1934): "In our last election, 1946, the Democrats did endorse and sponsor one candidate, but that situation was without precedent."

The testimony from the 45 others runs typically as follows:

MINOT, North Dakota, (16,577; 1933): "I do not believe that the Republican or Democratic organizations pay any attention whatever to the elections of city officials."

VISALIA, California, (10,363; 1923): "The Republican and Democratic committees take little if any interest in the city elections; they never express themselves publicly and since our town is only a little over 10,000 population and about evenly divided between Republicans and Democrats, the men run on their own merit and reputation for past civic service."

WATERTOWN, New York, (33,385; 1920): "It is an unheard of thing to have a Republican or Democratic city committee become interested as such in municipal elections."

II

In 22 of the 48 cities candidates usually or always just get on the ballot by petition as individuals and scramble for votes on their own initiative:

PITTSBURG, California, (10,841; 1919): "All councilmen in our city get on the ballot as individuals and scramble for votes on their own initiative. In some cases citizen groups select citizens and persuade them to run. Candidates do not get together and campaign as slates or tickets."

NACOGDOCHES, Texas, (7,538; 1932): "The candidates announce for office at their own discretion in most cases. To the best of my knowledge the practice of party or group sponsorship has never been followed in this city."

CORAL GABLES, Florida, (8,294; 1925): "Candidates merely announce and pay their qualifying fee before the final date. There are no parties and no groups sponsoring candidates. At one time there was a taxpayers association which sponsored a group of candidates but it no longer is in effect."

FORT ATKINSON, Wisconsin, (6,153; 1931): "To date no candidate has been publicly sponsored by a group or organization."

WAYCROSS, Georgia, (16,673; 1923): "In Waycross candidates announce as individual candidates in the Democratic primary, and nomination in the primary is tantamount to election. Slate of candidates is rare. Three candidates ran on an 'all for one—one for all' slate in the last primary, two years ago, and slate was defeated to the man."

MIAMI BEACH, Florida, (28,012; 1933): "Individuals who wish the honor of service on the city council and who usually have a 'cause' or two to promote, which they feel would improve conditions or correct what they consider municipal operation evils, announce their candidacies. Each conducts his own campaign, appearing before any groups who will hear him and participating in a series of rallies in various neighborhoods where local business or social groups arrange for the rally. There have been no candidates proposed by citizens groups. Since 1943 there have been no instances where candidates got together and ran as a 'ticket'; it is every man for himself."

III

The marked strength of incumbents when coming up for reelection under *Model Charter* conditions is a feature of this and other evidence. When all the incumbents seek reelection, they seem to enjoy a decided advantage, so much so that frequently no equally responsible candidates, and sometimes no candidates at all, take the field against them. The incumbents sometimes link arms and act as a team, defending each other, speaking from the same platform and letting themselves be listed together as a slate.

If a vacancy occurs in mid-term, they have power to fill the vacancy and the man thus chosen benefits by coming to the next election with the prestige of being an incumbent. Thus incumbents, filling the vacancies in their own ranks, may procure the persistent reelection of a slowly changing council in a considerable succession of uncontested or easily won perfunctory elections. These quotations illustrate the phenomenon:

SAN DIEGO, California, (362,658; 1932): "All of the city councilmen, except one, and the mayor have originally gained office by being appointed to councilmanic and mayoralty vacancies and have subsequently been elected while running as incumbents."

KALAMAZOO, Michigan, (54,097; 1918): "We have a 'slate' form of choosing candidates. As a general rule, some of the commissioners run again and they choose or ask others to 'run' with them. Labor usually puts up a candidate and may choose several of the present commissioners to serve on their 'slate.' There is an overlapping as a result."

So the evidence of this sampling is that under the conditions set up by the *Model City Charter*, nonpartisan elections are practical, voters need no partisan label and it becomes feasible for candidates and voters to transact their mutual business through ten to thirty years of biennial municipal elections without aid or intervention of political machines or even of organized leadership!

IV

However, there is evidence that in these simple and open political arenas a committee or civic association can perform high service and that in lack of it a city may elect mediocrities from a list of self-advanced mediocrities and provide the manager with dull-witted cooperation. A committee of citizens who have no private axes to grind and whose ability and selflessness are widely recognized, can under these conditions exert a wholesome influence by providing a little timely leadership. Of course, to be able to lead they must be leaders; the three tailors of Dooley Street can't do it!

The committee or the governing board of the citizens association must be of suitably mixed character, above wards and factions and beyond reproach. It can watch and review the performance of councilmen and, when election approaches, it can urge good incumbents to run again. It can single out citizens and ask them to run and engage to make the campaign easy for them by raising the campaign funds and providing experienced guidance.

The best men are unlikely to have the kind of brass it takes to seek office unasked. But a considered request from such a group is a fine compliment and able men will assent as they do when a nominating committee asks a member to be deacon of the church or treasurer of the hospital. The committee can assemble a balanced ticket and focus the good government vote on its candidates, preventing its scatteration to other good candidates, which might let in political adventurers.

The great effectiveness of a citizens committee to focus the good government vote is exhibited over 34 years by the experience of Dayton where the people have followed such leadership so consistently through eighteen successive biennial elections that committee-endorsed men have always constituted a majority of the council.*

Something of this sort is habitual or invariable in 23 of the 48 cities, and is thus described:

CITIZEN SLATES

HAYS, Kansas, (6,385; 1919): "I doubt seriously whether there has been a time when anyone has allowed his name to be placed on the ballot without more or less a promotion of a group of progressive citizens."

SAN DIEGO, California, (362,658; 1932): "In four of the six districts, alert civic-minded neighborhood organizations seek acceptable candidates, circulate petitions and finance the primary campaign. In two councilmanic districts, neighborhood interest is less evident. In these districts candidates must take more individual initiative and thus the primary campaign may be frequently lacking in civic zeal. These latter two present a city-wide civic problem because of the cosmopolitan character of the residents."

JANESVILLE, Wisconsin, (22,992; 1923): "Down through the years in Janesville very few have voluntarily submitted themselves as candidates. For the

* Reading H.

most part, the men that have served on council have done so at the insistence and inducement of a group of citizens interested in good government. In Janesville this group is called the Public Relations League. It is a voluntary group that operates without officers or memberships. In order to belong, the only requisite is to be interested in good government.

"When the time for filing for candidates comes around, any one of a number of persons may call a meeting of this group to discuss possible candidates. After the prospects have been thoroughly thrashed over, the committee will decide on certain prospects to fill the vacancies and then endeavor to induce their prospects to run. Once committed to run, the committee will back their choices with ads in the paper saying that they have been endorsed by the Public Relations League. They will also see to it that some leg work in the various wards is done for the men, if it is necessary."

. . . .

The largest of the cities reported on here is San Diego, 362,658 population. The principle alters when cities reach such size as Philadelphia or Boston for there is a limit to the area beyond which the mere size and cost of the task of conducting an effective canvass deter independents and amateurs and leave any standing army of political mercenaries with a monopoly of hopeful nominations.

SUMMARY

In the 48 medium-sized and small cities, this testimony covering over 500 elections demonstrates that politics without politicians is actually with us! It can be found in lucky cities under other types of charter too, no doubt; particularly in cities of homogeneous population like some of our suburbs and in stable old communities.

Under ideal *Model Charter* conditions the election process can run alone, it seems; that condition removes the adventitious powers of vested intrenched interests and facilitates appearance of natural leadership by making the duty and effort to lead less intolerably burdensome to capable responsible citizens who have other things to do.

Conditions in which the natural leaders of all groups who come forward to get a hospital built or to conduct a community chest drive can figure effectively in politics as candidates or sponsors are basic necessities to wholesomeness in the political scene. When such leaders neglect the new opportunities given them by the new political conditions, they are missing an opportunity to advance their towns. There can be no safety in letting the election process go without benefit of brains and leadership.

E.

NEBRASKA IDEA 15 YEARS OLD

One-house legislature no longer considered experimental;
people well satisfied with result of their pioneer move.

By Richard C. Spencer *

(From *National Municipal Review*, February, 1950)

Nebraska's experience with the unicameral legislature is now beyond
the experimental stage. The one-house system is well established and it
is possible to make a fairly accurate appraisal of its features. Seven regular biennial and three special sessions have been held. Some suggestions
for minor changes will go on the ballot in the 1950 general election, but
they do not call for any return to the two-house system.

Probably every session of any legislature pleases some people who are
affected by its enactments or by its inaction while it displeases others by
some of those same measures. Nebraska is not an exception in this respect but, regardless of expressions of disappointment at some of the
bills that become law, one does not hear now, certainly not from important political sources, any demand for reversion to two houses.

The constitutional amendment of 1934 provided merely for the abolition of the two-house legislature and the substitution of a relatively small
house of from 30 to 50 members. The size was fixed within these limits
in 1935 by the last bicameral legislature in providing for 43 districts, a
member to be elected from each, for the term beginning in 1937.

The biennial sessions were unchanged and so also were the relations
of the governor to the legislature by way of budget proposals, veto power
and the confirmation of gubernatorial appointments. The lieutenant
governor's duties as presiding officer were transferred from the old Senate
to the new body.

By statute the office of the clerk of the legislature was made permanent
and a legislative council with research and reference staff was established
to assist the legislature. These offices have been a distinct aid and the

* Dr. Spencer is professor of political science at Coe College, Cedar Rapids,
Iowa. He has taught political science at Western Reserve University and has
been visiting professor at the Universities of Cincinnati, Nebraska, and elsewhere. From 1942 to 1947 he was a government organization specialist with
the Governments Division of the U.S. Bureau of the Census.

fact that they need serve only a single house prevents confusion and waste of effort on their part.

The early accounts of the first two or three sessions of the new legislature seemed to some skeptics to be somewhat generous in praise of the new system but, in general, longer experience has proved the skeptics wrong. Some former political opponents who at first viewed the device with alarm or scorn soon became adjusted to the new idea, or even began to view it with approval or at least with some degree of optimism. A lieutenant governor who presided over the new legislature is numbered among the converts.

The 43 districts were rather equitably arranged on the basis of the population census of 1930 and, according to the 1940 census, no great change occurred to alter the picture seriously. But a further growth of the metropolitan communities could upset Nebraska's representation just as it has done in some other states. Any attempt to rearrange single-member districts, of course, could result in a gerrymander. The principal safeguard against such a contingency is that these legislators are elected on a nonpartisan basis. This nonpartisan, or "non-political," feature has been subject to some attack from partisans, at least during the earlier years, but no present proposals for change heed this criticism.

Election records show that voters are fully aware of their legislature and are interested in their representatives. Although legislative nominees do not have a prominent place on the ballot, about four-fifths of those voters appearing at general elections vote for legislative candidates. And between 80 and 90 per cent of those voting at primary elections vote for legislative candidates even though they are not on partisan sections of the ballot.

More than that, candidates elected are usually persons who have already won some local distinction, by long service on school boards or in city or county offices. A number have been presidents of their local chambers of commerce. Two-thirds or more of those elected each session have had previous experience in the legislature, some of them for a number of terms, so that Nebraska laws are not made by green legislators. Thus far there have always been a few members who had served in the former bicameral legislature.

Until now, at least, no member seems to have his district sewed up through local machine politics. Seldom are candidates without opponents, at least in the primary, and in some districts considerable rivalry develops.

Factors of Success

Internally, the factors that have contributed to the success of the unicameral legislature may be listed as: (1) knowledge of what goes on, that is, absence of the uncertainty so common under bicameral systems caused by not knowing what another chamber, its standing committees or committee chairmen or conference committees may do; (2) a bill procedure that is deliberate and democratic; (3) procedure that is clear, understandable, observable and easily reportable by the newspapers; (4) committee structure that promotes some degree of internal leadership and coordination; (5) a session that is not limited as to duration.

The preliminary examining or drafting of bills is real and not perfunctory. The rules requiring introduction of bills early in the session can be and are applied. Committees report bills only after each has a public hearing announced in the journals five days in advance and the report thereon adopted in a committee meeting held at a scheduled hour and a committee record made. A successful exposure of an attempted evasion of this rule late in the 1949 session indicates that rules on committee procedure are enforced. Newspaper reporters may attend executive sessions of committees.

The legislature itself has an adequate opportunity to debate each bill. Technical safeguards are provided so that there seems to be little opportunity to railroad a bill through, as so frequently happens in bicameral legislatures.

After the first general debate on a bill it is given a thorough review for technical accuracy, even rewritten if necessary. Then after a second consideration it is engrossed and reprinted by the same technical committee, and its draftsman, that had previously reviewed it.

Only then does it go on the calendar for final reading and passage. A bill may not be read finally for passage until at least five legislative days after having been submitted for review and two days after placement on final reading file and at least one legislative day after final printed copies have reached members' desks.

There are only eleven bill-considering committees, so that they do not get in each other's way. Their chairmen, as members of the committee on order and arrangement, prepare the daily calendar after the close of the period for free introduction of bills and thus can help coordinate committee action with the debate schedule of the house itself.

A further coordination of effort apparently is achieved through the influence of the budget committee whose chairmanship is recognized as one of the, if not the, most powerful positions in the legislature. The general appropriation bill, introduced early, comes to the floor for extended debate and amendment during the last two or three weeks of the session when the most difficult bills are in their final stages, and it is likely to be the last bill passed.

FEWER BILLS, MORE LAWS

All these things have had their effect on the total operation of the legislature. On an average the number of bills introduced in a session is about half that under the former bicameral system. The number of laws passed, however, is somewhat larger than in the bicameral legislature, but are felt by all concerned to be in better form technically and less subject to misinterpretation or to questioning as to constitutionality. As elsewhere, the number of laws needed is on the increase, also as elsewhere, most of them are corrective or amendatory of laws already on the books rather than of new substance. Regular sessions have increased in length somewhat, but this increase is less than 14 per cent, or by an average of about twelve legislative days.

The time-table of the session is rather striking. The deadline for the introduction of bills is enforced. Only seventeen bills in 1949 were introduced after the lapse of the first twenty legislative days, and a number of these were either recommended by the governor or were substitute or consolidated bills presented by committees rather than by members. The size of the job could thus be estimated early in the session.

In the 1947 session about three-fourths of the bills ultimately reported out of committee were so reported by the time the session was barely half over. Similarly, in 1949, something better than half the bills either to be passed or defeated in the session had already been disposed of when the session was half over, and about three-fourths of them were disposed of when the session was two-thirds of the way along. In general, only the difficult bills were left until late.

In striking contrast to the usual closing days of bicameral sessions, the last two weeks of the session saw only eight bills killed and 36 passed. The figures for the last week were two killed and six passed, and the only bill passed on the last day was the general appropriation bill. The number of bills on the governor's desk at the close of the session, therefore, is amazingly small compared with that usual in other states. Ordinarily the number is well under twenty.

The people of Nebraska have been well satisfied with their single-house legislature, at least until toward the close of the recent session, and they have enjoyed the distinction their state has in being unique in this particular.

There are now proposals for minor constitutional change in the system but no suggestion of returning to bicameralism.

. . . . . .

Perhaps one of the greatest assets of the Nebraska system is that operations, including those of lobbyists and members alike, are out in the open where newspapers may report them and keep the people of the state currently informed.

F.

HOW TAMMANY HOLDS POWER

*Democratic machine can smother all opposition because
New York primary laws permit party managers to barricade
themselves behind complexities.*

By Justin N. Feldman *

(From *National Municipal Review*, July, 1950)

Tammany Hall may consider the New York primary law a nuisance
but never an obstacle. The long cherished hopes of Charles Evans Hughes
which eventually developed into New York State's primary election system have been completely frustrated by failure of the law to prescribe
rules for the internal management of political parties.

How does the notorious Tammany Hall organization operate to perpetuate its control of the party's machinery despite a direct primary law?
It should be made perfectly clear at the outset that, while this story
deals with the Democratic party organization on Manhattan Island (New
York County), the techniques described and yes, even some of the in-
cidents, are often duplicated in the Republican party.

Tammany Hall is the popular name for the executive committee organization in Manhattan. Once the dominant influence over the party
organization in the entire city, Tammany has lost much of its power in
recent years because of its failure to offer any real service to the voters,
its loss of contact with the average Democratic voter for whom it pre-
sumes to speak, the emergence in the other counties within the city of
strong leaders, such as Ed Flynn in the Bronx, and the vehement de-
nunciations it has had to withstand from many respected citizens.

Still, it is Tammany Hall which, by controlling the party machinery,
designates the party's candidates for public office. It is Tammany which
sends large delegations to the all-important state and national nominating conventions. It is Tammany which dispenses whatever city, state

---

* Mr. Feldman, a New York lawyer, is a member of the new Manhattan
intraparty group known as the Fair Deal Democrats. Long active in public
affairs, he was formerly chairman of the speaker's bureau of the Democratic
State Committee and director of veteran affairs of the American Veterans
Committee.

and federal patronage falls to the Democrats. And it is Tammany which, under the election law, is authorized to make the rules by which the party in Manhattan is governed.

In Manhattan the Democratic vote regularly exceeds that of the Republican party. In most areas of the island a victory in the Democratic primary is tantamount to election. As less than 10 per cent of the Democrats in any given area of Manhattan ever vote in even the most hotly contested primary, Tammany, capitalizing on apathy, on its control of the machinery and on the obstacles it knows how to put in the way of insurgents, rules the roost.

Manhattan has sixteen assembly districts, each of which elects a representative to the lower house of the legislature. Each assembly district is divided into election districts (voting precincts) on the basis of the number of registered voters in the area. The number of election districts varies from 28 in the fourteenth assembly district to 105 in the fifth. The boundaries of the various assembly districts and of the election districts are set by the city council, which is commonly controlled by the Democratic party, and Tammany can thereby gerrymander the boundaries to suit its own convenience.

DISTRICT LEADERS

Each of Manhattan's sixteen assembly districts has one vote in the party's executive committee and is represented there by at least one district leader and a woman co-leader, sometimes more. The co-leader is entitled to divide the district's vote and cast her portion as she likes but by force of long tradition she usually remains in the background and exercises her vote in accordance with the wishes of her leader. The value of the district's vote on this executive committee depends further upon the number of leaders there are from that particular district. For the number of leaders and co-leaders who will be recognized and entitled to sit on this party executive committee with fractional votes is determined, not by statute or by the enrolled Democrats or by the geographical size or party registration of the assembly district, but by the whim or the carefully calculated design of the executive committee itself.

Most of the assembly districts in Manhattan have thus been carefully subdivided by the executive committee to the advantage of its veteran members. An assembly district may be represented on the executive committee or "in the Hall" by two, three or even seven district leaders and an equal number of co-leaders. The assembly district in which I reside, for example, has seven leaders and seven co-leaders on the Tammany executive committee; each of these leaders and co-leaders is entitled to $\frac{1}{14}$th of a vote.

The leader is an extremely important person. Aside from his county-wide power as a member of "the Hall," he helps control nominations in "his" county subdivisions which elect assemblymen, state senators, congressmen and certain judges.

But how is this key leader (executive committee member) chosen? In other counties of greater New York, Democratic district leaders are elected by the voters direct; likewise in other parties. But to make boss control of the party easier in Manhattan, the leader is not voted for in a party primary directly by the voters but is selected by the members of the county committee in his portion of the assembly district.

Now, let's look at this county committee. It is a massive barrier. By state law two county committeemen must be elected from each little election district. The party may by its rules provide such additional memberships on the county committee as its chairman deems desirable, so long as the additional membership for each election district is kept in proportion to the party vote for governor in the last gubernatorial race. So each election district in Manhattan elects some ten to twenty committeemen. The number of committeemen in each assembly district consequently comes to 1,125 or more! [1]

Most of the members of the county committee are friends and relatives of the party's election district captains (whom the leader appoints) and don't even know they are on the committee, much less what its function and power may be.

RAILROADED ACTION

In calling a meeting of the county committee members in his part of the assembly district, it is not uncommon for the leader to notify only those persons whom he knows to be friendly. Tammany Hall appoints the temporary chairman and secretary of the meeting. A script is prepared in advance and distributed to the "actors" who have been given particular parts for the evening. The chairman, working from a copy of his script, will only recognize those persons whose names appear on it although scores of other voters howl concertedly for a chance to speak or nominate. Often the meetings are held on the street. A truck is backed up in front of the local district club house. Passers-by are treated to a routine bit of mumbo-jumbo from the chairman on the truck. The stalwart Tammany committeemen who are present rubberstamp the top command's choice for leader. Who can prove that there, in the open air, no quorum of county committeemen was present?

[1] The whole county has about 20,000 county committeemen. Except for one occasion in 1933, however, no meeting of the entire county committee has ever been attended by more than 500 persons.

An insurgent seeking to elect sufficient county committeemen pledged to support him for leader has an almost insuperable task confronting him.

He must print and circulate nominating petitions bearing the names of a different slate of county committeemen for each little election district. If a name is misspelled on the petition, or if the signer uses an initial in signing instead of his full given name, or if the color of the petition differs in tint from the prescribed shade, or if the petition sheet uses an abbreviation in the name of an avenue or street, or if any one of several hundred pitfalls which have been read into the direct primary law are not avoided, the petitions will be whittled down and voided by the Board of Elections.

Under New York State law the Board of Elections is composed of four commissioners, two designated by the Democratic executive committees for the counties of New York and Kings (Brooklyn) and two by the Republicans. In all internal fights whereby the control of the dominant factions of the "regular" organizations is threatened, one hand very definitely washes the other.

If the insurgent candidate for leader succeeds nevertheless in getting his slates on the ballots, he must deal with the further difficulty that his name does not appear anywhere on the ballots, and the task of informing even an aroused electorate, so that they may pick out his ten or twenty supporters on the primary ballot, is extremely difficult.

Now, assume—if you can—that you have succeeded in electing a majority of the county committee in your bailiwick! Isn't that enough? Won't your candidate then be duly elected by the committeemen who have thus been pledged to vote for him? Surely if Tammany in calling the meeting has notified all of the persons entitled to attend, and if the persons whom you have elected attend, and if the Tammany-appointed chairman of the meeting acts fairly, and if the Tammany-appointed secretary of the meeting counts the votes accurately, and if the police repulse Tammany attempts to pack the meeting, you will elect the district leader? Oh no! Not so simple! There are many other obstacles which Tammany may put in your way. They may do any of the following under the rules they have set up since the law empowers them to concoct their own rules:

You Can't Win!

Suppose you run a candidate for district leader in an assembly district which contains 99 election districts. There have always been three leaders in that district and the fellow you are anxious to oust is in charge of election districts 1 through 33. You file your petitions for those districts.

You elect your slates for county committeemen in twenty of the 33 districts and are feeling pretty secure about the prospective meeting of the county committeemen when called to select the leader.

Tammany, however, has the right to decide *after* the primary that the man you opposed will now govern only thirteen safe districts and the remaining twenty, wherein you were successful, will be added to the territory of the fellow who previously had the 33 adjoining election districts numbered 34 to 66. You now control only twenty districts out of the revised group of 53!

Under Tammany rules, the executive committee—that is, the other leaders—may sit as judge of the qualifications of its own members and may veto the choice made by the county committeemen and substitute a man of their own selection. And this decision, again under the rules, may be made by the outgoing executive committee on which the leader you opposed is entitled to vote.

But this is not all. They have other devices! In 1947 a group of Democrats in the fifteenth assembly district organized to elect a district leader. After a hard and bitter fight waged against a leader who had been in control of that particular district for fourteen years, they elected a majority of county committeemen. Through the use of pressure on other party leaders they were able to get acceptance for their choice by the executive committee.

Some months later, however, the Tammany county leader, chairman of both the county committee and its executive committee, called a meeting of the county committeemen of that assembly district and, accompanied by some of his strong-arm men, attended this meeting which was chaired by his designee. When he walked in, he distributed copies of a script for the meeting to his accomplices and the meeting went off like a well rehearsed radio program.

Following a line by line recital of the script, the assembly district, which had heretofore had only one district leader casting a full vote in the councils of the executive committee, was declared split. A second district leader was selected—someone whom nobody in the district had heard of. The meeting was declared adjourned and the master light switch was pulled so that the meeting could not continue and objectors could not be heard.

A new henchman of the dominant faction of Tammany had been installed and from that time forward the leader chosen by the county committeemen of the district no longer enjoyed a full vote in the executive committee but was relegated to a half vote, offset, of course, by the half vote of the newcomer.

TRICKS OF THE TRADE

In the 1949 primary an insurgent candidate in the first assembly district filed petitions in the election districts covered by two incumbent Tammany leaders. He won a majority of the election districts in one portion of the assembly district, but not in the second. When the meeting of the county committee was called, he found that it was a combined meeting of both portions of the district and the majority he had in one section was completely swallowed up in the larger meeting.

There being sixteen assembly districts, one might think there would be a total of sixteen votes on the executive committee. But the chairman of the executive committee has an additional vote by virtue of his office. He has the further right to appoint—and remove—three sub-committee chairmen each of whom may cast a full vote in addition to his vote as a district leader. In this way the chairman controls four votes out of twenty.

All these extremely undemocratic methods are the result of a direct primary law which allows the party executive committee to make its own rules—rules that thus fortify tight clique control. It is in this way that a coterie of political leaders in Manhattan is able to frustrate insurgency, hold power for generations and select its successors. Those who are concerned with political and democratic techniques must turn their attention and that of the public to the important problem of ensuring democracy in the internal structure and machinery of parties.

G.

SELECTION OF JUDGES—THE FICTION OF MAJORITY ELECTION

Testimony that no elective process has worked well with judges.

By George E. Brand *

(Excerpt from *Journal of the American Judicature Society*, February, 1951)

Some years ago when control of the county *convention* in my county of Wayne was notorious, I undertook a study of county political party conventions in Michigan to ascertain the extent that electors in the rural areas participated in the selection of county delegates who, in turn, selected the delegates to the state convention.

In many of the upstate counties the county convention delegates ballot was a blank sheet on which only a few voters, haphazardly, wrote their choice. Their vote was hopelessly scattered. Any handful of voters acting in concert controlled the election of delegates. In other counties the politicians handed out a printed slate of names of delegates to be pasted on the blank ballot. Relatively few voters even then took the trouble to vote for delegates. In one county where the total vote for governor was 751, only a total of 63 votes were cast for all of the delegates. In a village casting 48 votes for governor on one ticket, 6 votes elected the delegate. On the other ticket 91 votes were cast for governor but 7 votes elected the delegate. This was not because many names were voted for— but because very few voted for delegates. In one rural township casting 41 votes two persons received votes for delegate. One received 2 votes and the other 1. (His wife should also have voted, or did she?)

Next, as to direct primaries:

Dissatisfaction with the *direct primary* as a means of judicial nomination has been pronounced in many of the states. I quote an appraisement made by the late President, William Howard Taft, that still holds true:

> . . . I affirm without hesitation that in states where many of the elected judges in the past have had high rank, the introduction of nomination by direct primary has distinctly injured the character of the Bench for learning, courage

---

* Past President, State Bar of Michigan.

and ability. The nomination and election of a judge are now to be the result of his own activity and of fortuitous circumstances.[1]

The reasons for this are not hard to find, nor do they pertain to any one state.

Detroit, located in Wayne County, has 18 circuit judges—elected at the same time. Following the landslide of 1932, the prospects for replacement of at least some of the 16 Republican incumbent circuit judges, by Democrats, seemed to be unusually bright. In the 1934 primary election there were 39 candidates on the Republican ticket for the 18 judgeships and 181 on the Democratic ticket, total 220.

Stuart H. Perry [2] has vividly described the melee of electioneering and publicity resorted to. Most of the candidates were unknown to the voters. Almost every billboard in the city was purchased by the candidates. Many of these displays reflected unethical and unfair statements and devices. Two brothers, both candidates, pledged, on billboards and in distributed literature, to remit $43,200 of their salaries, if elected. Another promised each day to give free legal advice to the public. Another promised a liberal construction of the law in keeping with the ideals of the New Deal. One advertised "Succeed with Successful Steiner." Another billboard ad portrayed a man evicted from his home as a preface to the assurance that such eviction would not have occurred had a named candidate been in office. Another candidate was accompanied to political meetings by barelegged girls in stage dress who distributed his cards. When the primary was run off it was found that 8 or 9 of the 18 Democratic nominees were of one racial-bloc-group. Few, if any, of the candidates previously endorsed on that ticket by the bar associations and the press were nominated. Fortunately, through an organized resistance, the attempt to raid the court failed, but what of the ordeal to which the incumbents were subjected by the aspirants? Michigan then resorted to the separate, nonpartisan judicial ballot at both primary and general elections as to county judges.

THE NONPARTISAN BALLOT

Next, as to *nonpartisan* elections:

That the direct party primary method was unsatisfactory may also be assumed from the adoption, in the last 30 years, of the nonpartisan plan in so many states.

Montana's experience with the separate nonpartisan judicial ballot is

[1] 38 A.B.A. Rep. 418, 422 (1913).
[2] *Annals of the American Academy of Political and Social Science,* September, 1935; *Journal of the American Judicature Society,* October, 1935.

interesting. It developed that many of the voters failed to vote on the separate judicial ballot. Consequently, in 1937, the law was changed so that a nonpartisan column was provided on the main ballot. Even this arrangement appears to have been unsatisfactory.

I think it is generally true throughout the country that the votes cast for governor at a general election greatly exceed those cast for judicial officers. I sampled the vote in Michigan in 1942 when the two persons were listed on a separate nonpartisan judicial ballot as contenders for the office of justice of the Supreme Court. A total of 1,193,555 votes were cast for the office of governor, as against a total of 660,302 for the judicial office. In other words only 55% of the voters who voted for governor voted for the high judicial office.

I have been furnished the figures showing that in 1944 a total of 538,896 votes were cast for governor in Nebraska as against a total of 445,184 for chief justice. Thus the vote for the Nebraska judicial office was about 83% of the vote for governor, and appears to be well above the average.

Pennsylvania adopted the nonpartisan plan of nomination and election in 1913. However, it was unsatisfactory and was repealed in 1921. Since then the Pennsylvania judges have been nominated and elected on party tickets.

Dissatisfaction with the Ohio nonpartisan plan adopted in 1911 could not be more authoritatively established than by the following statement by the late Honorable Newton D. Baker. In 1934 during a symposium on judicial selection,[3] Mr. Baker said:

Just before Senator Burton died, I happened to call on him in his apartment at Washington. He was very mellow. He knew he was approaching the end of a very long and very illustrious and useful public life. He had come to a time when he was very much more interested in making a political testament than he was in acquiring further distinction, and the reports I got of those who called on him at that time were that he loved to distill his experience and his observations for the benefit, particularly, of younger men who came to him as a sage for advice. In the course of the conversation he said to me: "Baker, you and I together drew the nonpartisan primary law in Ohio. Do you think we did the people of Ohio a service?" And I said to him: "No, Senator, I regret to say I think we did them a very great dis-service." He said to me: "Baker, I regard that as the most vitally wrong public act of my long career." And I was under no need of asking him why. I could see what was going on.

[3] *University of Cincinnati Law Review*, November, 1935; *Journal of the American Judicature Society*, October, 1942.

What Mr. Baker was referring to and what we know to be the picture was stated some years ago by Raymond Moley.[4] He said:

More recent attempts to keep out party politics by a nonpartisan ballot have roused the dogs of another kind of politics. Appeal to the people by a judge of anything except a very high court means appeal to race, religion and other political irrelevancies. It means cheap stunts for gaining publicity and slavery to the news-gathering exigencies of the city desk. This may be called politics of nonpartisanship. With every judge his own political leader, his ear must be to the ground constantly, instead of, as under the old system, at those fortunately infrequent moments when the oracular voice of the boss rumbled a veiled request or an unspoken order.

With obvious sketchiness I have touched upon the elective methods. I eliminate convention nomination as a basis of any improvement. I am satisfied that the nonpartisan feature has not cured the defects implicit in the elective system. It cannot be denied that the nonpartisan primary has multiplied the number of self-starters who plague an already vexed public in its efforts to secure the right kind of judicial timber. The nonpartisan primary has sheared off the responsibility of political party sponsorship and has left the judiciary without protection from the pernicious influences of private, individual and personal politics.

[4] Raymond Moley, *Tribunes of the People,* 1932, p. 247.

H.

IT'S A HABIT NOW IN DAYTON

*The pioneer council-manager city exhibits 40 years of
unbroken good government.*

By Richard S. Childs

(From *National Municipal Review*, September, 1948)

Dayton in 1913 was the first city of over 8,000 population to adopt
the council-manager plan. Its elected council of five (still called commission) acts as a board of directors, meeting once a week to sponsor and
oversee the city manager, who coordinates and directs all other municipal
employees.

. . . .

Dayton conducts other elections on the same day, however, choosing
three—or four—members of the school board and municipal judges, using
several separate paper ballots. Thus in 1945 there were four little ballots
covering twenty offices, including one for three city commissioners. Of
these offices the commissioners usually, but not invariably, attract the
heaviest vote, in accordance with their relative powers and importance.
The theory of the short ballot thus does not get ideal play; the candidates
for the commission are less solitary and conspicuous than the plan of
government is intended to provide.

In Dayton's history contests for the commission have frequently been
tame, even perfunctory, with no more than a third of the voters going to
the polls. In such years, if the commissionerships had been the only offices
up for election, the turnout might have been even smaller.

The situation reflects the fact that there are commonly no issues, no
outs disparaging the ins, making charges and countercharges or trying to
capture patronage. There is an incumbent or two up for reelection and a
new nominee sponsored by the Citizens' Committee on the nonpartisan
ballot, all good men. And there is a scatteration of self-nominated independents most of whom do not qualify at the primary election for a place
on the ballot at the final election, and who almost never get elected.
And there's nothing in sight to stir anybody's emotions.

There may be a cooling element in the fact that when two commissioners are to be elected they won't alter the balance in the council since

319

three others hold over; and when three are to be elected, one or two are incumbents up for reelection and fairly sure of it, so no earthquake is in sight. So the campaign frequently fails to make the first page of the newspaper from day to day.

No Complaints!

That Dayton has been well governed could, of course, be a legend waiting for some explosion of disillusionment, but if so the town is mightily fooled. There just isn't any complaint! Dishonesty in the city hall is as unthinkable as in a bank. Last year the city employed Griffenhagen and Associates to make an efficiency survey of the city services to look for chances to improve techniques. The Griffenhagen staff ransacked all departments for six months and offered some ideas, but they picked up one for themselves, for they volunteered this: "The city has an honest administration. Not once in the course of our studies here has the staff encountered even the slightest indication to the contrary. . . . Few cities are as free of what is best understood under the label of political pressure." And the mild mannered Dayton *News*, a Democratic newspaper, in an editorial on the outcome of the 1945 election, remarked: "Dayton has enjoyed 30 years of unbroken honest government."

Fred O. Eichelberger, then city manager, started for his office one day in 1946 and discovered that Dayton was starting to celebrate "Eichelberger Day," it being, as he learned, the 25th anniversary of his induction as city manager. In a floral scene in the city hall he was given a watch, a scroll, a handsome volume of letters of praise collected by the Chamber of Commerce and, of course, an earful of speeches. There were fifteen other city managers who in that year had served a single community for 25 years or more, but they were all in little places; Dayton had another "first" among the larger cities.

When Eichelberger resigned to retire in January 1948, he drove off to Florida in a new Cadillac, but there were no lifted eyebrows about that, for it was a surprise gift from a lot of Dayton citizens. Eichelberger has been a patient, diligent, thoroughly informed, self-effacing city manager who advised the council and deferred to its rare adverse decisions with unruffled serenity whether he agreed or not, executing them faithfully. A former mayor observes that the question of displacing Eichelberger for a new manager just never was brought up.

So I went to Dayton to see how a city of 260,000 has gotten along without partisan politics or ruckuses through eighteen successive elections, putting into the council an unbroken succession of good men and true who have given the town good government for 34 years.

Eighteen elections are too many to report on, but the outstanding fact is that few of them were heated or bitter; really pretty dull!

In 1913 the proponents of the new charter, headed by the vivid and eccentric John H. Patterson of the National Cash Register Company, kept their momentum after they secured adoption of the charter, formed a balanced committee to support selected candidates, and elected them. They spent considerable money—in the neighborhood of $20,000—in the campaign, and the Democratic and Republican party managements, recognizing that the voters had adopted nonpartisan elections, forebore to throw their weight.

OFF TO GOOD START

The first council included businessmen, a labor union officer and lawyers, and it promptly made a hit with history by finding for its pioneer manager Henry M. Waite, former city engineer of Cincinnati, who was one big man in any company. Big, gentle, soft-spoken and wise, he made the Dayton government a warm and human service. In later years he built the great Cincinnati railroad terminal and the Chicago subway, and his example in Dayton set the pace for the new profession.

In 1917 three members of the council were to be chosen. The Socialists organized aggressively and the Democratic party workers threw their weight for certain nominees.

The Citizens' Committee, favoring reelection of the three incumbents and undistracted continuation of a remarkable administration, put on a hard campaign and spent $23,000, mostly on printed and stereopticon publicity, to expound the achievements of those first four years which had won Dayton a national reputation. In the three-cornered primary fight they ignored the Socialists and set out to beat the Democrats, resulting in a combined vote of 20,545 for the three incumbents and 10,164 for the three Democrats. But the Socialists mustered 29,162 for their trio, three times their normal vote.

The eliminated Democrats, as expected, joined with the Citizens' Committee against the Socialists in the final election, and the novelty introduced by the possibility of a Socialist victory alerted the electorate, produced another $27,000 of campaign funds and brought out a bigger vote, of which the Socialists got 43 per cent. About $3,000 of the campaign money went to Democratic and Republican precinct workers.

The claim of a Socialist newspaper that its party's local growth rose from its anti-war attitude stirred up the Americanism issue, and much of the hysteria and heat of the final campaign dealt with issues that were extraneous and momentary. The heavy expenditures for publicity went largely to combat a shocking stream of sneering mendacity from the Socialist campaigners. City employees were successfully restrained from participating in the campaigns. The Democratic party never tried again.

In 1919, and on into the 20's, incumbents who had shared the glory of those early years were reelected by a Citizens' Committee, against scattering opposition, with ease. When new nominees had to be found the Citizens' Committee would tag some citizen and relieve him of the necessity of nominating himself or raising campaign funds.

The Citizens' Committee, of course, catered to the diverse elements of the population—the Catholics, the unions, the two sides of the river, and the Democrats and the Republicans. It balanced the council to keep it representative, and as long as both parties had some members of the council, the two party managements stayed out of the picture. But a new nominee was checked with the leader of each party and with the editors of the two leading dailies, and it is a fair guess that all four of those persons voted for every nominee of the Citizens' Committee.

No Need for Excitement

The committee's original membership of 50 dwindled to ten. So did the campaign funds—they became nominal amounts in some years—and all that the candidates of the committee did in some years was to accept invitations to speak at various club or civic meetings. It was not waning vigor or alertness—there was no need to do more. The Citizens' Committee candidates pooled their efforts in such ways as taking pains to support each other in the course of their speeches. Advertising was pooled and a single expenditures report was filed as required with the board of elections.

Thus they frequently survived the primary election easily and faced the highest of scattered independent and Socialist candidates at the final election without much fear except the hazards of a light vote.

Light votes—30 per cent—were frequent, but there were flurries and ructions. Dayton is an industrial city and so has some Socialist and radical labor elements which from time to time have flared into brief numerical importance. In 1921 in a light primary vote the three Socialist candidates reached the final elections and thereby alerted and alarmed the rest of the town, which raised and spent $20,000 and beat them by a substantial majority.

In 1933, amid the irritations of the depression, a labor leader named Breidenbach, with alarming manners and a tough attack, mustered the discontented and survived the primary. A few days before the election the Dayton *Herald* switched its support to him and he was elected. He became, in time, a useful and cooperative member in the council, but during the process he was disturbing and stormy.

When Breidenbach ran for another term without Citizens' Committee support, in 1939, there were only three candidates in the field. The *News,* in characterizing the two Citizens' Committee candidates, said: "Speice is understood to have Republican Chairman Brower's endorsement. Munger, elected to the legislature as a Democrat, will doubtless attract, although this is no partisan matter, a heavy Democratic vote."

Breidenbach's supporters in the three-cornered contest must have had to refrain from voting for a second candidate. The election was lively and the vote was: Breidenbach, 25,527; Munger, 32,706; Speice, 25,958. The total list of registered voters was about 130,000 at that time and the 48 per cent turnout compared with 30 per cent in 1937.

In 1941 "the campaign was a quiet one." Two incumbents and one new man, all supported by the "Nonpartisan Good Government League," were elected by a two-to-one vote. The *News* commented: "It shows a profound confidence in Dayton's city government, and what a relief to operate a city without partisan political campaigns!"

In 1943 only 30 per cent voted, with two to elect. Munger and Speice, Citizens' Committee choices, got 18,070 and 17,520 respectively; Smith, described as representing the CIO, got 11,615, and Beck, 9,270.

In 1945 large postwar bond issues, totalling $25,000,000, were put on the ballot and brought unusual interest to the election. The "All-Dayton Committee," succeeding the Citizens' Committee, wanted some fresh blood in the council. In consultation, the Democratic leader objected to a suggested Democrat; the man was a Democrat all right, but not a *registered* Democrat! It seems a narrow point, but the committee deferred to it rather than risk a fight, the town nowadays being 60 per cent Democratic.

PARTY LEADERS CONSULTED

In all such consultation with the party leaders, the deference to political opposition involved no trading or stipulations with party leaders; the latter kept out of the process of selection of nominees and dissent was rare. Obviously, the committee when it chose a Democrat needed to be sure that he could really draw Democratic votes, just as it would nominate a Catholic but make sure that the church rated him as a good one. The All-Dayton Committee published advertisements which were notable for their moderation of spirit and claims.

The 1947 campaign was described, however, as bitter. The All-Dayton Committee disappeared; this time it was "Citizens' Committee to Elect

Smith and Speice," there being two to elect this time. The CIO-PCA came to bat. Five organizers came in from out of town at the expense of the national organization and two leftish candidates were put up; one was a colored man and the other, a prominent CIO labor leader, was widely alleged to be, if not a Communist, at least a fellow traveler. Mr. Breidenbach, being AFL, turned up on the side of the current *ad hoc* Citizens' Committee. It was the left arraigned against the center and the right; the latter took alarm and heat again developed.

The radicals reported campaign expenditures of $1,345, but that did not include the work of the outside organizers and CIO union officers nor the prodigal space given by the CIO newspaper. The Citizens spent $8,331, which took no account of the fact that precinct workers of both the Republican and Democratic parties worked for their ticket and helped to bring out the vote. The Negro vote, which is extensive in Dayton, did not flock to the colored candidate.

On election day the radicals circulated handbills alleging that a 1 per cent payroll tax was to be imposed if the opposing ticket got elected, and the commission denied it as a barefaced lie.

The Citizens' Committee candidates, Smith, a first-time man, and Speice, running for his third term, got 51,631 and 50,410 votes; Sims, the CIO candidate, 19,942 and McLin, the Negro, 15,487. The *News* on the next day ran a cartoon picturing city hall with a huge flag on it—"The American flag still flies over Dayton's city hall."

I asked two former commissioners to tell me just how they got into consideration for public office. Mr. Brennan, former mayor and chairman of the 1947 citizens' group, had been an assistant prosecuting attorney (appointive) and had once run unsuccessfully for probate judge. The Citizens' Committee persuaded him to run and he assented—"that's all!"

Dr. Kneisly's case was an odd one. He was a dentist, but his political availability lay in the fact that he was president of the Federated Improvement Associations whose constituent local groups totalled 22,000 members. The Citizens' Committee asked him to run, the fact that he was reluctantly considering it leaked out and he was jocularly hailed as mayor by his friends on the street.

The Citizens' Committee finally settled on other candidates and issued its endorsements without setting itself right with him; just why, Dr. Kneisly never learned. His friends resented the mishandling and proceeded to nominate him and, on the wave of their indignation, he beat the committee candidate in the primary and was elected. Four years later he ran again without Citizens' Committee support but lost in the primary election.

So down the years public-spirited citizens of Dayton, drawn admittedly from the well-to-do, successful people who participate in community chest drives and other unselfish endeavors, have always seen their nominees constitute a majority on the commission. The $8,331 they spent in 1947 under the radical attack was larger than normal; their campaigns often cost no more than $3,000. They were like the nominating committee of a social club, buttonholing a new man now and then to persuade him to take a tour of duty. They catered to the natural groups and kept the council balanced.

Being in good repute, with no axes to grind, they were true leaders, as shown by the fact that the people followed. They never attempted to mollify the Socialists of the 20's or the current radicals by putting one of them on their tickets, and very likely would have been unable to elect them if they had. After each election the committees fold up and shut up and make no attempt as a group to influence city hall.

LABOR ISSUE

The AFL-CIO split extends to local politics and probably has diminished the concern the citizens have lest labor go solidly political on class lines; they cannot hope to cater successfully to that segment of labor and radicalism which wants all or nothing. Voters of Dayton come out and vote when there is an issue, as in 1947. In fact, the absence of issues in Dayton elections most of the time, except when the class struggle has lapped over into politics, can be proof of a real era of good feeling and mutual trust. "Happy is the land that has no history."

Commissioners in Dayton get a salary of $1,200 and the chairman (mayor) receives $1,800. The conditions of service obviously have been attractive to men who would never take the relatively trivial positions of councilmen under a mayor and council plan or the full-time service as a departmental head called for by the commission plan because they have business and professional careers too important to interrupt.

Just how unique Dayton's 34-year stretch may be is hard to say. Certainly there are cities with the older forms of government, as well as cities with managers, where decency and serenity rule. But it is more than a coincidence that since the adoption of the council-manager plan good citizenship has so easily and consistently been effective in Dayton!

WILL IT LAST?

How much longer can it go on so serenely? The factors to be watched are: (a) the possibility of increased class warfare and the arraying of "workers" against the rest; (b) the possibility of change in the newspaper situation, all three of the dailies now being almost invariably with the Citizens; (c) the fact that community leaders are silenced to an increasing degree by living now in growing suburbs outside the city's political boundary; (d) Dayton's new city manager Russell E. McClure, former manager of Wichita, may be less successful than Eichelberger in avoiding antagonisms; (e) another depression may substitute an irritated situation for the city's current thriving prosperity, with incidental repercussions against the town's present leadership.

If this story sounds like a prolonged domination of Dayton by its businessmen, be it remembered that the radical bloc gets every chance to challenge; indeed, the political stage is well cleared of false issues and well illuminated for their efforts—but voters of Dayton have remained stolidly unimpressed.

Leftist opposition to candidates of the citizens' committees is not extended to include opposition to the form of government. Once, in 1922, reversion to the old form was proposed by an initiative petition and the Socialists cooperated in the defeat of the effort by a vote of 26,000 to 17,000.

I.

FAREWELL TO THE POLITICIANS

They fought new manager charter every step of the way but Richmond's aroused citizens outvoted them six times.

By Hugh R. Thompson, Jr. *

(From *National Municipal Review*, October, 1948)

Richmond, capital city of Virginia, and one time capital of the Confederate States of America, last month abandoned one of the most cumbersome and outmoded charters to be found in the nation for one of the most modern and effective.

The change is no accident. It is the result of determined action by an irate citizenry with an effective medium for cooperative action and competent leadership.

From 1928 until 1946 only 3 per cent of the adult population participated in municipal general elections and only 9 per cent participated in municipal primaries. The low ebb came in June 1944, when only 2,987 votes were cast in the election of a mayor for the city, which has an estimated population of more than a quarter of a million!

Realizing the gravity of the situation, a meeting of civic-minded citizens was called by the Inter-Club Council of Richmond in February 1945. At this meeting an organization committee was named and Claude R. Davenport, a prominent businessman and civic leader, was elected temporary chairman.

During the months that followed the committee worked intensively to lay the groundwork for a truly effective city-wide, nonpartisan civic organization—the Richmond Citizens Association. In October 1945, this organization committee adopted a proposed charter and by-laws and elected its first officers and directors. Richard H. Hardesty, Jr., a local candy manufacturer, was named as first president of the new association, which was granted its charter by the State Corporation Commission in February 1946.

Almost simultaneously with the formal establishment of the association, the General Assembly of Virginia passed an enabling act which permitted the voters of Richmond for the first time to decide whether

---

* Mr. Thompson is executive secretary of the Richmond Civic Association. He was formerly news reporter for the Richmond *News Leader* and publications editor of the Virginia Transit Company. During the war he saw service with the infantry in the Philippines and Korea, retiring as major.

they desired to consider formally a change in their city's charter. Under the new statute it was necessary to secure some 4,800 signatures of qualified voters on petitions asking that a referendum be held. Each signature had to be notarized.

The infant association accepted the challenge. Within 90 days it secured 5,530 properly notarized signatures of qualified voters upon petitions for a referendum on the question "Shall this city take steps to frame and request the General Assembly of Virginia to grant to it a special form of government?"

The association then began work on a campaign organization. W. Moscoe Huntley, a prominent local attorney, was appointed general campaign chairman. A "personal contact" team of representatives of every section of the city was recruited to discuss the referendum question in every neighborhood; advertisements were run in the newspapers; folders, show cards and bumper strips were printed and distributed in large quantities; members of a speakers bureau appeared before scores of groups throughout the city; many prominent citizens were recruited to make radio talks; business, civic and fraternal organizations were encouraged to discuss the question at their meetings; thousands of letters were sent to prospective voters inviting their attention to the referendum and requesting them to post themselves on the question.

New Charter Supported

When the referendum was held on November 5, 1946, 20,840 qualified voters cast their ballots. Of these, 16,755 approved the proposition. On the same ballot seven candidates endorsed by the Richmond Citizens Association were elected overwhelmingly to compose a commission to draft a new charter for the city.

· · · · · · ·

Even before the judge of hustings court could announce that the proposed charter would be voted upon on November 4, 1947, Richmond's entrenched politicians served notice that they intended to use whatever means was within their power to stop the movement for a change in Richmond's government. Early in June they consolidated their forces and adopted a name as cumbersome and befuddling as the charter they were fighting to retain. They called themselves the "Organization for the Preservation of Our Democratic Form of Government."

Politicians Object

The City Democratic Committee fired its first shot in a resolution:

The City Democratic Committee of Richmond, having carefully considered the move now in full swing for the establishment of a city manager for Richmond and also for a nonpartisan council, takes this occasion to express its unequivocable opposition.

The Democratic party has been responsible for the city government for nearly a hundred years and has given the city a government that is efficient and without corruption. We feel that our party can continue to carry on in the future in the same way and to that end we pledge ourselves.

The insidious attempt to gain control of the city we regard as a reversion to old discarded things, to the dictatorship of a few who are to hold irresponsible power. We call upon all true Democrats to defeat at the polls this most undemocratic proposal.

This time the association knew it had a real fight on its hands. Step number one was to get the best general campaign chairman available.

Mr. [L. E.] Marlowe [1] went to his old friend Ed P. Phillips, one of Richmond's most dynamic businessmen and the most outstanding leader in the association's 1946 campaign. Knowing what lay ahead, he was hard to convince. He ran through all the usual excuses of why he couldn't accept the responsibility and then said that his health wouldn't stand it.

Marlowe immediately telephoned his own doctor and made an appointment—not for himself but for Phillips. He took Phillips to the doctor and said: "Give him a thorough physical and let me know if he's in condition to run our campaign for us."

The unique procedure took Phillips so much by surprise that before he knew it he was saying "Ah," having his blood pressure taken and submitting to thumps and listenings at various sections of his anatomy. His examination completed, the doctor pronounced: "It not only won't hurt him. It will do him good."

Having received this verdict, Mr. Phillips accepted the post and immediately dug into a work schedule which would have killed a lesser man. During the four-month period, July through October 1947, he devoted from fourteen to sixteen hours a day to the campaign.

.   .   .   .

Most amazing was the fact that the association was able to bring together on a common front the city's leading representatives of business, the Chamber of Commerce, the Junior Chamber of Commerce, the C.I.O., the A.F. of L., the League of Women Voters, the Junior League, Housewives League, Democrats, Republicans and other groups.

The City Democratic Committee, which had hastened to be the first to condemn the proposed charter, soon found that it could not make a party issue of the question and that many Democratic leaders were on the other side of the fence. This merely added fuel to the fire. The "old liners" fought with every weapon they could find. Their speakers

[1] President of the Richmond Citizens Association.

variously accused the charterites of being "big interests," the "silk stocking crowd," "communists," "fascists," and "reactionaries." Dr. J. Fulmer Bright, former mayor of Richmond for sixteen years, called the Citizens' Association "Richmond's Tammany Hall." Jesse M. Johnson, opposition chairman, charged that the Richmond Charter Commission had "outcommunized the Communist party."

VICTORY AT LAST!

By election day there were few residents of Richmond who were not personally in the thick of the fight. This time 29,672 qualified voters—the largest number ever to vote in a municipal election—went to the polls, 21,567 of them to vote in favor of the charter drafted by the commission.

Despite this decisive vote the opposition again waged a bitter fight against the proposed charter when it was introduced into the 1948 Virginia General Assembly as House Bill Number 1. Led by Archie C. Berkeley, chairman of the City Democratic Committee, and former State Senator John J. Wicker, Jr., they fought it in committee and on the floor of both houses. After almost a month and a half of debate and delay the bill was approved by the General Assembly with only a few minor changes.

The old charter which Richmond has tossed into the ash can provided for a bicameral council of 32 members elected by wards, 20 serving on a common council and twelve on a board of aldermen. . . .

Richmond's new charter has streamlined the city's legislature to a single body of nine members, elected at large. This council is given the responsibility of establishing policy but must leave administration in the hands of a city manager whom it appoints.

. . . . .

To serve on its first nine-man council and to establish policy under its new form of government, the voters of Richmond, on June 8, 1948, elected nine men who had publicly supported the charter change. Eight of the nine were endorsed by the Richmond Citizens Association.

. . . . .

What's happened to Mr. Phillips, the reluctant campaign chairman? Oh, he was elected president of the Richmond Citizens Association and says he never felt better in his life!

[Postscript: The council recruited one of the ablest of the city managers. The Citizens Association again elected eight of its nine candidates two years later in 1950. R. S. C.]

Part IV

Outlines of the National Municipal League's Model Laws

A. MODEL STATE CONSTITUTION
5th edition, revised 1948
A short constitution—confined to structure and powers

Executive

An elective governor
  for a 4-year term (as in 32 states)
  elected in nonpresidential years (as in 16 states)
  with appointive power over all the other administrative officers (as in New Jersey and the U.S.)
Integrated state administration, all appointees, present and future, to be grouped in a limited number of departments (preferably single-headed) as in New York, Missouri, and New Jersey
Administrative manager to assist governor
Merit system throughout the civil services

Legislative

Single-house legislature (as in Nebraska and in Canadian provinces)
  two-year terms
  elected by proportional representation from a few large multi-member districts
Legislative Council of members of legislature with staff for between-session research and expert preparation of major measures (as in 28 states)
Secretary of the legislature, elected by the legislature, as chief of its service staff with power to appoint and remove other legislative employees

Judicial

A simple unified court system (as in New Jersey and the U.S.)
Chief Justice elective for term of 8 years, to appoint all state judges from lists submitted by a judicial council chosen partly from bar association nominees. Popular vote on retention of each judge after four years' trial; 12-year term

Cities and Counties

Self-executing home rule for cities; i.e., right to draft and adopt new charters by local action (as in about 20 states)

Extension of similar home rule privileges to counties and elimination of county officers from mention in the constitution

Liberal grants of powers to cities and counties, minimizing recourse to the legislature for special acts

Initiative and Referendum

Governor may submit to referendum bills which failed of passage and majority of legislature may submit bills vetoed and not repassed by ⅔ vote. Popular petition may suspend new laws pending referendum or may submit proposed new laws or constitutional amendments to referendum

Revision and Amendment

Constitution amendable by two passages through the legislature and approval at the polls, or by initiative

Constitutional convention callable at any time by legislature submitting question of having a convention for approval at the polls. Automatic submission of the question every 15 years

Purpose: Short ballot for voters; integrated, responsible administration; strong, truly representative legislature; simple, visible political scene; short, flexible basic constitution; practical (instead of complicated) democracy!

B. MODEL COUNTY CHARTER
1952 Edition in Preparation

Elective Officers

County Council of 5 to 9 members
elected at large
for terms of 2 years (keeping clear of national and state election dates)
by proportional representation, or by primary election with runoff election three weeks later if necessary to insure majority selection
on nonpartisan ballot
with nominations made by filing petition of ten electors with a deposit
of money returnable if candidate gets certain percentage of the votes
or by petition signed by large number of electors

Appointive Officers—by the County Council:

County Manager, to serve at the pleasure of the council, subject to
suspension at any time and removable after 30 days' notice, with
statement of reasons and public hearing if manager desires
Auditor for post-audit
County planning commission

Appointive Officers—by the County Manager, without confirmation by
the County Council:

County clerk (unless county council chooses to appoint him)
All department heads and other non-judicial officers

Up to 1952 no county had shortened its ballot and integrated its administration with the completeness proposed in this model, the reason in
some cases being provisions in state constitutions requiring election of
numerous county officers.

References:

Model County Charter (under revision 1952), National Municipal
League.
The County Manager Plan, 24 pp. 20c. National Municipal League.
Digest of County Manager Charters and Laws, 65 pp. $2.00. National
Municipal League.

335

C. MODEL CITY CHARTER
(5th ed., 1941, 4th printing, 1948, 173 pp.)

All the powers of the city vested in a Council
> of 5 to 9 members
> elected at large
> for terms of 2 or 4 years (keeping clear of national and state election dates)
> by proportional representation, or by primary election with run-off election two weeks later if necessary to insure majority selection
> on nonpartisan ballots
> with all nominations made by filing petition of ten electors with a deposit of money returnable if candidate gets 5% of the votes, or by petition signed by large number of electors

Council empowered
> to appoint city manager
> to suspend the city manager and to remove him on 30 days' notice by a resolution giving reasons with public hearing thereon if manager requests
> to establish and alter administrative departments except finance
> to investigate any department
> to adopt the budget and issue bonds
> to appoint personnel board, planning commission, and zoning board of appeals
> to adopt plats, master plan, official map and zoning restrictions, and 6-year capital improvement program
> to provide for independent post-audit
> to select city clerk
> to select one of its members as chairman with courtesy title of mayor without loss of vote in council

City Manager
> not necessarily a resident before appointment
> with indefinite tenure
> head of administrative branch of city government, with power to

336

appoint and remove department heads and employees subject to
civil service rules and rights
to prepare the budget for council
to control budgeted expenditures and purchasing

Department of Finance with all financial functions, subject to independent post-audit

Annual budgeting by uniform procedures and publicity

Capital improvement budgeting on 6-year schedule

Department of Personnel
headed by a director
to conduct civil service examinations for appointments and promotions
to recommend rules of employment conditions to personnel board,
and enforce rules
Personnel Board, 3 with 6-year terms expiring in rotation
hears appeals of removed employees and advises city council and
personnel director

Planning Commission, 5 members
to draft official map, master plan, and zoning for approval by council
to draft for city manager 6-year list of desirable capital improvements
in order of preference

Director of Planning appointive by the city manager to manage staff
and service to the commission

Initiative to propose or veto ordinances signed by 10% of the voters
compels referendum

Amendments
submitted by a charter commission to referendum
or by ordinance submitted to referendum by council
or by initiative petition signed by 10% of the voters and submitted
to referendum
and passed by majority of those voting thereon

THE REFORMER

A Reformer is one who sets forth cheerfully toward sure defeat. It is his peculiar function to embrace the hopeless cause when it can win no other friends and when its obvious futility repels that thick-necked, practical, timorous type of citizen to whom the outward appearance of success is so dear. His persistence against stone walls invites derision from those who have never been touched by his religion and do not know what fun it is. He never seems victorious, for if he were visibly winning, he would forthwith cease to be dubbed "reformer."

Yet, in time, the Reformer's little movement becomes respectable and his little minority proves that it can grow and presently the Statesman joins it and takes all the credit, cheerfully handed to him by the Reformer as bribe for his support.

And then comes the Politician, rushing grandly to the succor of the victor!

And all the Crowd!

The original Reformer is lost in the shuffle then, but he doesn't care. For as the great band-wagon which he started goes thundering past with trumpets, the Crowd in the intoxication of triumph leans over the side to jeer at him—a forlorn and lonely crank mustering a pitiful little odd-lot of followers along the roadside and setting them marching, while over their heads he lifts the curious banner of his next crusade!

R. S. C.
in *National Municipal Review*, July, 1927

INDEX

Kales, Albert M., 126

Kansas, 119

Kansas City, Mo., better governed than Jackson County, 4; plan of selecting judges, 127; council manager experience, 165; manager's career, 173

Kellogg, Wilbur R., 164

Kentucky, attempt to shorten ballots, 86; reorganization effort 1934, 1951, 106

Kerwin, Henry and, 225

Key, V. O. Jr., xvi, 52

King County, Wash., 67

Kings County, New York, 19

Knoxville, Tenn., returned 10% of tax levy, 151; council-manager ousted by legislature, 266

L

Labor, Oregon Federation of, supported single-house legislature 1912, 119; supported Nebraska single-house legislature 1933, 122; Pennsylvania Federation of, for council-manager plan, 139; Pennsylvania Federation of Labor flouted, 175; C.I.O. supported council-manager in Bayonne, N. J., 177; Democrats in labor unions, 252

La Grande, Ore., 147

La Guardia, Fiorello, 296

Lane County, Oregon, 207

Lausche, Gov. Frank J., Ohio, 273

League of Women Voters, does not tire (Cleveland), 160; Cleveland 1931, 162; does 80% of the work, 177

Lee, Mrs. Frances G., 231

Lewis, John L., 254

Lincoln-Roosevelt League, California, 87

Lindsay, Ben B., 90

Lister, Gov. Ernest, Washington, 120

Livermore, N. H., 263

Lockport, New York, first council-manager draft, ix; Board of Trade sponsored optional law 1911, 145

Long, Huey, ticket maker in Louisiana, 44

Long Beach, Calif., elects nine councilmen, 16; recall of manager, 185; "Vote for nine," 283

Los Angeles Calif., unwieldy constituency, 51; strong mayor, 133; no progress toward simplification, 189

Los Angeles County, Calif., transfer of functions, 68; incident in charter board, 199; progress in 1912, 200; county manager structure, 205; county executive successful, 205; incomplete managership 1938, 211; appointive coroner, 230

Louisiana, reorganization permitted 1921, 107; no city managers to 1952, 174; county managers possible, 209; elects state board of education, 217; elective state school commissioner, 217

Low, Seth, 83

Lowden, Governor Frank O., reorganization in Illinois, 98; reorganization in retrospect, 116

Lowell, A. Lawrence, 151, 220

Lucas County, Ohio, Short Ballot amendment carried in, 1912, 96; county manager proposed 1935. 202

Ludington, Arthur C., 90

M

Maine, Governor is only elective administrator, 92; cities and villages with managers, 174; rural managers, 209, 213; University of. trains managers, 214

Malden, Mass., 130

Manchester, Conn., 172

Mainstee, Mich., 147

Mapp, G. Walter, Virginia, 113

Marlowe, L. E., Richmond, 329

Marquis, Don, 130

Maryland, one unit of government for 10,000 population, 67; legislature ignored vote for constitutional convention, 118; slow progress in counties, 201; county managers possible, 209; medical examiner service, 231; Governor reapportions one house, 264

Massachusetts, reorganization 1919 107; protected tenure for managers 181; medical examiner service 231; opposition to P.R., 249; Plan E blocked, 266; office-group bal lots, 273

McCloskey, John J. Jr., 296

McClure, Russell E., 326

McCooey, "Boss" John H., 34

McMinn County, Tenn., 210

Medford, Mass., 184

Memphis, Tenn., xiv, xvii

Merriam, Charles E., 235

Miami Beach, Fla., 300

Michigan, 4% know name of state treasurer, xiii; poll on awareness of voters, 23; 15.8 governments for 10,000 population, 67; Governor urged Short Ballot 1913, 88; Bil to shorten ballot 1913, 96; reorganization efforts 1921, 1935, 1938, 1950, 107; eighty-four cities with managers, 174; county government reform 1920–1928, 1934, 1936, 1942, 1944, 202; elects state board of education, 217; elective state school commissioner, 217; restrictive constitution, 260; awareness of state officers, 291; low vote for Justice of Supreme Court, 317

Milton, Washington, 36

Milwaukee, Wisc., 191

Minneapolis, 123

Minnesota, Progressives endorsed Short Ballot 1912, 88; reorganization efforts 1925, 1951, 108; single-house legislature urged by governor 1914, 119; poll on single-house legislature 1945, 123; county managers possible, 209; Morlan Report quoted, 225

Minot, No. Dakota, non-partisan ballot, 300

Missouri, attempt to shorten ballots, 86; reorganization effort 1945, 109; initiative for single-house legislature 1945, 123; plan of selecting judges, 126; plan of selecting

judges adopted 1940, 127; satisfaction with judges, 128; county managers possible, 209; can abolish townships, 213

Mississippi, reorganization effort 1950, 109; county managers possible, 209

Mitchel, John Purroy, Mayor New York, 229

Mitchell, John, 90

Model State Medico-Legal Investigative System, 231, 279

Model City Charter, complies with Three Rules, 141; revised 1915, 151; tenure of manager, 184; silent on schools, 224; includes P.R. as first alternative, 246; in National Municipal League program, 279; outline, 333

Model Direct Primary Election System, 239, 279

Model Election Administration System, 279

Model Registration System, 279

Model County Charter, possible in twenty-one states, 201; partially adopted in seventeen counties, 207; in National Municipal League program, 279; outline, 333

Model County Manager Optional Law, 1930 version, 207

Model State Constitution, influenced Nebraska, 121; follows Kales' idea of selecting judges, 129; includes P. R. for legislature, 246; malapportionment averted, 263; in National Municipal League program, 279; outline, 333

Moley, Raymond, 318

Monroe County, N. Y., protected tenure for managers, 183; County Manager 1936, 211

Montana, county managers possible, 209; non-partisan judicial ballot, 316

Montclair, N. J., 137

Montgomery County, Md., 211

Morgan, Daniel E., 161

Morganton, No. Car., 147